PENGUIN BOOKS

The Puppy and the Orphan

The Puppy and the Orphan

SUZANNE LAMBERT

PENGUIN BOOKS

PENGUIN BOOKS

UK | USA | Canada | Ireland | Australia
India | New Zealand | South Africa

Penguin Books is part of the Penguin Random House group of companies
whose addresses can be found at global.penguinrandomhouse.com.

First published 2017

001

Copyright © Suzanne Lambert 2017

The moral right of the author has been asserted

Set in 12.5/14.75 pt Garamond MT Std
Typeset by Jouve (UK), Milton Keynes
Printed in Great Britain by Clays Ltd, St Ives plc

A CIP catalogue record for this book is available from the British Library

ISBN: 978–1–405–93248–6

www.greenpenguin.co.uk

Until one has loved an animal,
a part of one's soul remains unawakened.

Anatole France

Although this story is fictional, the orphanage and the people within it are very real. I arrived at the doorstep of Nazareth House as a tiny baby, and it was my home for many years. There, I was taken under the wing of a remarkable woman called Nancy, who cared for the little ones in the nursery, and I am proud to be able to call her my mother. Over the years, she shared many stories with me about the orphanage – and I have poured many into this book.

Contents

CONTENTS

CONTENTS

Stars in the Sky

Little Billy Miller was five years old. He was sitting on the floor watching the toy train puff its way around the track in a circle. He had no idea how long he had been there and didn't care anyway. He could hear murmuring from the room next door. The adults were talking quietly – now and again he caught a snatch of what they were saying. Many of the words he didn't understand or had never heard before. Whatever they were talking about wasn't good: that much he knew. Mummy had told him never to whisper, it was rude, but she wasn't here any more: she had gone to be a star in the sky with Daddy, they had told him.

After the car crash that had taken Mummy and Daddy away, Billy had moved in with his grandma Miller. Grandma had tried her best but Billy could hear her crying at night after he had been put to bed. She had painted his little bedroom pale blue and cut out silver-paper stars and stuck them to the wall. On Billy's first night in his new room he stayed awake, staring out of the window at the stars, waiting to see Mummy and Daddy. He had called and cried out to them until his throat hurt.

Early in the morning, exhausted, he had ripped all the stars off the wall. On his first morning in his new home

Grandma Miller had found him lying fast asleep on the floor, surrounded by stars. She had had to turn away and force back her own tears. Why, God? she said to herself. Just look at him. Find a way to make this better, please.

Sadly, the heartbreak in old Grandma Miller's heart was too great. It was only a few days later that she, too, left Billy to be a star in the sky.

Billy was in the neighbours' house now, playing with their son's train. Everyone knew how much Billy loved trains. Daddy had bought lots of books about them and together they had learned all about the different kinds of trains, what they were called and how they worked. Daddy was very proud of how much his Billy knew about trains. 'One day we'll go on a train journey together,' he had promised. He had swung Billy onto his shoulders, then run around the room making train noises until Mummy told them to be quiet before they disturbed the whole street.

Daddy had pretended to drop Billy, catching him at the last minute, and Mummy screamed, 'I do wish you wouldn't do that!'

'Always catch him, though, don't I?' Daddy laughed, and Mummy just smiled.

These were moments Billy was trying hard to remember. He would squeeze his eyes tight shut and try to see their faces. Sometimes he could, but more often now he couldn't. Maybe when they had been stars in the sky for a long time he wouldn't be able to see them at all . . . and they would forget about him.

The voices next door were louder now and Billy had no idea what was going to happen to him or where he would be taken. He began to shiver and then the tears came once more.

It was only six in the evening, but it had been dark for hours. It was freezing cold outside and the sky was clear, showing the brightly shining stars. Suddenly Billy remembered Mummy telling him that Christmas was a time for magic and miracles. It was when they were putting the tree up last year and Daddy had lifted him high to place the star at the top.

Now Billy jumped up and ran to the window. 'I forgot to make a Christmas wish! That's why Mummy and Daddy couldn't hear me.' He knelt on the floor, closed his eyes, made a wish, then got up and pulled open the curtains. The he fetched a chair, climbed up and pushed the window up with all his might. When it lifted, he stuck his head outside. 'Mummy! Daddy!' he called. 'Oh! I forgot the prayer.' Every single night Billy and Mummy had sung it together at bedtime but he never had since Mummy and Daddy had turned into stars. He squeezed his eyes tight shut, then quietly began to sing:

> '*Goodnight, Man in the Moon,*
> *Up in the sky so high.*
> *Goodnight, Man in the Moon,*
> *Watch over me tonight.*

God bless Mummy, God bless Daddy,
God bless my family,
God bless everyone I know,
Then please, God, bless me.'

Billy opened his eyes, leaned out of the window, stared up at the stars and waited. 'Mummy said God always keeps His promises,' he whispered, and he began once more to call to them.

He was still there when the adults came to find him. They were all shocked and grabbed him, pulling him away from the window.

'What on earth are you doing, Billy? You're freezing.'

'You could have fallen!'

But Billy wasn't listening. He was never going to sing again. It hadn't worked.

He was pushed hastily into a warm coat and they fussed about with a hat and scarf. It was time for him to leave for his fourth home in as many days. The front door slammed as little Billy Miller was taken away.

The house fell silent. Upstairs the breeze blew the curtains in the room, the stars twinkled, and the man in the moon looked down.

Had God been listening? Of course He had.

Nazareth House, December 1953

Nazareth House Orphanage in Jesmond, Newcastle upon Tyne, was full to the brim this year. Nancy was busy going through all the presents that had been donated for the children during the past few weeks. It really was going to be quite wonderful, she thought, remembering past Christmases when there had not been enough toys for the children. She smiled, remembering the long-ago Christmas Eve when, tired and exhausted, she had finally got all the little ones settled and tucked up in bed. She was reaching for the light switch when one of the children had whispered, 'My friend from school is getting a ragdoll for Christmas, can you imagine?'

Nancy's heart had almost stood still, but she smiled now, thinking about it. She had gathered all the rags, wool and buttons she could find and sat up all night making rag dolls for the children. 'Christmas magic,' she whispered.

Nancy was now thirty-three and couldn't have been happier. She had the kindest and brightest blue eyes and light brown hair that fell in soft waves around her face. Her favourite colour was blue and she always wore the prettiest blue apron with a little pocket where she kept her handkerchief, rosary beads and comb. When Nancy smiled at the children, it was as though a little bit of sunshine touched their hearts. Nancy dreamed of a world in which children never cried – and tears were always hastily wiped away with the corner of her pretty apron. 'There now,' she would say, 'all is well.'

She often sat at the big table in the television room and looked out of the huge window at the driveway that led to the big iron gates. Had it really been twenty-four years since she had arrived in 1929 as a frightened and cold nine-year-old child. With every step she had taken down the long driveway through the snow she had prayed to go home.

Now Nazareth House was her home and she loved it. In fact, she had refused to leave when her father came to take her home. She had grown up to have a wonderful way with the children, and eventually she had decided she, too, wanted to become a nun. How-ever, when Nancy turned nineteen, during the Second World War, the Sisters of Nazareth were not accepting new postulants, so she continued to look after the chil-dren. She was the heart and soul of the nursery department, and Mother Superior had been heard to say on more than one occasion, 'Whatever would we do without her?'

Nancy remembered how much the children loved snow, how excited they were when the first flakes fell. This year, so far, there had been none and they were very disappointed indeed. The radio kept reporting that it was on its way but so far there had been no sign of it. Yesterday, Nancy had distracted the children by decorating the playroom. She had gone up to her treasure trove in the attic for the materials they would need to make new decorations – she never threw anything away. She was well known for it. Her eyes would light up at an empty box. Years ago she had rescued a battered basket on its way to the dustbin. 'That might come in handy for something.'

Someone had dared ask, 'In Heaven's name, Nancy, what for?'

When it turned out that there was no crib for the baby Jesus in the nativity play, Nancy had produced her battered basket and had sat proudly through the play.

There had been times when she had felt the pain of grief, and fear had gripped her heart. She had been only nine when her mother died and the family was split up. Her brothers stayed at home with their father, who was grief-stricken at losing his wife. Her youngest sister, Mary, was sent to a home that took babies, while Nancy and her other sister, Margaret, had been brought to Nazareth House. At that time it was a convent school for girls. Some years later, the nuns had closed the school and opened its doors again as an orphanage. Nancy had stayed on to care for the children. There were many reasons children came to Nazareth House. For some it was a short stay while a parent was in hospital or otherwise unable to cope with them. Others were orphans and would be adopted.

That was the hardest part of the job for Nancy. She tried not to get attached to the children but it was one of the things she just couldn't manage. There was always plenty of love to go around, she would tell everyone, and always made time to cuddle the children and sit them on her knee. She told the children wonderful and magical stories, and they would laugh and clap and make up songs about the stories.

Recently, three children had been adopted, twin girls and a little boy. Oh, the excitement in the nursery when the twins had arrived. The children had gathered round, staring at them, trying to tell them apart, until they had burst into tears and clung to each other. It had been impossible to separate them so Nancy had let them share a bed and sit next to each other at mealtimes. They had brought with them a case full of matching clothes but Nancy put different-coloured ribbons in their hair to ensure she knew which was which. Nancy grew fond of them very quickly; they were such sweet little girls, yet there was a sadness as they continued to cling to each other. Their mother had died, and when Nancy asked the children's officer about their father, there was simply a shake of the head. He had left, she said, shortly after the girls were born. They were to be adopted by a doctor and his wife, who were arriving this morning to take the girls to their new home before Christmas.

Nancy thought that was wonderful. She loved to see the look on the adopters' faces when they left Nazareth

House as parents. Young Robert went to a couple from Manchester. They had made the three-hundred-mile round trip four times already to spend time with the little boy and get to know him before all the adoption papers had been signed.

Usually Nancy had watched from the window upstairs as the children began their new life. She would wave to them as they walked up the driveway until she could no longer see them. Nancy had felt extremely tearful when she realized the doctor had a car, and by the time she reached the window, the car was gone. There would be no waving goodbye to them that day.

It was the strangest mixture of emotions, Nancy thought. Of course, she was thrilled to see the children with a new mummy and daddy at the start of what she hoped would be a wonderful new life. Yet there was sadness in the knowledge that she would never see them again.

'I want you to come too, Aunty Nancy,' Robert had said, looking nervous, with tears in his eyes. Nancy had thought her heart would break. She had swept him onto her knee and wiped his eyes with the corner of her apron. 'Well now,' she said, 'I'll always be there with you because you, like every single child who leaves here, will take a tiny piece of my heart that will love you wherever you go.'

Little Robert had stopped crying, then giggled. 'Aunty Nancy, you must have a very big heart.'

9

It was her job to prepare the children, support and encourage them until the day they were taken for adoption or went downstairs to the junior department.

Nancy had no time during the run-up to Christmas to dwell on how much she missed her little ones. There were plenty of others to keep her busy. Considering how many children she had in her care, the nursery was a fun yet perfectly organised place to be. Well, most of the time: there were always a few occasions when everything went horribly wrong. Nancy, of course, never admitted that those days ever happened.

One summer it had rained for days and the children couldn't play outside. Soon they were squabbling and crying for no reason. Nancy had walked into the nursery to tears and tantrums. She found a chair and sat down. 'Gather round,' she told them. 'I have something to tell you. It's a very special secret.' One by one the children stopped crying and began to gather round her. Works every time! Nancy smiled to herself.

'Well, children,' she said, 'did you know I had magic knees?' There was a pause and a few gasps. Nancy leaned forward. The children did too. Nancy told them about her very special knees and how she could balance a hundred children on them at any one time. There were howls of laughter as the children imagined such a sight.

Then, of course, there was her magic apron. Apparently, if you were crying and Nancy wiped your tears on the corner of her apron, you immediately felt better. 'Isn't that just so?' she asked them.

There were shouts of 'Yes, Aunty Nancy!' They nodded to each other.

'Ah, there now, that's better,' she said. 'Peace restored.' Isn't imagination a wonderful thing? she thought. 'Mind you, I also have eyes in the back of my head, so don't be thinking you can be up to no good when I'm not looking,' she told them, with a twinkle in her blue eyes.

It was one of the children's favourite games to creep up on her to try to find the eyes in the back of her head. 'If only she'd go to sleep,' they said. Young Martha told the others she didn't think Aunty Nancy ever went to sleep. She was always there. If you knocked on her door day or night, she always seemed to be ready to handle any emergency immediately. Aunty Nancy was very special indeed.

That particular December evening Nancy was having a much-needed break from the boxes of toys kindly donated by the people of the north-east. Every year their kindness never failed to warm her heart. It had been a long day and she was enjoying a cup of tea and the slice of cake Cook had given her.

The room was warm and her eyes closed. Her head nodded forward. She dozed, happy in the knowledge that she could relax now. Everything was in hand. No catastrophes or last-minute panics expected this Christmas.

As Nancy slept, though, she became aware of the

strangest feeling that something wasn't right. Somewhere a child was crying.

Outside the window, the velvety sky, the moon and the stars looked down on Nancy as she dozed.

Slowly, and ever so gently, in her dreams Nancy's fingers moved and reached for the corner of her apron.

The Very Special Biscuit Box

It is not known exactly how many young children stood, terrified, at the gates of Nazareth House, wondering what life held in store for them. There had been many tears cried at the top of the driveway, and on more than one occasion a child's sobbing could be heard by people passing on Sandyford Road.

Today there was no sound at all. Maura Rogers, the local children's officer, had tried to chat to the little boy whose hand she was holding. It was a freezing cold day and she wanted to be inside quickly. It had taken an age to get to Nazareth House, and the trolley bus was draughty. As kindly as she could, she had tried to explain that he was going to an orphanage with lots of other children who had no mummy or daddy. It was then that Billy had stopped talking because he was unable to talk. His throat had closed. He hadn't understood much of what she was telling him but he knew what an orphan was. Daddy had read him a book called *Oliver Twist* last year. Oliver had been an orphan. Was Billy going to be all dirty and have to steal like the children in the book just so he could eat? Mummy and Daddy would be very cross indeed.

Standing at the top of the driveway, Maura looked at

the young child, who was completely silent. Billy's eyes were squeezed tight shut, terrified to look and see this awful place he was going to. He began to shake and his eyes were filling with tears and spilling down his cheeks, no matter how hard he tried not to let anyone see. 'Come along, Billy,' was all Maura could think of to say. 'They're expecting us, and I'm sure there'll be a lovely hot drink for you and something to eat.' Billy couldn't imagine anything he felt less like doing than eating. In fact, he thought he might be sick.

Maura didn't know that the phone lines were down so her office hadn't been able to contact Mother Superior. Nobody had any idea that they were on their way.

Billy's legs were shaking and he stumbled more than once, trying to walk with his eyes shut. When the lady had told him about the orphanage, she had said, 'Won't that be nice?' Billy wasn't sure that there was anything nice about it at all.

When they reached the bottom of the driveway he dared to open one eye, then the other. He had never seen such a huge house in his entire life. All those windows. To his left there was a wooded area with trees. To his right he saw a statue. Billy didn't know what it was, yet some tiny spark of hope ignited inside him. Many before him had felt that too. He lifted his eyes to the stars – but it was no good. Mummy and Daddy weren't there. He wasn't sure he believed they were in the sky at all. They certainly couldn't hear him because when he talked to them, they didn't answer.

Maura hurried to the large oak door, rang the bell and waited. 'Heavens, what an age they're taking,' she said, but Billy wasn't listening. His eyes kept being drawn to the room the moon was shining into. He began to tremble again as Maura once more put her finger on the bell and held it there. The sound made Billy jump, and once more he squeezed his eyes tightly shut.

Inside, there were hurried footsteps at the frantic ringing of the bell. Mother Superior opened her door and joined Sister Mary Joseph at the large oak door. That was when they saw Billy for the first time. A young child, obviously upset and frightened, with his eyes squeezed tightly shut.

The children's officer and her charge were invited in and, after Mother Superior had explained about the telephone line, Maura told her that the child would have to be left in their care. She had all the paperwork and there was simply nowhere else for him to go.

Mother turned to Sister Mary Joseph, but she was already running upstairs to the nursery department. 'Nancy,' she was muttering. 'We need Nancy.'

Mother started to tell her not to run but stopped when she saw the child open his eyes. Tears were trickling down his face yet he wasn't making a sound. She thought it was one of the saddest sights she had ever seen, and she had seen many.

She invited Maura and Billy into her room and asked them to sit down. Maura opened her bag and took out some papers, wanting to get this over and done with so that she could get home to her nice warm flat. Billy sat quietly with his head down, his tears no longer running down his cheeks but dropping straight from his eyes onto the carpet. Mother breathed a sigh of relief when she heard the nursery door open and more hurried footsteps.

A moment later, Nancy walked straight into the room.

'Thank you for knocking, Nancy,' Mother said, but the sarcasm went straight over her head.

Nancy looked at her. 'Parents?' she mouthed. Mother slowly shook her head.

Maura had stood up to leave, but Nancy took no notice of her. She went to Billy, knelt in front of him and lifted her apron to dry his tears. Billy looked into the most beautiful blue eyes he had ever seen. So soft, gentle and kind. The lady was smiling at him but not speaking. He liked that. He didn't want to talk.

Maura cleared her throat but nobody spoke. Mother was watching Nancy weave her magic, not for the first time, but it never failed to amaze her.

Maura was now tired and fed up. She had done what she came to do and she coughed again. 'I must be on my way,' she said. She looked at Nancy. 'Just needs taking out of himself,' she added, pulling on her gloves.

There was quite suddenly an icy silence. Nancy stood up and went over to Maura. Those soft and gentle eyes were now cold and hard as ice. 'Excuse me, taken out of himself? Oh, well, I'm glad that's all there is to it.'

'Well, erm, I just meant . . .'

'Yes, go on, do tell me,' said Nancy, coldly.

Mother Superior swiftly stood up and hustled Maura out of the room, thanking her for bringing the child and promising to sort out the necessary paperwork. They'd speak on the phone when the line was back in order.

Billy was watching Nancy and had stopped crying. She didn't seem scary at all and she was really nice and clean, not at all dirty like he had imagined. She reached down, scooped him up in her arms, then placed her hand gently on the back of his head, easing it down onto her shoulder. She felt his lips quivering on the side of her neck. She held him perfectly still for a few moments, then slowly rocked him from side to side.

Mother Superior watched Nancy carry the child up the parlour stairs in total silence to where Sister Mary Joseph was waiting in the nursery doorway. She had already prepared hot milk and biscuits for him, and a bed had been freshly made.

Nancy sat in the little kitchenette at the top of the stairs and put the radio on. 'Songs add a little warmth I always think,' she told Billy. She sat him on her magic knees and wiped away the last of his tears with the corner of her apron. 'There now, drink your milk,' she said, expecting to be obeyed, 'and we'll all have a biscuit.'

Sister Mary Joseph smiled at Nancy. 'Our favourites, do you think, Nancy?'

'Oh, indeed I do! Maybe even . . .'

'Not the chocolate ones. After all, they're for the very best occasions.'

'Mm, you have a point, Sister. Let me think.'

Billy was watching them, fascinated, as he sipped his milk.

'Yes, Sister, I really do think this calls for the very special biscuit box.'

Sister Mary Joseph reached up into the kitchen cupboard and lifted down the chocolate biscuits. 'Now, Nancy, how many do you think?'

'Half a biscuit each, would that be sufficient?'

They looked at Billy, who shook his head ever so slightly.

'Very well then. One each,' said Nancy.

'Surely two biscuits, don't you think, Nancy, as this is a very special occasion?'

'Three!' Billy shouted, then clapped his hand over his mouth.

Nancy burst out laughing. 'Very well,' she said. 'Three it is.' She hoped fervently that they wouldn't make him sick.

Billy drank his milk and ate his biscuits. Never before had he been allowed three biscuits before bedtime.

'Heavens above,' Nancy said, 'I've never seen biscuits gobbled up so quickly and not a crumb dropped. You'll eat us out of house and home at this rate!'

There was a small movement that Nancy did not miss. Little Billy had very nearly smiled. Nancy gave him a quick hug. 'Come along, darling,' she said, and they left the kitchen to walk along the corridor. Billy stopped as they passed the television room and peered out of the window. He glanced at Nancy, then turned back to the window.

'What is it?' she asked.

Billy let go of her hand, ran to the window and looked out.

Nancy turned off the big light, switched on the pretty Christmas-tree lights and went to stand behind him. She placed her hands gently on his shoulders and followed his gaze to the stars in the sky. Words were pointless, she knew, but one day he would tell her all about it. She had never failed a child yet and she wasn't about to start now.

Down the corridor in the little kitchen, the radio continued to play and a choir was singing 'Hark! The Herald Angels Sing' as the first flakes of snow fell onto the roof of Nazareth House.

Billy looked up at Nancy and smiled.

Her fingers touched the rosary beads with the Holy Cross that always lay in her apron pocket. She too looked up to the sky. 'Nice timing,' she said.

Snow at Last

The next morning, there was great excitement when the children discovered not only the snow but a new little boy in the nursery department. Nancy watched as they gathered around him, telling him about the playroom and asking what his favourite toys were. 'Trains,' he whispered. Sometimes it was the children themselves who helped ease the little ones into their new life.

Billy was smiling now but since that one word in the kitchen last night he had not spoken again until now. Oh well, it was Christmas in a few days and that would be a distraction for him. Nancy was sure there must be a toy train somewhere and promised herself she would have a look. This morning she'd wrap the little ones up warm and they could go out to play in the snow. Then this afternoon she'd get her treasure trove box out and they could make some more decorations. Nancy had all these thoughts running around her head as she prepared breakfast for the children. She'd find a special part for Billy in the nativity play on Christmas Eve. They were having a practice next week; she would think of something. In the meantime, tomorrow they would all go to the chapel to practise their carols. All of the children loved singing. Surely that would help cheer up the poor little mite.

'Usually Nancy's magic has worked by now,' Sister Mary Joseph told Mother Superior. 'The little lad still hasn't spoken.'

'His grief is deep, Sister,' Mother Superior replied. 'I fear it may take more than a little hot milk and a few biscuits to bring happiness back to his heart. Nancy will know what to do, and we can pray.'

Sister Mary Joseph made her way up to the nursery to help put hats, coats, scarves, outdoor shoes and gloves onto thirty-two children, which was no mean feat. It took nearly half an hour, and the noise as they clambered down the stairs that led to the garden could be heard in the chapel, where Mother Superior was praying quietly.

Mother thanked the Lord for the kindness of the people in the north-east. Every child will receive a present this year and today she had received a letter saying that a local company would like to put on a Christmas party for them at the orphanage. Even Santa would be there. Mother was so grateful. The children would be thrilled. Hopefully, this would cheer little Billy up.

She bent her head and carried on in silent prayer, thanking God not only for the gifts but for Nancy, who never asked for anything for herself. Not for the first time Mother wondered if she expected too much of

Nancy. She felt distracted this morning. She closed her eyes and tried to concentrate on her prayers. Suddenly she heard the children coming down the stairs and Nancy's voice shouting to them to be careful. Then came squeals of delight as they ran outside to play in the snow. Mother could see Nancy in her mind's eye, cheeks flushed, eyes sparkling as she ran around with them, loving every single moment of it. Her heart warmed and her mind wandered. Heavens above! she thought. This will never do. Once more she bent her head in prayer, but she was smiling.

Out in the garden, just as Mother had imagined, Nancy was chasing the children around the great oak tree. The tree had been there as long as anyone could remember. Later in the year the children sat beeneath its great branches, had picnics, gathered conkers and, on very special days, Nancy sat with them telling stories of magical adventures. Nancy, with a twinkle in her eyes, told the children it was a magic whispering conker tree and if you placed your hands on the great tree trunk and listened very carefully it would tell you stories.

The snow lay thick and as the children's voices carried all the way around the grounds, the tree looked on and shook in the breeze, its branches covering the children with snow, making them squeal even louder with excitement. Billy stood in the middle of the playground watching the children, stopping to look upwards every now and then.

What was it with the sky? Nancy wondered. She could help if only he would tell her what was bothering him. Yet she had the feeling Billy could not be hurried. He would tell her in time. Maybe he would tell Santa at the party. She hoped fervently that he would be talking by then. She left the children running around, went to him and took his hand. Together they began to make a snowman and his eyes were shining. He was even smiling, but still not talking. Nancy chatted to him, telling him about the party and how excited the children were about the nativity play.

After lunch, the children played with the bits-and-bobs box, making decorations for the nativity. Yesterday Nancy had been upstairs in the attic and brought down the box of figures for the crib. She had taken care of them lovingly. She had never forgotten December 1945 and how it felt to be back home: she had been evacuated to Carlisle with the children to be at a safe distance from the bombing. That was the first Christmas after their return and it was hard to tell who was the most excited, Nancy or the children. The chapel was once more full of happy children, alongside the crib, the Star of Bethlehem above the stable, Joseph with the wonky head and the three-legged donkey. Nancy had never seen anything so wonderful in her entire life and she would never forget it as long as she lived. Many offers had been made to buy a new set of figures but Nancy was adamant in her refusal. Every year out they came a little more battered and glued together than they had been the previous year. They were perfectly wonderful; 'Nancy's treasures', everyone called them.

This afternoon the children were covered with glitter and glue but, most important, little Billy was joining in. They would have the last of the decorations ready before it was time for carol practice. Nancy tipped out the bag in her hand onto the table. 'Now then,' she said, 'who wants to help make the Christmas stars?' Lots of the children jumped up excitedly, but Billy burst into tears.

Nancy did all she could to stem the flow as she sat him on her knee and rocked him back and forth. What on earth was it with the sky and the stars? 'I know,' she said, suddenly thinking about the nativity play and how he could take part. 'Listen, Billy,' she said. 'I've just thought of something special that you could be in the play. It's not something everyone can do. It's an extremely important job.' She saw that she had his attention and he had stopped crying.

'Billy, are you listening to me?'

He nodded.

'Oh, I forgot! Billy, you have to be able to smile. Could you try that for me?'

Billy looked up at her and gave her a very small smile, which melted her heart.

'Well now, Billy darling, how would you like to be the Bethlehem Star?'

Little Billy Miller's screams could be heard all along the orphanage corridors.

The Boy Who Could Not Sing

Sister Mary Joseph had looked everywhere for Nancy. It was unusual for her not to be exactly where she always was, in the nursery. Sister Mary Joseph knew Nancy was upset at what had happened that afternoon. It had taken quite some time to calm Billy down, and in the end he had cried himself to sleep. Nancy had sat on the edge of his bed, stroking his hair, until she was sure he was settled.

Her heart was heavy as she made her way to her own bedroom at the end of the corridor. She loved her room. The window looked out onto the chapel roof and the bell that rang every morning at six o'clock. To the left of the window stood a large built-in cupboard full of Nancy's treasures and her very special button box. To the right there was a large wardrobe where her clothes hung in perfect order. Her bed, with the pretty blue counterpane, stood in a corner. A small table occupied the middle of the room, with a chair at either side. Today, Nancy's eyes strayed to the dressing-table with the little holy pictures stuck on the mirror.

She sat on her bed and looked at them. 'I give up,' she told them. 'I have no idea what to do. Heavens above, the things I've had to do over the years, the ideas

I've had to come up with. Magical singing ironing boards, mermaids, enchanted clocks. Never have I let a child down, ever.' Nancy began to feel sad. 'Come on then,' she said to her pictures, 'give me a helping hand. It's Christmas, a time for magic and miracles, so get on with it please.'

It was getting dark and Nancy had no idea how long she'd sat in her room feeling sorry for herself. She lifted her apron and dabbed at her eyes, then went down to the chapel. As she passed she heard the children in the dining room having tea. Sister Mary Joseph was an angel, she thought. Nancy never had to tell her how she was feeling or what needed to be done. They had lived and worked together so long there was no need.

Nancy opened the chapel door and closed it quietly behind her. Only the altar lights were on and some candles were flickering in the darkness. She made her way over, lit another candle, then went to kneel at the altar. She didn't bend her head in prayer, instead she looked directly up at the Cross of Our Lord. 'Help me,' she said. 'You've never let me down before. Please don't let me down now. This child has nobody. He has lost his parents and grandmother. There is absolutely no one else. He looks to the sky constantly and I need to know why and, dear God, please tell me what I said to upset him today. I'm failing him, Lord.' She stayed for a while in the chapel, then returned to the nursery. When she got there, she found that Billy had woken and Sister Mary Joseph had given him his tea. He seemed a little happier.

She was determined that she would find a way to persuade little Billy to tell her what was bothering him. The children had all had a wonderful time today, and were now about to go to the chapel to practise their carols. Music always cheered people up, Nancy thought. Billy walked with the other children into the chapel and took his place alongside them by the altar.

Cook popped into chapel to tell the children she had an enchanted wooden spoon that simply whizzed round the bowl to make cakes when they sang. The problem was, she told them, it was a very thick wall between the kitchen and the chapel. They would need to sing really loudly because the louder they sang the faster the spoon would spin round. Billy's eyes, like those of all the other children, were wide and sparkled with images of an enchanted wooden spoon. Nancy smiled at Cook and mouthed, 'Thank you.' It was working at last. The Lord had answered her prayers.

Nancy nodded at Sister Mary Joseph who hurried upstairs to take her place at the organ. 'Now then, children, as loud as you can so that Cook can hear you sing.' The organ boomed out the introduction to 'Away in a Manger' and the children began to sing.

Cook's heart was full of joy as she whipped up fairy cakes, but Nancy's was sinking fast. Little Billy had opened his mouth to sing and Nancy almost held her breath. Nothing came out. He tried again, but still nothing happened. Little Billy Miller could not sing. It took all Nancy's resolve not to rush forward to the altar and grab him in her arms. Instead she brought the practice to an end and hustled them all upstairs to the dining room to enjoy their cakes.

Goodness knows how long Nancy stayed in the chapel afterwards, going over everything that had happened since Billy had arrived. 'I've missed something, Lord,' she prayed aloud. 'I've tried my best, you know I have. It's over to you now.'

She stood up, smoothed her clothes and patted her hair. She walked down the aisle but stopped when she reached the door and turned once more to face the altar. 'Don't forget now. Send something to cheer him up.'

As the chapel fell silent, the moon shone through the stained-glass windows on a lone figure sitting quietly in the darkness. Mother Superior looked up at the cross, but just as Billy had been unable to sing, she was unable to speak for the lump in her throat. Her lips moved in silent prayer.

As the snow fell over Newcastle that night, and the stars continued to twinkle in a velvet sky, there was no way of knowing how all their prayers would be answered.

The Doll's House

It had been a busy week and by eight a.m. on Christmas Eve Nancy felt worn to a frazzle. 'Happy Christmas Eve,' sang Sister Mary Joseph, bouncing into the dining room. 'Ooh, who's excited about Santa then?' she said to the children.

They all shouted at once.

'Me! Me!'

'Oh, I am, Sister.'

'Hooray for Christmas.'

'Santa's coming! Santa's coming!'

'I'm going to ask for a doll's house, Sister.'

Nancy momentarily closed her eyes and took a deep breath. 'Thank you, Sister. I've only just in the last five minutes managed to calm them down enough to eat their breakfast.'

'Oh, Nancy, come on now, surely you're excited about Santa coming.'

Nancy looked around the room at the excited children. She walked slowly to Sister Mary Joseph and placed her hands on her shoulders. 'Santa swans in here to the children's Christmas party, ho-ho-hoing, with a sack of presents to excite the children even more on Christmas Eve when, dear God, it's hard enough to get them to sleep. The girls have all been wanting their hair plaited since six this morning, and the boys got out of control while I was trying to do it. We're all late for breakfast, and you know how cross Cook can get. Now, Sister, if you can have a word with the big man and tell him to get here early, throw off his lovely red cloak, dress the children for the party, play with them and help out with the other million chores that have to be done today instead of swanning in and plonking himself down on a chair for an hour, I'll be more than pleased to see him.'

Sister Mary Joseph giggled. 'Oh, Nancy.'

'Never mind oh-Nancy. Here,' she said, handing her a large serving spoon. 'You serve breakfast while I calm them down.'

Nancy usually loved Christmas Eve, full of promise and excitement, but Santa Claus arriving meant only one thing and her heart had sunk when she had been given the news. The nativity play, which was traditionally first performed on Christmas Eve, had taken place the night before and Nancy wasn't pleased. She liked to stick to tradition and be organised. Still, the local company was giving the children a party and Nancy was not ungrateful. It was a wonderful idea, of course it was, except for the one thing nobody had thought of.

All around the world children were whispering to Santa their hopes, wishes and dreams, and their parents would try their best to ensure their little ones had exactly what they wanted in the Christmas stockings hanging at the end of their beds. How could you do that for a nursery full of children? It was impossible. Nancy had spent many Christmas Eves at Nazareth House and knew that every child would want something different. She had tried hard over the years until she had come up with a solution. Each year she would go through the toys that arrived and pick out something quite special. She would then begin to place the idea in each child's mind that 'It would be wonderful to have a whatever-it-was' from Santa. Usually it worked quite well. It was perhaps a little unfair, she supposed, but it would be worse for them to think Santa hadn't sent what they had asked for.

Two weeks ago Nancy had seen a big van coming down the driveway and wondered what on earth it could be. She'd hurried along the corridor and peered down the staircase to see what was going on. Mother Superior was making her way towards the oak door when she called, 'Nancy, please don't hang around on the staircase. Come down and see what treasures we are to receive today.' It seemed Mother Superior, too, had eyes in the back of her head.

Mother had received a telephone call earlier that day asking if donations of gifts could be dropped off for the children. When they arrived, the van driver and his mate were offered tea but graciously declined. 'Just happy to bring these along,' they said, and Mother thanked them. She never ceased to be amazed at people's generosity. Nancy and she between them carried all the boxes into the parlour but the last was too heavy so old Mr Bell, the caretaker, had been summoned.

'What is it, do you think?' Nancy had kept asking, as he pushed it into the middle of the parlour and began to open the box. Nancy and Mother stood together, almost holding their breath, as they waited. Mr Bell carefully sliced all around the top of the box until finally the sides fell down.

Mother and Nancy gasped. It was the most beautiful doll's house they had ever seen. Nancy dropped to her knees and Mother leaned forward to watch as Nancy held the tiny door handle and the house opened. The nuns by now had heard the commotion and were all hurrying across to the parlour and gathered around Nancy. There were gasps of 'Oh!', 'How on earth do they make furniture so small?', and 'Oh, Nancy, look at the tiny beds! It's just like the nursery.'

Nancy simply sat staring at the most beautiful doll's house in the world.

There was silence as they all stood in the parlour, looking for all the world like they were frozen in time, until eventually Nancy sat back then turned to them. 'Well,' she said, 'I am absolutely lost for words.'

'That must a first,' said Mother Superior, and all the nuns burst out laughing.

'And the last,' said Nancy, laughing with them.

'This is a wonderful day,' she said to them all. Old Mr Bell was looking extremely uncomfortable. He didn't like being in the parlour. He was asked to put the doll's house somewhere safe until Christmas Eve and was relieved to get away.

Nancy almost skipped up the stairs. This would be the special present that the children could ask Santa for, she thought, and straight away began to plant the idea in their heads. Over the next few days she told the children stories about doll's houses, the tiny beds and other furniture just like theirs, and waited. Eventually, it was Martha who said, 'Ooh, Aunty Nancy, wouldn't it be wonderful if Santa brought us a doll's house?'

The children all began to agree at once. 'Like the one in the story you told us,' they said. 'Tell it again.'

Nancy was extremely pleased with herself. After story time she leaned forward and said to the children, 'You know, there is only one way I can think of that we could get a doll's house in the nursery for Christmas.'

'Tell us!' they cried.

'We need to get some paper and a pen and write a letter to Father Christmas asking for one. Shall we do that, children?' The next couple of hours in the playroom went quickly as, first, Nancy wrote the letter and then the children covered themselves in glitter and glue as they made pictures to send to Santa with the letter. Nancy walked around the playroom, happy in the knowledge that this particular dream would come true for them. 'We can ask Santa at the party for a doll's house just to make sure,' she said.

Sister Mary Joseph smiled when she walked into the playroom and saw Nancy beaming from ear to ear, her bright blue eyes sparkling. 'You look even happier than the children,' she told Nancy.

'Oh, I am, Sister,' she replied. 'Isn't Christmas just wonderful?'

'Aunty Nancy,' Tommy shouted, from the corner, his arms folded.

'Yes, darling,' sang Nancy.

'I don't want a doll's house. I want a bike.'

Sister Mary Joseph and Nancy looked at each other in stunned silence, then slowly turned to Mother Superior, who was standing in the doorway.

'Well, that's wiped the smiles off your faces,' she said.

Old Mr Bell

Nancy was not going to be beaten easily. Something would turn up.

The very next day, Sister Theresa came hurrying along the corridor, calling Nancy's name. 'Come quickly! Come and see what has arrived! God has blessed us.'

'What on earth is going on?' Nancy said, steadfastly refusing to move from her room where, for once, she was enjoying a quiet moment and a cup of tea.

'Come along, Nancy! Hurry!' said Sister Theresa again.

'What is the hurry, may I ask?' Nancy said with a sigh.

'We've had a delivery of second-hand toys.'

Nancy ran along the corridor and down the stairs to where the pile of toys was lying in the middle of the parlour floor. All eyes were on Nancy as the nuns stood waiting to see what she would think.

'Oh my,' was all Nancy could think of to say.

There, in the centre of the room, were two old wooden children's bicycles.

The nuns turned when they heard Sister Mary Joseph coming down the stairs.

'I've heard all about it! Oh, is that it? Nancy, where did they come from?'

'Some scrapyard, I imagine, Sister. What do you say, Mother?'

'Well, they are just a little battered, Nancy.'

'A little bit battered, Mother! Battered, bruised and broken would be a better description. Please will somebody tell me what in God's name I'm supposed to do with them?' Nancy had to give the Lord credit. She had prayed for a bike. But these were not *quite* what she'd had in mind.

The nuns all looked at each other but nobody had any answers. 'Oh, for Heaven's sake!' Nancy said, exasperated, and had to be reminded that she was in the nuns' parlour.

'Peace and order, Nancy.' Mother smiled, but suddenly Nancy was gone. Mother hurried to the window and watched her running up the driveway to disappear into the wood. She sighed. They would all simply wait for her return. How she loved Nancy. A force to be reckoned with – and sometimes, she had to admit, difficult to handle, yet she had managed to weave her way into the hearts of everyone at the orphanage, most especially the children. It was always all about the children, Mother knew that, which was why she forgave Nancy so much. Just a short while later Mother watched Nancy currying back down the driveway, then enter the parlour with a huge grin. 'All in order,' she said, a little out of breath.

A few moments later Mr Bell shuffled in, as usual looking most uncomfortable at being in the nuns' quarters. He liked his cottage and the grounds. He had a little workshop there and saw no need to go to the big house unless some maintenance task was needed.

Nancy pointed at the bicycles. 'Well?' she said. 'What do you think?'

Mr Bell grunted. He folded his arms and stared at the two battered objects.

A few more minutes passed and Nancy was getting fed up. 'Well?' she said again.

There was still no answer. Mr Bell continued to stare at the bikes. Mother gave her a warning look. Except for the tick-tick-tick of the hallway clock there was utter silence in the parlour as they all stared at the broken second-hand bikes. Mother jumped and Nancy let out a little squeal when suddenly Mr Bell leaned forward, grabbed the bicycles and marched across the parlour and out of the door a bike in each hand.

'Well I never,' said Mother.

'All will be well now, I think,' said Nancy, and returned to the nursery.

Old Mr Bell's cottage, with a weathervane on the roof, was behind the wooded area that ran down the left-hand side of the driveway. Nobody could say how long he had lived there or what his own story was because he had never told them. There was sadness in his brown eyes, yet there was a kindness and gentleness too. There was nothing Mr Bell couldn't fix. The heating system at Nazareth House ran perfectly, and he would mend broken pots, burned pans, anything electrical, and replace tiles on the roof. He dealt with frozen pipes, too. His cottage had no central heating but he had a roaring coal fire in his living room and another in the bedroom. In the kitchen, he would put his oven on to heat the place up. His favourite place to sit was in front of the living-room fire with his boots off and his feet on the hearth as the flames crackled. Then he would listen to his wireless and light his pipe. There was a photograph of a young child on the mantelpiece and sometimes he would stare at it for hours before drifting off to sleep.

For three days nobody saw or heard from him, and Nancy was losing patience. She had knocked on the door more than once but old Mr Bell had ignored her. Nancy was in the garden getting a little fresh air one day when she saw smoke billowing from his chimney. He must be so lonely, she thought, yet he never sought company. Suddenly, his door opened and, seeing her, he beckoned. At last, she thought, hurrying over to the cottage. 'Do I come in?' she called. Mr Bell stood aside.

'I will take that as a yes then,' Nancy said, and for the first time she stepped into Mr Bell's home. He gestured towards the living room and followed her. Nancy went in – and there they were. Her eyes filled with tears and for the second time in a week she was unable to speak. Together, side by side, Nancy and Mr Bell stood in front of his fire, and in the light of the flames there stood two of the most beautiful bright blue wooden bikes. Not only had he fixed them, he had also painted them. He spoke suddenly. 'Blue for boys,' he said. 'Yes?'

'Oh, yes!' said Nancy. 'Yes, yes, yes.'

Nancy ran all the way down the driveway and burst into the parlour, breathless. 'All in order, Nancy?' Mother asked.

Nancy's smile said it all.

'Thank you, Lord,' she whispered. 'Now, about little Billy . . .'

Nancy went back to the nursery to continue with the party and Christmas preparations. All was going well yet something was nagging at the back of her mind and she simply couldn't think what it was. Then she stopped what she was doing. 'Well now,' she said to herself. 'I wonder who that child in the photograph was on Mr Bell's mantelpiece. There's a story there, no doubt.' But Nancy felt it would be too intrusive to ask. 'Well now, I wonder,' she whispered again.

Santa Comes to Town

Christmas Eve dawned and somehow Nancy had the children all washed, dressed and ready before the party started at three o'clock.

It had been a long day for the children, who were now beyond excited at the thought of jelly and ice cream, as well as a visit from Santa Claus. Even Billy was smiling and seemed to be enjoying himself.

Earlier that day cars had arrived laden with toys, games and prizes for the children, and Nancy had helped to sort them out for the girls and boys. The party was to be held in the large juniors' room downstairs and Santa's grotto was in one corner covered with tinsel and red paper. Cook had been up since five, making cakes, jelly and sandwiches for the children, and at three o'clock, when Nancy came to see how she was getting on, she was in a state of collapse. 'Oh, Cook,' Nancy said, laughing, 'you look like you've been dragged through a hedge backwards.'

'Oh, really?' Cook replied. 'Says the woman standing in front of me with red tissue sticking to her shoe, covered in glitter, and I do believe that's a piece of jam on your cardigan.' They looked at each other and burst out laughing. 'Take the food and get out,' said Cook, throwing a tea towel at Nancy.

By the time Nancy returned to the room the children from the junior department and the nursery were all there and the madness and mayhem were in full swing. The people who had arranged the party were running round in circles, trying to keep some sort of order. Nancy thought it was hilarious and went to sit at the table with Mother Superior and the nuns. A slice of cake and a cup of tea while they watched the children have the time of their lives: what a wonderful way to spend an afternoon.

Most of the party games were a great success, but persuading the children to sit in a circle for Pass the Parcel was not. Nancy had to intervene. 'Really, children!' she exclaimed. 'Circle now.' The children all sat down.

'How does she do it?' Sister Mary Joseph whispered.

'No idea,' said Mother, smiling.

At four thirty the children were told Santa was on his way but they had to sit very quietly or he wouldn't come. There wasn't a sound in the room and every eye was on the door. Mother took Nancy's hand and squeezed it. The children sat completely still, their eyes as big as saucers. This was Christmas magic at its best. 'You see, Nancy?' Mother said. 'Maybe having the party on Christmas Eve wasn't such a bad idea after all.'

'You know, Mother, you might just be right on this one occasion,' Nancy replied.

Mother raised her eyebrows. 'Just this once, Nancy?'

At that point the room erupted into screams that

could be heard as far as Sandyford Road as Santa made his entrance.

The helpers were trying desperately to get the children into an organised line – not a job for the faint-hearted – and Nancy hurried forward to help. The noise was so loud you had to shout to be heard. 'At least they'll get it all out of their systems and be worn out by bedtime,' Nancy yelled to Sister Mary Joseph.

The room was awash with wrapping paper as the children ripped open their gifts from Santa. Nancy, naturally, was running around picking it all up. One of the helpers tapped her on the shoulder and said, 'Please let us do that. We can tidy up afterwards.'

'Tidy up?' said Nancy. 'I'm not tidying up! I'm gathering all the paper to make decorations next Christmas.' She hurried off to her attic of treasures to put it all in a box. Waste not, want not, was Nancy's motto.

She made it back in time to see the last of the nursery children receiving their gifts from Santa. Mother Superior and Sister Mary Joseph stood at each side of his chair so they could hear the children telling him what they wanted for Christmas. Nancy made her way over with a question in her eyes and Mother nodded. All had gone to plan. One by one they had whispered their hopes and dreams to Santa.

'A doll's house, please, Santa.'

'Please can I have lots of pretty doll furniture.'

'A doll's house, Santa, just like in Aunty Nancy's stories.'

'Furniture with little beds, please, Santa.'

'A blue bike to ride around the playroom.'

Nancy stretched her hand out to Billy, who was last in the queue. 'Go on, darling,' she said.

Billy stood for a moment, then walked right up to Santa.

'Well, young man, what would you like for Christmas.'

Billy grinned and his eyes twinkled for the very first time since he'd arrived at the orphanage.

'Oh, how wonderful,' said Mother, making the sign of the cross in thanks.

'Oh, isn't Christmas just magic, Mother?' said Sister Mary Joseph.

Santa smiled at Billy and leaned forward.

Mother and Sister Mary Joseph leaned in closer as Billy whispered in Santa's ear. 'Please, Santa, I would like a train for Christmas.'

Everyone looked at Nancy.

'Oh, joy,' she said.

Answered Prayers

After the party there was pandemonium. The children were all overexcited, except the two who were asleep on pillows in the corner. Nancy hurried over to them. Sister Mary Joseph saw the look of thunder on her face and tried to escape, but bumped into Mother Superior. 'Sorry, Mother – have you seen Nancy's face? This means trouble, although I can't think why.'

Nancy was waking the sleeping pair, who began to cry as all the other children took the opportunity to begin running around the room.

Sister Mary Joseph bravely turned to her. 'I thought they needed a little sleep.'

'Oh, did you, Sister? And on the one night of the year, you know, it being Christmas Eve, when I struggle to get them off to sleep, with all the excitement, you thought it would be good to let them sleep just before bedtime, did you?'

Sister Mary Joseph's shoulders sagged and Nancy felt ashamed. She hadn't any idea how she would manage without Sister Mary Joseph, especially as Dolly, her helper, was away visiting family tonight. 'Come on, Sister,' she said, 'let's get the children upstairs without getting battered and bruised if we can.'

The children all clambered up the stairs leading to the nursery. As they started up the stairs, there were cries of 'Aunty Nancy, I feel sick!' and 'I need carried,' and 'She kicked me!' and 'I don't want to go to bed!' And so it went on. It took a back-breaking two hours to get them all bathed and into their pyjamas and Nancy was feeling out of sorts. Normally she took everything in her stride.

Sister Mary Joseph wondered what was wrong, but they were so busy there was no time to ask. Maybe when the children were settled they could have a much-needed cup of tea together and put their feet up. 'Feet up and a cuppa,' she said. 'How wonderful.'

'Yes, about midnight that will be, at this rate,' shouted Nancy, over the din.

Eventually, after a lot of fuss and many tears, the children went to the dining room to choose biscuits and a glass of milk for Santa and the reindeer. There was an argument as to which biscuit was best, and then someone spilled the milk. Nancy closed her eyes and counted to ten. 'Just remind me whose idea it was to have a Christmas party today,' she said, but she was smiling. 'Come along, children,' she called. 'Santa will be here again in no time at all and those not in bed won't get presents.'

'What if he doesn't come back?' one child, Mary, asked. 'He might forget us tonight if he's already been here.'

Normally Nancy would have come up with a

plausible explanation as to why he would not forget, but not tonight. 'You see, Sister Mary Joseph, what happens when you go against tradition?'

Mary opened her mouth to ask again, but Nancy swept her up and into bed, kissed her and said, 'It's magic and that's that.'

As the children settled, Nancy's eyes turned to Billy. He was smiling and her heart sank. Was it because he thought Santa would bring him a train? she wondered. He was still hardly talking. How would he feel if he thought Santa had forgotten him? She still hadn't found out why the sky fascinated him. What on earth am I to do? she worried, as she fussed about getting the children tucked in. Really, this year had been sorted out. There had been no worries about toys for the children because plenty of donations had come through. All the gifts were wrapped. 'How can everything go so wrong?' she muttered to herself. She sighed, then went down the corridor to the kitchen where Sister Mary Joseph was waiting for her.

'Kettle's whistling,' Sister called, when she heard Nancy's footsteps, but after a couple of minutes had passed and Nancy hadn't appeared, she popped her head around the door. The corridor was empty. Sister Mary Joseph checked everywhere, the dormitory, the playroom, the television room, the dining room, then knocked on Nancy's door. No answer. Where on earth could she be?

At that moment the door at the top of the nursery stairs opened and Mother Superior came through. 'Is something wrong?' she asked.

'Oh, Mother, it's Nancy. She was walking down the corridor, then disappeared.'

'Ah,' said Mother. 'I think I know where she may be. I heard a bit of a commotion in the attic as I was walking up the stairs. Maybe we should check there.' Slowly they made their way up the stairs as the crashing and clattering above them got louder. 'Nancy,' Mother called, as she reached the top of the attic staircase.

Nancy was sitting among what seemed like hundreds of boxes full of old toys and anything else she had decided shouldn't be thrown away. She was covered with dust and her face was flushed. 'Nancy, whatever is the matter?' Mother said. She tried to get closer to Nancy to comfort her, but it was impossible with all those boxes on the floor.

Nancy looked up. Mother's heart hurt to see the expression on her face. 'Oh, Mother, I can't find a train. There isn't even a book about trains. I should have remembered Billy told the children his favourite toys were trains when he first arrived. Now he's asked Santa for one and I simply don't know what to do. Oh, poor Billy.'

Mother Superior pushed aside the boxes and reached for Nancy's hand without a word. She understood how she felt. That was enough.

Mother and Sister Mary Joseph insisted on helping Nancy to clear up as she wouldn't leave her treasures in a mess, and after a good half-hour everything was back in order. The three made their way to the nursery kitchenette for a fresh pot of tea. It should have been an evening of laughter and excitement but it was a sad threesome who sat quietly together.

'He still doesn't say much,' Nancy told Mother. 'I can't get him to talk to me. I've never failed a child yet, Mother, and I don't want little Billy to be the first.'

Mother patted her hand. 'God will find a way,' she said.

'Well, He'd better get a move because it's Christmas Day tomorrow,' Nancy said angrily. They cleared up together and Mother told Nancy they would all pray at the service later that night, then made her way downstairs with an extremely heavy heart.

It was dark in Nancy's room so she lit the little lamp in the corner, then sat on the edge of her bed looking at her holy pictures. She bowed her head in prayer. 'Help me,' she said.

Later that evening she made her way downstairs and through the big door that led to the chapel. It looked so peaceful. There were lots of candles lit all around her and the nativity crib stood on the altar. Nancy sighed as she made the sign of the cross and went to sit beside Sister Mary Joseph at the front. The sound of the nuns in prayer was soothing as she gazed up at the cross above the altar. It's Christmas Eve. Please help me, she prayed, over and over again. A short while later, when the prayers were over, Mother told the sisters to leave and have their supper. 'I will follow shortly.'

There was silence in the chapel as Mother went to sit next to Nancy. Nancy cares so much, she thought, but then she always had. Mother had lost count of all the times Nancy had been called on to calm an unruly child, wipe their tears and make presents out of nothing but rags and buttons. Experience told her that no words would comfort Nancy: it was a miracle they needed. They sat quietly for a while until Mother patted Nancy's hand. 'Come along. Come and share supper with us. We cannot have you with a heavy heart on Christmas Eve.'

Mother looked around her. 'The chapel looks especially splendid this year, Nancy. You've done a wonderful job. The decorations are beautiful. The children have all worked extremely hard. You must be so proud of them.' Mother knew the only thing that calmed Nancy was to talk about the children. 'I'm sure the lady mayor will thoroughly enjoy the nativity play. There are more people than I imagined coming this year.' Mother continued to chat as they made their way up the aisle. 'We may even have to bring in some extra chairs,' she said.

Suddenly Nancy stopped and grabbed Mother's hand. 'Chairs!' she shouted. 'Oh, Mother, chairs! Thank you, God, thank you, thank you, thank you.'

'Really, Nancy!' Mother was shocked. 'Please remember where we are!' But Nancy was gone. Mother stood alone in the silence. She turned to face the Cross of Our Lord and smiled, then bowed her head and left for her supper.

The Ragdoll Express

Nancy's heart was beating fast. As she raced up the nursery stairs she had to stop and take a breath. She burst through the door and found Sister Mary Joseph, ready to join the other nuns for supper. She saw Nancy's flushed face. 'Oh, Nancy, whatever now?'

'Chairs, Sister Mary Joseph! Chairs.'

'Chairs, Nancy?'

Nancy was grinning as she grabbed Sister Mary Joseph's hand and dragged her towards the dining room. Once there, Nancy picked up two of the little chairs and put them beside each other. Then another two behind them, and she repeated the process until suddenly Sister Mary Joseph squealed with delight. 'Oh, Nancy, how clever of you.' She picked up her rosary beads and kissed them.

'Come along, Sister, we have work to do,' said Nancy. 'I promise you tea and an extremely large piece of Cook's cake for supper in the kitchen afterwards.'

'Well now,' said Sister Mary Joseph, 'who could say no to that?'

Sister Mary Joseph was on lookout at the door of the dormitory as Nancy quietly carried the chairs one by one into the long corridor, placing them in a line, two by two, with one special chair at the front. As the children slept soundly, Nancy wrote each child's name on a slip of paper, then put one on each chair. Only one name was missing. Nancy smiled and wrote it down, then placed it on the seat at the front. Together Sister Mary Joseph and Nancy crept up and down the corridor draping tinsel along the sides of the chairs. They stood back and admired their handiwork. 'It's missing something,' Nancy whispered, and together they stood looking at the train, wondering what it could be. 'I know,' Nancy mouthed, and hurried off. Sister Mary Joseph closed her eyes and dreamed of a hot cup of tea and a slice of cake. She leaned against the passage wall, opened her eyes and looked longingly down the corridor, hoping Nancy wouldn't be long.

Ten minutes later, Nancy was back, waving something in her hands. 'Remember summer, Sister, when we had all the games in the school playground? Well, look what I found!'

'Well done!' Sister Mary Joseph said.

'Come along now, Sister,' Nancy whispered. 'Let's go and have that cup of tea.'

'Not forgetting the cake!'

Nancy laughed. 'Definitely not forgetting the cake, Sister.' She turned the big lights off in the corridor, leaving only a dim lamp at the end. As they walked away, Nancy paused only once, to place the very special gift on the chair at the front.

*

It was nearly midnight when they washed up their cups and plates. 'Happy Christmas, Sister,' said Nancy, but Sister Mary Joseph was already yawning, on her way to the nuns' quarters and her much-needed bed.

Nancy went to her room, far too excited to feel sleepy. The moon shone through the many windows along the corridor and lit the tinsel, which sparkled in the dark. There it stood in all its glory: 'Welcome aboard the Christmas train,' she said, smiling.

As she got ready for bed she looked upon her holy pictures. 'You cut that one a bit fine,' she said. She lay down, thinking she would never sleep. Nancy was wrong. She was asleep almost as soon as her head hit the pillow.

She was woken at six by the bell ringing from the chapel roof outside her bedroom window and jumped out of bed. She dressed hastily, then ran along the corridor to see to the children. There was great excitement as they leaped up to grab the beautifully decorated socks hanging at the end of each bed. Nancy had sewn pretty ribbon onto them and a little bell. Oranges and sweets for everyone, handkerchiefs for the girls, little toy cars for the boys. Then the children's eyes fell upon the presents in the middle of the floor.

Sister Mary Joseph arrived just as Martha shouted, 'Look! It's a doll's house!' The children all ran over to it, shrieking with delight over the tiny furniture. Meanwhile the boys had spotted the bikes and were now riding round the dormitory, squealing with excitement. Billy sat on his bed and watched. Nancy thought she had never seen a sadder sight in her entire life. She hadn't the heart to disturb them yet so she let them continue to play for a little longer, then went over to Billy's bed. 'You know, I do believe I heard Santa in the corridor last night. I can't think why he was there, can you?' Billy shook his head. 'Maybe he was leaving something special for you.' Still no answer. Nancy picked Billy up and swung him around. 'It's Christmas Day, little Billy Miller, and I know for sure there's something just outside this door that's for nobody but you. Now, do you want to know what it is?' Billy nodded. 'Then tell me,' Nancy said, and waited.

'Yes, Aunty Nancy,' he replied quietly, but with a little smile.

Nancy gathered the children around her. 'There is something very special in the corridor. Come along, children, hurry now.' She put Billy down, grabbed his hand and together they made their way into the corridor.

Nancy almost held her breath. The children were all shouting at once but she hushed them. Billy walked slowly forward and touched one of the chairs. Then the children began shouting once more.

'Santa must have been ever so quiet!'

'Can we play with it now?'

'What is it?'

Billy turned to face them all with a huge grin 'It's a train,' he said. 'It's a train, it's a train, it's a train!'

There was chaos and excitement as they ran around in the corridor, Nancy and Sister Mary Joseph helping them to find their names on the labels and sitting in their own seats on the Christmas train. Billy ran up and down, looking more and more puzzled that no one had taken him to his seat. He went up to Nancy, who took his hand and led him to the seat at the front of the train. 'Do you know what that word says?' she asked Billy. He shook his head. 'It says "driver". That's you, Billy.' There was only a moment's pause before Billy sat down. There was one more surprise. It was on the seat beside him. He looked at it, then back at Nancy. 'It's on your seat so it must be for you. Go on, Billy, open it.' The children all leaned forward, trying to see what the special gift was. He ripped the paper off and held it up for them all to see.

'It's a whistle!' the children shouted. 'Go on, Billy, blow it!' There was a piercing shriek as little Billy blew it for all he was worth, and Nancy hastily covered her ears. He still had little to say but he was smiling and his eyes were bright with joy for the first time since he had arrived.

'What's the train called?' the children were shouting now.

Nancy thought for a moment. 'How about the Ragdoll Express?'

'Yippee!' the children shouted, as Billy blew the whistle once more.

Nancy could not have been happier. The children were

all still in their night clothes but were having the time of their lives. For the first time in the history of Nazareth House, Christmas breakfast would be late and Cook would not be pleased, but Nancy didn't care one jot. She walked over to Billy and ruffled his hair. 'Where to then, Billy?' she said.

Billy turned his head to look out of the window and pointed to the sky.

Nancy understood perfectly.

'To the stars in the sky it is then.' She smiled as Billy lifted the whistle to his mouth and blew it again.

To the Stars and Back Again

Nancy had no idea how long the fun on the train went on for. They travelled round the moon, visited the zoo, journeyed to the other side of the world – the train crossed the seas on enchanted railway tracks – then whizzed up a mountain and whooshed down the other side. The excitement of the children echoed off the walls as they sang and called out where they wanted to go next.

It was the frantic ringing of a bell that brought Nancy to her senses. In the dining room a dumb-waiter lift carried food from the kitchen. Cook would ring the bell downstairs to let everyone know breakfast was ready and Nancy would pull a rope to bring up the food. Cook had been ringing furiously for a good half-hour and was now extremely angry. The breakfast would be getting cold, and with lunch to prepare she was not going to heat it again. Now the ringing of the bell could be heard all around the house.

Mother Superior, who was in the chapel, raised her head and wondered what on earth was going on. She'd thought she'd heard a whistle blowing earlier and a bell ringing. Now she heard the bell again and sighed as she left the chapel to find out what was happening.

At the same time Sister Mary Joseph was running along the corridor, shouting to Nancy that Cook was ringing the bell and sounded very angry. Nancy simply laughed. 'Look at their little faces, Sister. See how happy they all are.' Sister Mary Joseph and Nancy looked at Billy, who sat at the front of the train as the children called out destinations. He would then blow the whistle, signalling their departure on a new journey. His eyes were bright, his cheeks glowing, yet still he hadn't said much. 'It's an improvement, Nancy,' Sister Mary Joseph said. 'Now, please can we get the children to breakfast?'

The children were not happy to have their game interrupted but one by one they were shepherded into the dining room for their Christmas breakfast. Each of the little tables was decorated with tinsel and naturally more pandemonium ensued when they realised that all their chairs, which made up the train, were still in the corridor. 'You take the children to get the chairs, Sister, while I bring up the breakfast before Cook blows a gasket.' She laughed, but little Billy began to cry and then the others were joining in.

'We don't want to spoil our train, Aunty Nancy,' they cried in unison. It was at this point Mother Superior arrived. Never in the history of Nazareth House had she seen the nursery department in such disarray.

'Nancy?' she asked questioningly.

'Hush, children, please,' said Nancy, sternly, and they turned to look at her.

Mother gazed at Sister Mary Joseph. 'Well?'

'Mother, Nancy saved the day. You see, we made a train.'

'A train?'

'With the chairs from the dining room. Oh, Mother, you must come and see.'

'Oh, yes, please do, Mother,' the children chorused. 'Please come and see our train. It's so special and Billy's the driver.'

Nancy was watching Mother, who looked over at her now. She nodded at Nancy, smiled, then turned back to the children, who were standing still, waiting. 'Very well, children,' she said. 'Let's see this special train of yours.'

The children didn't need telling twice and all ran ahead, Nancy shouting at them not to run, without success.

Nancy turned to Mother. 'I can explain.'

Mother took her hands. 'Please don't, my dear, there is no need, but I do think we should bring up the break-fast before Cook explodes.'

Nancy ran back to the dining room and shouted down the lift's hatch, 'Morning, Cook! Happy Christmas.'

'Don't blame me, Nancy Harmer, if lunch is an hour late. That's all I can say,' she shouted back.

'It's Christmas Day and, for once, I'm going to break with tradition, Mother,' said Nancy. She was piling toast onto plates to carry down for the children to eat aboard the Ragdoll Express.

'Billy must have been thrilled, Nancy.'

'Oh, Mother, his face was a picture. I've never seen him look so happy.'

'Is he talking?'

'Not quite yet, Mother.'

Mother sighed. 'God will show us a way to help him. Now we had better feed the children.'

As the snow fell on Nazareth House Orphanage that Christmas Day, the children played happily on the train, visiting places that existed only in their imaginations. It was an incredible day. Everything ran late for the first time ever. Nancy didn't care.

Before lunch the children were taken into the play-room where they fell eagerly upon the doll's house and bikes, while Nancy and some young girls who were helping her that day cleared the corridor and prepared the dining room for Christmas lunch.

By teatime the children were all rather hot and bothered. The younger ones were crying and Nancy thought that the excitement had been too much for them and decided on early baths. At six thirty they were all settled in bed and even Nancy was yawning. There were cries of 'Goodnight, Aunty Nancy,' as she reached to switch off the light.

Nancy made her way to the television room and popped her head round the door. The set was switched on but her young helpers were fast asleep. Nancy went to the kitchen to make herself a pot of tea, which she took to her room. Sitting down, she closed her eyes for a moment and wondered what it was about Christmas that made everything seem magical. She saw in her mind's eye the children having fun. It had been a perfect day, and they would never forget it. At least, she hoped not. Once more she wondered what life held in store for them. Would they remember her? Would she grow old and forget them? Never, she thought. The cup of good strong tea on the table in front of her began to grow cold as her head nodded.

She was woken suddenly by a child screaming and jumped up, knocking over the cold tea. She grabbed the tablecloth and dabbed at the spill, then heard more voices shouting. She dropped the cloth and ran out of her room, down the corridor. 'I'm on my way, children,' she called, slightly out of breath, then stopped as she reached the dormitory.

The sight that met her eyes rendered her speechless. Nancy was completely dumbfounded.

The children had managed to push the heavy sash window up just enough for them to put their heads out and they were yelling towards the sky. Billy was at the front, shouting the loudest.

Twice Nancy tried to speak and failed. Eventually, she found her voice and yelled louder than any of the children. 'Children, what in God's name are you all doing, hanging out of the window?' She hurried across and tried to drag them inside so that she could close the window.

'Don't close the window! They won't be able to hear me!'

'Please, Aunty Nancy, Billy says we have to make them hear.'

Nancy looked around the room at the children, her eyes finally resting on Billy. 'Very well. If you can tell me all about it, I won't close the window,' she said, sitting down on a chair as the children gathered round her. They all began talking at once. 'Stop,' Nancy said. She reached out and lifted Billy onto her knee. 'I believe this is your story, Billy, and if you want that window left open I'm afraid you're going to have to tell me what you told the children.'

'Go on, Billy,' the children said. 'Tell Aunty Nancy what you told us.'

Nancy cuddled him close and almost held her breath. There was total silence in the dormitory and the cold winter breeze ruffled the curtains as they all waited.

Billy looked at Nancy, then at the window again. Nancy asked Tommy to turn the light off and in the darkness they all turned towards the dark night sky.

'My mummy and daddy are stars in the sky,' he whispered.

Nancy gulped back tears as she saw all the little faces looking up at her. 'My mummy and daddy died and then they were stars in the sky, and I thought if I shouted really loud they might be able to hear me. I know they could hear me out of my bedroom window at home. Mummy told me that Christmas is magic and I thought that because it was Christmas this might be the day they could hear me and call back. Aunty Nancy, I don't know if these are the same stars as out of my window at home and I might have to shout even louder. Can they really hear me?' The words came tumbling out until Billy fell silent.

Nancy shivered as she, too, gazed up at the stars. 'Into bed, children, before you all catch pneumonia,' she said, and slowly the children, with disappointed faces, returned to their beds and waited.

Nancy continued to look out of the window so the children could not see the tears in her eyes. There was, once more, complete silence in the room as they lay in their beds, wanting to believe that somewhere out in the midnight sky their parents waited to hear them call so they could send their love back to them.

'It's true, children,' Nancy told them. 'When we love someone and they love us back, we're surrounded by something called for-ever magic. That means that no matter where those we love go to, no matter how far away it is, their love is still with us, and if we close our eyes, we can feel it always.'

'Can my mummy hear me?'

'Oh, yes, Lucy, darling. She can see you, hear you and be with you in your heart every time you call her.'

'Does God let them see us sometimes, do you think, Aunty Nancy?'

'Oh, yes, Martha, I'm quite sure He does.'

'I like going to the stars on the train, Aunty Nancy. Can we do it again tomorrow?'

'We'll see, Billy. Settle down now, children.'

'Do you think just for tonight you could leave the window open in case they want to call to us?'

'Well, just for a little while longer,' Nancy said, feeling choked. 'I shall sit here with you.'

'Will you sing us to sleep, please, Aunty Nancy?'

Nancy went to sit beside the window and leaned on the sill as she looked up at the sky. It was the clearest of nights and the sky was particularly beautiful. Very softly she began to sing:

> 'To reach the stars and back again,
> Jump aboard the Ragdoll train.
>
> Whisper ready, wait, and then
> Close your eyes and count to ten.
>
> Make a wish to make it start,
> Then place your hand upon your heart.
>
> Imagination, not too much,
> A pinch of magic, just a touch.
>
> Then suddenly the whistle blows,
> A toot and then away it goes,

Beyond the clouds and past the stars,
Around the moon, then twice round Mars.

Sing out loud, then shout hooray
While spinning round the Milky Way.

There's Christmas magic all around.
Listen now, don't make a sound,

For in the sky so high above
A place exists that's filled with love.

Believe they're there and when you do
That's when you'll hear them calling you.

Sweetly you will hear them call,
Sending kisses to you all.

Feel their lips upon your cheek
To bring the comfort that you seek.

Then feel that spark inside your heart
That says you'll never be apart.

As long as you see just one star,
They'll hear your cries, it's not that far.

Listen well for that's not all,
Often you may hear them call,

"Little ones, we love you still.
We always did, we always will."

Bless you, children, come again.
Just jump aboard the Ragdoll train.'

Nancy shivered. She looked at the children, listened to their gentle breathing as they slipped into their world of dreams, and smiled. Well, stars or not, this window would have to be closed and locked securely. Nancy looked up once more at the stars, then pulled the window down firmly. She tiptoed quietly across the room and paused briefly in the doorway to look back into the dormitory.

She glanced towards the window and frowned. I'm getting fanciful, she thought. I could swear I heard a dog barking in the garden.

Michael and Jennifer

Jennifer looked in the mirror, thrilled with her new hairdo. It had been a Christmas present from Michael. 'A treat for you,' he told her, 'to cheer you up.' It would take more than a hair appointment to do that but she was determined to make an effort this Christmas after the horrors of last year. Michael was so sweet, and Jennifer knew how lucky she was: everyone had told her so until she was sick of hearing it. She had known he was the one for her from the moment they'd met.

Jennifer sat on the edge of her bed and looked at the wedding photograph on her bedside table. Three years they had been married, and it had been perfect except for the one thing that threatened to ruin it all.

Jennifer remembered the first time she'd danced with Michael. That day she had left work with her friend Julia and they'd hurried home to get ready for the local dance, which started at seven o'clock. Jennifer was so excited – she couldn't wait to wear her new dress and shoes. The dress was blue with little white spots and a bow at the back. She had new nylons and a pair of stunning stilettos too. 'We'll be the belles of the ball,' Julia had said, laughing, 'and naturally we'll have the pick of the boys.'

Jennifer said nothing. She was remembering the boy she had seen a few weeks ago at the dance hall. He had caught her staring at him. Jennifer had immediately blushed. Then he winked and turned away. That had been it. No dancing, no chatting, just a wink, and her heart had done a double flip. She had looked for him every week but never seen him again.

Julia broke into her daydream. 'You, young lady, are going to dance instead of spending the whole night looking for your winking man. Anyway, he was a good bit older than us. I want to have lots and lots of fun tonight.' With that she swung Jennifer round and they laughed. They saw the trolley bus in the distance – 'Run!' shouted Julia, and together they ran.

They chatted about the dance all the way home, until Jennifer got off, calling, 'See you later.'

Mum had driven her crazy that night, making her stop to eat tea when all she wanted to do was get ready to go out. He would be there tonight, Jennifer just knew it. At six thirty she was in her new dress and shoes. She even had an early Christmas present from Mum, a pretty handbag that matched her shoes perfectly. It was a cold evening but Jennifer was too excited to care. She hurried to join Julia in the queue outside the dance hall and, after many compliments to each other on how lovely they looked, Jennifer glanced around.

'Stop it,' shouted Julia. 'What did I tell you? Tonight we're going to dance with lots of boys and thoroughly enjoy ourselves. The music will be brilliant and we, yes we, Jennifer, we are going to enjoy ourselves.'

The dance had been in full swing for a good half-hour when Jennifer was dragged onto the dance floor by a boy she had seen a few times before. Might as well, she thought. He isn't coming. I probably won't see him again. She laughed as she saw Julia being swung around the floor.

Her partner said something, but she couldn't hear him over the noise. 'Sorry, what was that?' she shouted, but he grabbed her hand and together they began to dance. Jennifer realised she was beginning to enjoy herself. The boy was spinning her around when suddenly she glimpsed the winking man. She stopped too quickly, lost her balance and the man reached out to grab her. 'Hey,' her partner said, 'she was dancing with me.'

Michael had smiled and said simply, 'Not any more, I'm afraid. This young lady is all mine.' He had taken her hand, and a thrill ran through her. He put his arm around her waist and she held her breath. The music started up once more, and he smiled, then swung her around and around, and Jennifer was dancing and laughing. Never in her whole life had she felt such happiness. This was simply going to be the best Christmas ever.

They stayed together the whole evening, and at the end, he walked her to the edge of the dance floor and pointed upwards to where the mistletoe hung. 'Be rude not to,' he said, then leaned forward to kiss her. Jennifer thought her knees were going to give way but he held her so close that she couldn't have fallen.

They had met again on Boxing Day and Michael told Jennifer about his work as a railway apprentice, a job he loved. 'I'm going right to the top,' he said. He and his parents, Judith and William, lived in Jesmond and he was their only son. 'I was a late baby,' he told her, 'so I'm afraid I've been very spoiled.' Jennifer frowned. 'Just kidding,' he said, laughing. 'My parents are wonderful people and they'll love you just as much as I do.' There, he had said it. He loved her. Sometimes it just happened that way, she supposed. The fact that he was eight years old than Jennifer, who was twenty-two, didn't matter to her in the least.

He was the one, and Jennifer was walking on cloud nine from that day. A year later, Jennifer and her mum and dad, Alfie and Peggy, were invited to Michael's parents for lunch on Christmas Day. Her mum had made such a fuss: what to wear, what to say, what not to say. After all, if they lived in Jesmond and one of his uncles had his own business, they were obviously well-to-do. Peggy was a little worried. Jennifer was too happy to care and Peggy's words floated over her head.

As it turned out, Judith and William were kind, friendly people and had made them all welcome. When they were settled in the lounge after tea, Judith handed round the sherry. It was then it happened. Oh, what a moment! Jennifer would never forget it. Michael got to his feet and stood in front of the roaring fire, facing them all. 'Is something wrong, dear?' Judith had asked.

Michael had turned to Jennifer's father. 'Sir,' he said, 'I would like your permission to receive your daughter's hand in marriage.'

There was a complete hush in the room. Everyone looked at Alfie as he stood up and shook Michael's hand. Suddenly everyone was shouting words of congratulation and offering their good wishes. William was sent to open a bottle of champagne and eventually Michael shouted over the noise, 'Excuse me, but I didn't actually hear Jennifer say yes.'

All eyes had turned to her as she opened her mouth to speak. It had come out in a whisper, she was so overcome with emotion. 'Yes.' That was it, one word and her whole life changed.

They were married that summer and that was when the whispers started from both sides of the family. Babies. As both of them were only children, there was great excitement at the prospect of grandchildren. Michael's uncle, who was Judith's elder brother, had decided to sell his business and gave them his house to live in. His health was poor and he was moving in with his sister. Jennifer could hardly believe it – their very own house! It was something she could never have dreamed of. Most of the young married couples she knew were struggling financially. It was the best start to married life. 'Now for the grandchildren,' they all said and waited hopefully.

Jennifer and Michael thought the whole thing was hilarious. There was plenty of time. The look on her mother's face every time she went to visit was a huge joke to the pair of them. There would be questioning glances, and Michael and Jennifer would laugh all the way home. It seemed, however, that their prayers had been answered when in November, just five months after they had been married, Jennifer began to feel unwell. 'Can't put my finger on,' it she told her friend Julia.

'Oh, Jennifer, you silly girl, you must be pregnant.'

'Definitely not,' she had replied. 'I haven't been sick and, anyway, I would know.' After two weeks she eventually went to the doctor. She was indeed pregnant. 'Honestly,' she complained to the family, 'you'd think I was the first woman ever to be in the family way, the fuss you're all making.'

It had been a whirlwind year: Christmas proposal, wedding in June, and now a baby on the way. They would spend their first Christmas as a married couple with everyone at Michael's parents' house. Jennifer was now feeling better and getting carried away with all the excitement. They were surrounded by a constant clicking of knitting needles, arguments as to who would buy the christening robe, and so it went on.

Jennifer and Michael let them get on with it. Some days she could hardly believe that this was her life now. She had met Michael, fallen in love and got married. They had a little house to live in, which the whole family had helped decorate. Now she was to be a mother. Oh, what a beautiful word that was. Mother. She wondered what her child would look like. Somehow she felt it was a boy. He would be a proper little smiler, ruined by the grandparents if she wasn't very careful, but, oh, how loved he would be. What did I do to deserve such happiness? she often wondered.

On Christmas Day 1952, Michael's parents were up early. William was at a loss to understand why as Michael was at work – the railways were running as usual even though it was Christmas – and dinner wasn't until four. The table had to be extra special this year, and far too much money had been spent on it, as far as William was concerned. When he saw the amount of food for the two families, he asked if the whole street had been invited. Judith smiled. 'It's special this year.' William shook his head but he was just as excited as everyone else about the new baby.

In the early hours of Christmas morning, Jennifer woke when she heard Michael get up for work. She tried to stand up but couldn't. Her legs were shaky. 'Something isn't right,' she said.

'Don't worry, it'll be all those mince pies we got through last night,' Michael said, laughing.

Unfortunately, it was more than mince pies. Much more. Jennifer had miscarried and lost the child that had been so wanted. Christmas Day wasn't celebrated in Judith and William's house that year, after all. The table remained half decorated, the food uncooked. Jennifer had lost a lot of blood and had been taken into hospital, where Michael sat in the corridor alone, wondering how life could change so rapidly.

In Jesmond, as Christmas evening approached, families slept in chairs around their fires, full of food, sherry and far too much chocolate. Except in two particular households.

Jennifer's parents, Peggy and Alfie, sat in front of their fire drinking tea. Neither had eaten. They sat in the dark staring at the flames. 'Today should have been so different,' Peggy whispered, and began to cry.

Judith had decided to go for a walk along Sandyford Road, just to blow away the cobwebs. She couldn't cry in front of William. That wouldn't help at all. She'd known how things could go wrong. She herself had waited so long for a baby, and given up hope and then out of the blue Michael had come along. That was the way of it, thought Judith. Something had gone wrong for Jennifer and the next time would be fine. She had wrapped up warmly, and her feet took her past the local orphanage. She heard the chapel bell from the other side of the wall.

As it rang out, the children of Nazareth House Orphanage raised their voices in song, and the sweet sound carried all the way to Sandyford Road. Judith paused, then leaned against the wall and began to cry.

Wagging Tails and Big Brown Eyes

Jennifer sat staring into the fire. There was so much to be done, yet she was sitting there thinking back over things that couldn't be changed. At least nobody mentioned babies in her presence now. A whole year later, another Christmas Day and still no baby. Michael had thrown himself into his job, and Jennifer worked hard to make their home a happy, comfortable place. Only when she was on her own would she allow her thoughts to wander. Would she ever be a mother and hold a baby in her arms? They had so much to give a child. She couldn't help but work out how old her child would have been now. She must stop doing that because it was pointless. A new baby would have taken her mind off it . . .

Why? she wondered, over and over again. It must be her fault and that was the worst of it. She was the one who didn't carry her baby to full term. What was wrong with her? There were people she could ask, of course, and tests that could be done. Appointments had been made, but Jennifer had always made excuses to cancel them. At least if she didn't know it was impossible to have a child there was hope. Without hope . . .

Michael deserved better. He deserved to be a father.

He would be home from work soon and they were going to his parents for Christmas dinner. Her mum and dad would be here soon to drink a glass of sherry before they made their way to William and Judith's house together.

Time to stop being miserable and move on, she thought. Michael was very excited about something this year, which had made Jennifer laugh. 'What are you up to?' she asked, before he left for work. 'I know that look, Michael Harrison, and you know I don't like surprises. Best tell me what's going on.'

Michael had picked her up swung her round and kissed her. 'You're a lucky girl, Mrs Harrison. Christmas dinner cooked for you, presents under the tree and a very special gift later on.'

'Tell me now,' Jennifer had insisted.

'You, young lady, will just have to wait and see what it is.' He ran out of the door and hurried down the street, waving and laughing.

Jennifer's heart was warmed. I love him so very much, she thought.

It had been a bittersweet Christmas Day. Michael had arrived from work just as the turkey was being taken out of the oven. They had all enjoyed themselves quietly yet there was an undercurrent of what should have been. It should have been Michael and Jennifer's child's first Christmas. It was impossible not to imagine what the day would have been like if their little one had been with them. How could people not understand? It wasn't just something that went wrong. Someone had even commented that it hadn't even been a baby at that early stage of pregnancy when Jennifer had miscarried. Well, it was, she thought angrily. From the very first moment she'd known she was pregnant, it had been her baby and she was a mother.

Christmas had brought it all back to her, yet Judith and William had tried so hard to make it lovely for them all, and Jennifer was grateful. There was only that one time, just after tea, when she'd had to make an excuse to leave the room: a children's choir had come on the wireless. Everyone had begun talking at once to cover the embarrassment.

Later that evening Michael and Jennifer walked home. Michael knew exactly what was on her mind because he was thinking exactly the same thing. He hoped so much that she would like the special surprise present he had for her. It would cheer her up no end, he was sure. He was moving up the promotion ladder at work and the shifts were getting longer. He loved his job and it was secure. They wouldn't be rich but they could pay their bills and manage nicely, and he was happy with that. No matter what the shift pattern was, he would work it. He never let them down and he was well thought of.

When they arrived home, Jennifer hurried to light the fire. Tonight they would sit in front of it and listen to the wireless. A whole night together, no night shift, and Jennifer was looking forward to it very much indeed.

The fire was just taking hold when Michael announced he was popping next door and winked, which still made her heart flip.

She was kneeling in front of the hearth when Michael walked in with a big box. 'Goodness me! Whatever is that?' she asked, but got no further. There was no need for explanations. Jennifer stared at the box which was now rocking from side to side in Michael's arms and . . . barking.

Jennifer leaped to her feet and opened the lid. Her heart melted. A gorgeous little yellow Labrador puppy, with the biggest brown eyes Jennifer had ever seen, was peering up at her. His little tail was wagging furiously, banging against the end of the box. Michael watched as Jennifer picked up the puppy, laughing as it began to lick her and bark at the same time. 'Well?' said Michael, hopefully.

'Oh, he's absolutely perfect. I love him.' She put him down and immediately he was barking to be back in her arms, jumping up and down, and gazing at her with those adoring eyes. Jennifer gathered him up and began dancing round the room. Michael watched as the sparkle returned to his wife's eyes. 'Thank God,' he whispered.

The Lost Puppy

'I've got other things,' Michael said later, and hurried out. He brought back a basket and dog food the neighbours had kept for him. 'I don't know a thing about dogs,' he said, 'but I expect we'll learn as we go along.'

'We'll love him and take care of him. That's all that matters, I expect,' Jennifer replied. The rest of the evening was spent trying to calm down the noisy, excitable puppy. The water bowl was knocked over more than once, and at one point the dog food ended up all over the kitchen floor. Jennifer didn't care: she hadn't been so happy in ages. 'Let's take him for a walk,' she pleaded.

Michael looked outside. 'It's beginning to snow – it could turn nasty,' he said, but Jennifer was already putting on her coat, boots, scarf and hat, ready to face the elements.

'Come on, Michael,' she said. 'Hurry now.'

He was glad to see her so happy – and who was he to spoil it? They made their way through Jesmond and along Sandyford Road. The little puppy was thoroughly enjoying himself. When they passed the gates of the Nazareth House Orphanage, his tail was wagging fast, and he pulled on the lead when he saw all the trees inside the gates that led to the main house. 'For one so small he's mighty strong.' Jennifer giggled.

They enjoyed their walk until the puppy was tired. Jennifer picked him up and tucked him into her coat, his little face sticking out. 'Oh, Michael, just look at those eyes,' she said, but it was her eyes that Michael was looking at. Shining, sparkling and happy. It had indeed been the perfect present.

Michael sat in front of the fire, feeling wonderfully relaxed, while Jennifer prepared supper. In the background he could hear the clattering of pots and pans in the kitchen but the heat of the fire had made him drowsy. There was barking and the sound of voices. Michael's head nodded and he dozed. In his dream someone was screaming. It woke him up. It was Jennifer. He ran to the kitchen where he saw Jennifer outside, standing in the snow, shouting, 'Come back! Come back.'

Michael's heart froze. There in the darkness, just ahead, the puppy was racing down the street. It took him a moment or two to grab his boots, and then he was outside in the freezing cold to chase the puppy. But it was no good – the puppy was too fast. Michael tried to follow his tracks but the snow was falling heavily now. He carried on looking and calling for more than an hour, to no avail.

When he returned he was hoping against hope that the puppy was back at home. He walked into the kitchen and listened, but heard no sound at all. He kicked off his wellingtons and went into the living room to see Jennifer kneeling in front of the fire. She looked up, and Michael shook his head.

'It's my fault,' she whispered. 'I opened the door to put the milk bottle out and he just ran past me. I didn't even give him a name. I couldn't call his name. It might have helped. Where is he, Michael?'

Michael had no idea. He knelt beside her, shivering. Jennifer continued to stare into the fire.

Just half a mile away on Sandyford Road, for the first time in the history of Nazareth House, it wasn't a young child who stood at the gates, wondering what life held in store for them. The puppy looked around, wagging his tail. This looked good, with all those trees.

He thoroughly enjoyed himself scampering through the wood and around the trees, but then he shivered. The nice lady who had cuddled him was gone. He gave a weak bark. It wasn't so much fun now. There were lots and lots of trees and some of the smells around the wood were good, but it was cold and he yelped.

His ears pricked when he heard a door opening somewhere behind him.

Light came from the caretaker's cottage where smoke was billowing out from the chimney. Old Mr Bell shone a torch into the woods and spotted the puppy shivering in the cold. 'Where have you come from?' he said. The puppy ran to him and jumped up, whimpering.

Mr Bell stepped out into the cold and shone his torch around, calling, 'Is anyone there?' The puppy must be with somebody, surely. He hurried back to the cottage but the puppy was gone. Mr Bell shivered and closed the door. Must have gone home, he thought, as he walked into his living room to put more coal on the fire.

'Well I never!' he exclaimed. 'What on earth do you think you're doing?'

The puppy had settled himself in front of the fire.

Mr Bell looked at him. 'One night,' he said. 'You go home tomorrow, do you hear?' Off he went to see what he could find to feed him.

The puppy closed his eyes and basked in the heat of the fire. Think I'm going to like it here, he thought.

The Dog with No Name

Boxing Day was always a let-down after the excitement of Christmas Day. This year Nancy was glad that all the fuss was over and she could expect a more peaceful day. The day after tomorrow the children would perform their nativity play for the lady mayor but today, thankfully, should be quiet enough. They had their breakfast and were sent to play with their new toys and everything seemed to have returned to normal. Nancy watched them for a while, and was happy that Billy seemed to be joining in the games, even though he still didn't talk much. She had hoped after last night he might be a bit chattier but he seemed to have gone back into himself. Time will help him heal, she thought. All we can do is wait.

Before lunch the children were asking to go outside and play in the snow and Nancy agreed, thinking a run-around would do them all good. It seemed to take for ever to get them into their coats, hats, gloves and wellingtons. Eventually, they were all ready and went outside to play with the helpers, who always came on Boxing Day to give Nancy a break.

She stood and watched them out of the window as they ran into the garden and listened to their squeals of delight as they threw snowballs. She made her way downstairs and went into the kitchen. 'Got the kettle on, Cook?' she called.

'Nancy Harmer, what a question!' came the reply. Together they sat on either side of the large range and drank tea with a very large slice of cake. 'It is Christmas, after all,' Cook said.

Nancy couldn't have agreed more and they sat in silence as they munched through Cook's wonderful Christmas cake.

Outside, Billy was feeling sad. The train had been wonderful, and Nancy was kind. Yet deep inside him there was a hurt that would not go away. Every time he wanted to talk, it resurfaced and he would stay silent. He wanted his mummy's arms around him, then he wanted to be swung high into the air and sit on his daddy's shoulders. He didn't want to play trains any more – it wasn't a real train anyway. Billy closed his eyes and remembered how the real trains sounded, the hissing they made, and the smell of the smoke. Daddy had taken him on the trolley bus to the station to see the trains and then they had gone into the café opposite to have a cup of cocoa. Billy could almost taste it now.

He wandered away from the other children until he was standing at the bottom of the wooded area to the side of the driveway. Head bent, he kicked at the snow, then stopped suddenly when he heard a noise. He stood very still and waited. There it was again. In the wood something was moving about. Billy thought it was very strange that he wasn't frightened. He stepped into the wood. He saw movement behind a clump of trees and moved slowly forward. He heard a bark, and a little puppy ran out from behind a tree. Billy jumped into the air. 'Hello,' he said, and waited.

The puppy began barking and running in circles around him. 'Come here,' Billy said, and the puppy jumped into his arms, licking him and wagging his tail so furiously that Billy lost his balance and landed flat on his back in the snow. The puppy jumped on top of him and Billy laughed as they rolled around in the snow together. 'Where have you come from?' he said. 'You can't stay here, you know. We could play for a little while, though. Would you like that?'

Billy had forgotten he couldn't talk.

'Come on then,' he said. 'Race you to the top of the wood.' He sped off through the trees, the puppy bounding after him until they were both worn out. Billy cleared the snow off a big rock in the middle of the wood and sat down. The puppy immediately jumped up and settled on his knee.

'Did you get lost? Have you got no mummy and daddy like me?' Billy knew some dogs had names around their necks, but although the puppy had a collar there was no name. 'Tell you what, I'll give you a name. How about Bob?' The big brown eyes continued to gaze at him. 'Scamp?' Still nothing. 'I know! Daddy read me a book called *Oliver Twist* and he was an orphan just like you and me. How about I call you Oliver?'

The puppy barked and wagged his tail, then jumped down and ran around in circles. 'That's settled then,' Billy said. He heard his name being called from the garden.

'Billy, where on earth are you?'

'Got to go, Oliver,' Billy told him, and ran back through the wood towards the other children. Oliver followed him every step of the way. 'You can't come with me,' Billy told Oliver sadly. 'They'll take you away.'

Oliver sat down and looked up at him with sad eyes.

They were still calling to Billy and he was worried. If he ran into the garden, Oliver would follow him and that would be that. He would never see him again. He looked around him and saw smoke coming from the caretaker's cottage. He remembered there were old outhouses that had once been stables where horses had been kept in the olden days. Aunty Nancy had told him all about the days when horses and carriages came down the driveway and the horses were put into the stables. 'Come on, Oliver,' he said.

Together, they hurried through the wood, trying to keep out of sight of the house, then ran for the stables. The door was slightly open and Billy managed to squeeze through it, pushing it a little wider. It was a bit cold inside but Oliver didn't seem to mind. He was running around, sniffing and enjoying himself. Billy took off his hat and coat, then grabbed Oliver and wrapped him up. He put his woollen hat on Oliver's head and laughed. 'You do look funny. Now stay there. I'll try and get you something to eat.'

He crept out of the stable and pushed the door almost shut. He glanced around to make sure no one had seen him, then ran back to the garden.

Billy was wrong. Somebody had seen him. Cook had been standing at the sink washing up when she had looked out of the window. What in the world is little Billy up to? she wondered. And why was he outside in this weather without a hat or coat? He couldn't be trying to run away because he was coming towards the garden. Something's afoot, mark my words, she thought.

When Billy got back to the garden he was asked why he wasn't wearing his hat and coat. He couldn't think of anything to say so he hung his head and refused to speak. No amount of coaxing would tempt him to talk and by then it was time for all the children to go inside for lunch. It was such a performance getting them back upstairs to the nursery, their coats and boots to contend with, that Billy's missing coat was forgotten.

They trooped along to the dining room and sat at their places waiting for Aunty Nancy to bring them their lunch of meat sandwiches and potato slices. Billy had an idea. Nobody took much notice of you when you were eating as there was too much going on. When his plate was put in front of him he picked at the food, every now and again pushing a morsel into his pocket.

Fortunately, biscuits were handed round after lunch, with juice. Oliver would like the biscuits, he thought.

Nancy was no fool and thought Billy looked somewhat distracted in the playroom after lunch. 'Can we go out to play, Aunty Nancy?' he asked.

'Oh, Billy, darling, that's the most you've said to me all day.' She laughed.

'I like being outside, Aunty Nancy, and running round in the snow.'

Nancy was thrilled and decided to take a few of the older children with them. Only one problem: where was Billy's coat? Nobody seemed to know and Billy's face became red every time Nancy mentioned it. She was not about to let a missing coat spoil the moment. This was the longest conversation she'd had with him since he'd arrived. She borrowed another child's coat for him and they made their way outside.

In the garden, Billy shouted, 'Hide and seek!' then darted away from them. The children all ran in different directions and Nancy stood under the great oak tree and counted to a hundred, then called, 'Coming, ready or not.' It was one of the children's favourite games but Nancy had never known Billy want to play before today. It was Christmas magic, that's what it was, and she was absolutely thrilled to bits.

When Billy turned up after ten minutes, Nancy wanted to tell him that he had been away too long and she had been worried, but the smile on his face stopped her. They played outside for another half an hour before the clouds gathered and it began to look like rain or snow. 'Come along inside quickly now, children.' They all skipped towards the house except Billy. 'Did you enjoy that, Billy?' Nancy asked, taking his hand. She was disappointed when he didn't answer. He looked worried. Nancy squeezed his hand. Oh, well, she thought, small steps.

Boxing Night

All around the city of Newcastle upon Tyne, people enjoyed the festivities and children played happily with their new toys. There was, however, one sad face in Nazareth House. Billy had spent the whole day worrying. Oliver would be hungry and frightened. It was only because he was away from the house in the stables that nobody had heard him barking. Billy thought he had heard him but most people would think the sound was coming from Sandyford Road. He would be in terrible trouble if anything happened to Oliver, and it would be his fault. Maybe he should tell Aunty Nancy. Yet he knew that, even if she understood, Oliver would be taken away, and Billy remembered how he himself had felt, all happy, when he had held the puppy in his arms. It was quite strange, really. It was like being made to feel all warm inside. Billy could talk to Oliver and he knew that Oliver understood every word he was saying. Maybe nobody wanted him – after all, he had been alone in the wood when Billy had found him. He remembered the soft brown eyes and another part of the cold inside him was warmed. He smiled, remembering how Oliver had followed him everywhere he went . . . No, he couldn't tell anyone – he couldn't risk the grown-ups taking him away.

Billy lay awake listening until all the children were asleep. Then he crept out of bed and put on his dressing-gown and slippers, walked quietly across the room and peeped out of the door into the corridor. He could see the flickering light from the television room as he began to walk slowly down the corridor. Every single step seemed to take a lifetime and the corridor seemed to be a million miles long. When he eventually reached the end, he went round the corner to the nursery door that led downstairs to the garden. Very carefully he turned the handle, his heart thumping. He tiptoed down the stairs, hoping no one was around.

Once he reached the bottom of the stairs, the door to the garden was on one side of him and the door to the kitchen on the other. Billy almost jumped out of his skin when he heard Cook burst into song. By this time his knees were knocking together and he was absolutely terrified of being caught out of bed. The door to the kitchen was open: Cook had been baking and the smell was beyond wonderful, Billy thought. Bravely, he peeped into the room. There, on the table, was a plate of biscuits and a glass of water. Billy never knew what gave him the nerve to do it but he ran in, grabbed the biscuits, pushed them into his pocket, then picked up the glass and was out again in seconds. He waited for a moment, then moved to the garden door, which was always locked at seven thirty sharp. Billy closed his eyes in prayer, pleading for it not to be seven thirty yet.

He reached up for the handle, took a deep breath,

turned the handle and opened the door. Then he ran for all he was worth through the snow, slipping and sliding, until he reached the stables. When he went inside, Oliver jumped up at him, spilling some of the water. 'Get down, silly!' he shouted.

Oliver lapped at the water, then ate Cook's biscuits. Billy hugged and kissed him, holding him tight and stroking him. Then he took off his dressing-gown and wrapped it around the puppy. Whatever am I going to do tomorrow? he wondered.

He settled Oliver down and hurried back to the house. He reached the door and paused, his heart racing, in case he would find the door locked. Very slowly, his fingers curled round the handle and he turned it. Click. His heart was now hammering in his chest and he opened the door, hurried inside and closed it. He swallowed, and wondered if his legs would take him any further as he was now shivering, whether from the cold or fear he didn't know. He crept up the stairs, then ran quickly to the nursery door. There were tears in his eyes now and he was very frightened indeed. He opened the door and was once more back in the nursery department. He had made it. He listened carefully, then raced along the corridor to the dormitory.

He was only halfway there when he heard Aunty Nancy frantically calling his name and ran into the toilet. He heard her footsteps and his name being called again. He was so frightened but he shouted bravely, 'I'm here, Aunty Nancy.'

There was a pause, then, 'Billy?'

He had done so well but it had all been too much for him. He sat on the floor and began to sob.

Nancy opened the door and saw that his slippers and pyjama bottoms were soaking wet. 'Oh, darling,' she said, 'it's okay, please don't cry. Let's just get these off you and find you some nice clean dry ones.' Nancy had Billy changed and into bed within moments. 'It really is fine, Billy,' she said, tucking him into bed. 'Little accidents happen sometimes when we're upset, and we don't think about them for a moment, darling.'

Billy had been so naughty and here was Aunty Nancy being so kind to him. It was simply too much and he burst into tears once more.

Oh, Heavens, thought Nancy, what on earth have I said now?

Downstairs, Cook was very pleased with herself. She had all the meals prepared for tomorrow and now it was time to go and sit down with a nice glass of water and a biscuit. She reached to turn off the big light and switch on the night light, then went to fetch the glass and the biscuits she had put ready.

I must be overtired, she thought. I could have sworn I left a glass of water on the table . . . and where, in God's name, are my biscuits?

Away in a Manger,
No Basket or Hay

On Boxing Night, as Billy and the children slept, the local church was holding a carol service for the local community. The church looked beautiful: all the candles were lit and the Christmas tree was splendid. The ladies of the parish had surpassed themselves, the priest had told them. The children had all visited the nativity scene at the side of the altar, then been given a decoration to hang on the tree, an annual tradition. It was a lovely service, and afterwards there would be mince pies, tea and juice in the church hall. Many of the younger children were asleep as the congregation stood up to sing the final carol, 'Away in a Manger'.

Half a mile away, in the grounds of Nazareth House, the moon and stars shone down on a very different stable from the one the congregation were singing about.

A new story was beginning. It would be a story of challenges, loss, sadness and joy. The Star of Bethlehem in the Nazareth House chapel was twinkling as it caught the light of the moon through the stained-glass windows. So many Christmases had been spent here. In 1945, Nancy had sat there with a smile on her face after returning home with the children at the end of the war.

They had been away for six long years. As she had watched them sing their carols her heart had almost burst with happiness. It was what she had dreamed of and planned all during the war years.

Tonight the chapel was silent as it waited. New stories were unfolding. The Cross of Our Lord hanging above the altar was also caught in the light that shone through the windows.

In Jesmond's parish church, the voices raised in song were carried on the breeze as snowflakes once more began to fall upon the roof of the stable where the puppy, with no basket or hay, was snuggled up in a little boy's dressing-gown.

A new story had just begun.

Straw Knickers

It was the morning after Boxing Day and Martha woke early. She looked over at Billy, who was still fast asleep. Martha sensed that something was going on that involved Billy. She had heard him being brought back to the dormitory last night. She jumped out of bed and began waking some of the other children. They all began whispering to each other, trying to work out what Billy had been up to. 'He must have been very naughty,' they agreed. He had been out of bed at night, which none of them would have dared to do. They all stared at Billy's bed.

'Do you think he tried to run away?'

'Don't be silly! He had his pyjamas on.'

'But where's his dressing-gown and slippers? They were there when he went to bed.'

They all pondered this puzzle for a moment.

'Maybe he was sick.'

'We would have heard him.'

'Somebody should just ask him.'

They all looked at Martha. 'Well, you started this.' They pushed Martha in front of them and all stood behind her. 'You ask him.'

Lots of little heads nodded in agreement as they

pushed Martha forward. Martha made her way over to Billy's bed and all the children stood round her. She gently tapped on Billy's shoulder.

'Harder,' said Tommy.

Martha leaned over and tapped on his shoulder again.

Suddenly Billy woke up, saw all the faces staring at him and screamed.

'Sssh, Billy,' the children said, looking around to see if anyone had heard.

'You'll wake everyone up,' Martha said.

'Why are you staring at me?' Billy asked feeling worried.

They all looked at Martha. 'Well' she said, 'we want to know where you went to last night.'

Billy sat up, and all the children gathered round, some jumping onto his bed. 'You'll tell,' he said.

'We won't.'

'You will. I know you will.'

'Promise Billy, we wouldn't ever tell.'

'Promise?'

'Promise, Billy,'

'Nobody, mind. Not even Aunty Nancy.'

'Not even Aunty Nancy.'

Billy sighed. 'I found a lost puppy.'

The children's eyes lit up. They hadn't expected anything so exciting.

'A real puppy?' asked Martha.

'Yes.'

'A real live one that jumps about?'

Billy laughed. 'Yes, he jumps about all right. I got scraps for him to eat and some water. And I had to take some biscuits from the kitchen.'

'Ooooooooh, Billy, you must be very brave indeed.'

Billy didn't feel brave, just worried that Oliver would be hungry and thirsty again by now. He told the others how he had wrapped the puppy in his winter coat and dressing-gown. 'I don't know what to do – he needs a dog's bed, but if we tell, I just know they'll take him away,' he said.

'Billy,' Martha asked, 'how do you know it's a boy?'

'I don't know, but I called him Oliver. What are we going to do? Remember, you promised.'

They all looked at Martha. 'We have to be very careful,' she said, trying to look important. They all continued to stare at her. 'I know one thing, though.'

'What, Martha?' they asked.

'I know where we can get some straw for Oliver's bed . . .'

That morning there was a great deal of whispering among the children and knowing glances that Nancy would never have missed, had she not been called to the parlour. A new child had arrived a day earlier than expected.

'Aunty Nancy's gone to see the new girl,' Norman told them.

'Good,' said Martha. 'She'll keep her busy.'

'But Aunty Nancy knows everything.'

'Mary,' said Billy, near to tears, 'we have to keep him warm and feed him. You promised!'

The children all agreed they would have to keep their promise. 'Do you remember,' Martha said to everyone, 'Aunty Nancy told us never to make a promise we can't keep?' Five little heads nodded. 'So Billy, Tommy, Mary, Norman and me will do what we said.'

It was agreed that the plan would go ahead.

'Wonder who the new girl is,' said Martha.

Josephine

The child at the big iron gates that led to Nazareth House was the first not to be held in somebody's arms or be standing waiting to take their first steps towards their new home. Josephine was in an ambulance that only paused briefly as it turned into the gates. She was looking straight ahead, yet seeing nothing. She was remembering home.

Josephine Jones had bright green eyes that sparkled and the longest brown hair in the street where she lived. It was the envy of many little girls. She also had the most enchanting laugh, if Maggie Jones, her mother, was to be believed. Apparently, she had smiled and giggled as soon as she was born and had never been a moment's bother to anyone. 'Giggles more than she cries,' a proud Mrs Jones would tell the neighbours. 'A real treasure.'

One of Josephine's favourite games was dancing on Daddy's feet. He would place her feet on top of his and together they would spin around the room and Josephine's laughter could be heard all down the back lane. 'We're so lucky,' Maggie told everyone. 'She's a delight.'

Ernie loved nothing more than to come home from

work and sit by the fire watching Maggie brush Josephine's hair. 'Prettiest girl in the world.' he told her over and over again. He was so very proud. He had hurried home on the day he had been promoted at work. He burst through the door, lifted Josephine into his arms and promised her that one day soon they would go to Newcastle together and he would buy her the brightest ribbons in the whole shop. That night, after Mummy had brushed her hair and plaited it, holding it together with a piece of elastic, Josephine dreamed of the prettiest ribbon in the whole world. Life was very exciting indeed.

Everyone said Josephine's plaits had a life of their own. They would quiver even when she was standing still. It was a constant source of amusement for her parents. Josephine was hardly ever still. She was always running, skipping, dancing, doing cartwheels across the yard, and was often found upside-down doing handstands in the back lane. There was always a group of children around her and all of the girls were jealous of Josephine's long plaits.

She was very proud of them indeed. When the children played on the roundabout in the local park, Josephine's plaits would fly out either side of her. After Maggie washed Josephine's hair she would spend hours in front of the fire brushing it dry as Ernie watched them smiling. Yes, life was wonderful for the Jones family. Until that day. For many weeks afterwards, Maggie told the neighbours, she could still hear the knock on the door, not matter how hard she tried not to. One day she had been so angry and upset that she'd taken a hammer to the knocker, banging and banging until it had fallen off. The neighbours had tried to stop her until she'd collapsed to the ground, screaming, and nobody had known what to do.

The whole neighbourhood felt so sorry for Maggie and young Josephine. They had been shocked when they saw the police car outside the house. They had looked through their net curtains wondering what had happened. Maggie's screams told them it was something terrible.

Ernie had been on his way home from work on his motorbike when he was hit by a wagon. He hadn't stood a chance. Their perfect world was shattered. Mrs Nelson from next door came to see if she could help, and she later told the people in the street it was the saddest sight she had ever seen. Little Josephine, who never sat still, was on a chair at the table, looking straight ahead. 'Looked like a little statue,' Mrs Nelson told them, 'white as a sheet. Even her plaits weren't moving.'

'Ooh,' said the women. 'Poor little lamb. It can be a sad, cruel world.' They all nodded in agreement.

But there were yet more challenges for the Joneses to face. Over the next few weeks everyone agreed that Maggie wasn't taking care of herself or Josephine properly. 'Walks around talking to herself,' they said.

'Never cleaned the doorstep for weeks,' said another.

The next time Mrs Nelson called, she was shocked

not only at the state of the house but at Josephine, who sat in front of the fire, her tangled, matted hair around her shoulders. Mrs Nelson had brought them some broth and stayed until she had seen them both eat it. She sent Maggie off to bed for a good rest, then cleared up and put more coal on the fire. She lifted Josephine onto her knee and began to brush her hair.

For a while, Josephine sat perfectly still. Then she turned so sharply that Mrs Nelson jumped. 'Where's Heaven?' she asked. Mrs Nelson paused with her hand in the air, twiddling the brush round in her fingers. 'Can I go there?'

Mrs Nelson sighed and put her arms around the child.

Josephine grabbed Mrs Nelson's hand and looked up at her. 'Mummy said it's a lovely place and we can go there too one day and see Daddy again. I know Mummy will feel better when we go. Can we go tomorrow, do you think?'

Mrs Nelson was shocked to the core. 'Goodness me, I hope not, Josephine.'

'Why not?' asked Josephine, with tears in her eyes. 'I want my daddy.'

'Oh my, there now,' said Mrs Nelson, not knowing what on earth to say. She sat staring into the fire, rocking the sobbing child until eventually she fell asleep. She carried Josephine to the sofa and covered her with a blanket. Then she crept upstairs to check on Maggie, who was lying on top of the bed sleeping. There was a small cross on the bedside table and Mrs Nelson walked over to look at it. She had never been one for going to church but it had given her an idea. She went quietly downstairs, checked Josephine again, and closed the door. She would pop along to the local church and ask Father Brian to call in and see them. Maybe it would help. It certainly couldn't do any harm. Talking about Heaven was his domain. Hers was making sure they both ate and kept their strength up.

Maggie had been a funny colour today. Can't put my finger on it, she thought, but she really hadn't looked well at all. 'Just the shock, I expect,' Mrs Nelson told her neighbours later.

It was extremely fortunate that Father Brian called one evening later that week. Nobody ever locked their doors so after he had knocked once or twice he had gone in. He had found Josephine crying and Maggie lying on the floor. It had been more than shock that had made Maggie look so pale, and she was rushed to hospital. She had polio and six weeks later she went to join the husband she missed so badly, leaving Josephine alone.

'She shouldn't have died,' Mrs Nelson told the neighbours. 'Many people are crippled by polio but they don't die.'

Maggie Jones, it seemed, had simply lost the will to live. 'We've saved worse cases,' the nurses at the hospital had said. They agreed that Mrs Jones had had no fight in her, and some had tutted on being told she had a young daughter. But the grief that had lain so heavily inside Maggie Jones had engulfed her.

The challenges for that family were not yet over. The condition of the house had deteriorated so much that Josephine had also been taken to hospital, where it was found she, too, had polio. The people in the street talked about nothing else for days and Mrs Nelson cried endlessly. She had been boiling her sheets, clothes and towels, cleaning her whole house just in case. 'Poor child asked me if she could go to Heaven to see her daddy. Looks like she might just get her wish.'

'Surely not,' the neighbours said, standing round the street in huddles.

Later that night Mrs Nelson got down on her knees beside her bed. 'Don't know much about this praying stuff,' she said, feeling quite ridiculous, 'but spare this little child, please. She is only five years old and she'll make a lovely daughter for some poor childless couple. There now, wouldn't that be a reason for all this? For the life of me I can't think of another.' Mrs Nelson struggled to her feet and walked over to the window to close the curtains. She looked up at the sky. 'Don't forget now,' she said.

It was a few weeks later that Josephine left hospital. A quiet child, they said, no bother at all, except that she refused to walk. She could stand perfectly well – it had been a mild case of polio – and the callipers would help. It was almost as though Josephine Jones had decided not to get better. As soon as they stood her up, she would cry and plead to sit down again. 'You'll get better,' they kept telling her. 'You'll be as healthy as the next child if you just do as we tell you.'

'Bit more encouragement, that's all it'll take,' said Annie, the nurse who was to accompany Josephine in the ambulance. 'Needs to be forced out of that chair and made to walk. It was a good recovery and she won't need those callipers on her legs for ever – but we can't get the child to walk,' she told her colleagues. Annie looked at Josephine, who sat completely still, looking straight ahead. She sighed and patted the little girl's shoulder.

Josephine looked up, smiled weakly, then continued to look straight ahead. Annie was handed a small bag. 'All her treasures,' the ward nurse said. 'Never lets it out of her sight.' And then she hurried off to her busy ward. Josephine smiled at Annie and asked if she could carry the bag herself. She hugged it to her as she was pushed down the long corridor.

Annie looked down at her and felt a tug at her heart. Poor little soul, she's clutching that bag as though her life depended on it. Annie leaned forward and asked if there was anything she would like. A glass of water before leaving, something to eat maybe? Suddenly Josephine turned round. 'Please can I have my hair in plaits?'

'Well, of all the things . . .' Annie said.

Josephine's eyes filled with tears.

'Don't cry,' said Annie. 'I have nieces with plaits and

I've seen how to do it. Shall we give it a try?' On a seat at the entrance to the hospital Annie sat and tried to remember how her sister did it.

Josephine opened her bag and took out her brush. Not any old brush, the one Mummy had used every night in front of the fire. Gradually the plaits took shape until suddenly Annie said, 'Oh, I haven't anything to tie them with.' Josephine smiled, opened her bag again and pulled out two bits of elastic. 'Well I never,' Annie said. 'So that was your treasure, was it?'

It took a bit of time to get the plaits tied but eventually Annie had finished and was extremely pleased with herself. 'There now, how wonderful they look,' she said. Josephine looked up at her. There was a twinkle in her eye and she was smiling. Annie had only recently qualified as a nurse and was thrilled. She had made the child smile, which no one else had been able to do. There was a spring in her step as she pushed the young child out of the doors. She had known exactly what to say and do to make the child feel better. Yes, Annie Foster was very pleased with herself indeed. 'Here we are, Josephine,' she said. Josephine was placed in the back of the ambulance and Annie sat beside her. 'Pleased with your plaits?'

'Oh, yes,' replied Josephine. 'I want to make sure I look nice when I see Mummy and Daddy again.'

Annie's smile disappeared and her hands shook. Surely the child hadn't been told she was going to see her parents. Oh, dear God, surely they'd told Josephine her parents had died. Annie went through everything she had been told. The child knew her father had died in an accident. She had definitely been told that her mother had also died. What was she talking about? Annie opened her mouth to ask but in the end said nothing. She hadn't a clue what to say.

The ambulance turned into the gates of Nazareth House. Josephine's plaits lay perfectly still. Not a hair moved. Josephine had not heard a word of Annie's chatter on the way there. She had better things to think about. Daddy had promised he would never leave her and had told Mummy over and over again about how they would all be together for ever and ever. When Daddy had gone to Heaven, Mummy had said it was where good people went when they died and that God would look after him until they could go too. Mummy had gone to Heaven now so of course they would send for Josephine soon. Josephine had been very excited until the doctor had said she was well enough to walk now and wasn't sick any more. When she asked if she was going to Heaven, the doctor had laughed and said, 'Most definitely not.' He had told her how lucky she was, that when she was fully fit she would be able to walk again.

Josephine knew that if she got well enough to walk she would never be able to go to Heaven so she had refused to walk and would continue to do so. Josephine Jones was a bright little girl.

She was lifted out of the ambulance and sat in her wheelchair looking up at the house in front of her. Staring straight ahead, she missed the sight of the wood to her left and the beautiful statue of Our Lady of Lourdes.

Josephine didn't move. There wasn't a tear in her eyes. She was too numb inside to cry. Annie squeezed her hand, saying, 'It's all right, you're here now.' Josephine remained completely still. Even her plaits refused to move.

She stared towards the huge house in front of her, terrified. 'It's so big,' she said, looking at all the windows. Josephine tried to count them but couldn't.

'Be a brave girl now,' Annie said.

Josephine was tired of being told to be good and to be brave.

'These kind people will make you better, Josephine,' added Annie, but Josephine didn't want to get better so she continued to stare at her new home. A gentle breeze blew around her, making her feel her hair was being stroked, like Daddy used to do. Something stirred inside her. Josephine didn't notice that she had begun to cry.

Nancy walked along the long corridor and felt a familiar tug at her heartstrings that told her a child was crying. She stopped, listened, then went slowly to the window to look down onto the driveway.

*

Josephine looked up and saw a face. Suddenly, from nowhere, a spark of hope and warmth began to ease the chill inside her.

Nancy's fingers reached for the corner of her apron as she looked at the child and smiled.

Heaven

Nancy's first sight of Josephine was confusing. Hundreds of children had been in her care and most of those little souls were frightened and crying when they arrived, but this was different. At her age Josephine would normally have gone downstairs to the junior department, but because of her mobility issues Nancy had been asked to take her into the nursery.

Josephine sat in her chair, staring at the floor, and when Nancy lifted her chin, she looked into her eyes. Well now, Nancy thought, what's this? The tears were gone but it was easy to see the child had been crying. There was a flush of colour on each cheek and Nancy knew what it was. This child was very angry indeed. 'This is a first,' she whispered to Mother Superior. Nancy had read the notes and knew Josephine's history. The little girl had turned six on Christmas Eve. She had lost both parents and had suffered ill health herself. Maybe she had every right to be angry, thought Nancy, but she certainly couldn't be allowed to remain so. It wasn't right.

Mother Superior took Josephine's hand and said, in her best soothing voice, 'We're here to help you, Josephine.'

Josephine Jones had been taught good manners by Mummy and Daddy. She had never answered back in all her six years but today a numbness inside her had been replaced by something she had never felt before. Her cheeks burned red.

Mother Superior looked at Nancy, then patted Josephine's hand. 'Well now, here we are, yes, here we are.'

Nancy was amused: poor Mother had no idea what to say. Tears I can deal with, she thought, but anger? She decided to tackle it head on. 'Josephine, darling, you look a little bit angry. Would you like to tell me why?'

'I didn't want to come here.'

'Well, many other children have said the same and they're upstairs now having great fun in the playroom after running about in the garden this morning. We have some lovely books and toys.'

'I wanted to go somewhere else. Mummy promised.'

Nancy knelt in front of the child, who looked as though any minute the anger would be replaced by tears. 'Where did you want to go, my darling?'

'Heaven!'

'Where?'

'Heaven!'

There was a stunned silence in the parlour and the only sound that could be heard was the ticking of the clock that hung high up on the wall.

'God decides when we go to Heaven, darling.'

'But Mummy promised we'd be able to go and see

Daddy one day and Mummy went without me and I want to go there now. If I get better I can't go.'

Nancy swooped Josephine out of the chair and held her close as Josephine gave way to the tears that poured down her face onto Nancy's neck.

'Please can I go?' Josephine sobbed. 'Please let me go to Heaven.'

It was not known at this point who was most upset, Nancy or the young child she held in her arms. Nancy carried Josephine up the parlour stairs and made her way through the door into the nursery. Mother paused for a few moments before making her way to the chapel. She knelt at the altar steps. 'Heaven,' she said, well it was the first time a child had asked that. Mother looked up at the cross. 'There is a reason for everything and only you know what it is,' she prayed. 'It is for us to carry out your will. Help us soothe this young child's pain, dear Lord.'

Upstairs Nancy tried to coax Josephine into drinking some milk and eating a biscuit without success, but at least she was no longer crying. Nancy carried her to the dormitory and tucked her into a bed for a nap. The child looked exhausted and she was asleep before her head hit the pillow.

Nancy walked over to the window and prayed for help. 'I've got one child who won't talk and another who won't walk. Please could I bother you for another miracle?'

Stolen Straw and Guilty Faces

Josephine was still asleep and Nancy was in the dining room, preparing for lunch thinking all in all it had been a lovely Christmas. The nativity play for the lady mayor was over and she would be able to relax a bit. It was a yearly tradition to hold a special nativity service for the lady mayor and dignitaries between Boxing Day and the New Year. All had gone well this year after the panic on Christmas Eve had been averted. Now Nancy heard Sister Mary Joseph hurrying along the corridor to help the children wash before lunch and decided she had time to pop along to the kitchenette for a cuppa before the children made their way to the dining room. They'd be here soon.

Sure enough, ten minutes later, feeling refreshed, Nancy made her way to the dining room. 'Hello children,' she said as she watched them taking their seats at the tables. Good as gold, she thought as they all replied.

'Hello, Aunty Nancy.'

Nancy smiled, but only for a moment. Hm, she thought. What are they up to? Nancy was no fool. 'Is everything all right, children?'

'Yes, thank you, Aunty Nancy.'

There's something I can't put my finger on, Nancy thought, watching them. After lunch they usually ran off to the playroom but instead Martha, Billy, Norman, Tommy and Mary stood in front of the serving table where Nancy was stacking the dishes.

They pushed Martha to the front.

Ah, Nancy thought. I knew there was something. 'Yes, Martha?' she said, but it was Billy who answered. Nancy was both shocked and thrilled. It was the longest sentence she had heard from him.

'We wanted to be extra good to help you and we want to do some of your jobs today because it's Christmas and you told us that being kind to others was the most special gift ever.' Four little heads nodded.

Nancy was so moved she almost dropped a serving dish. 'Oh, my darlings, come here,' she said, gathering them around her, their little angelic faces gazing up at her.

'Please, Aunty Nancy, could we go and bring the milk up for you.'

'Very well,' she said, 'but be very careful. I don't want any glass broken.' They all hurried out of the dining room but got no further than the door when Nancy shouted, 'Wait, children. You can't all go storming down at once.' She chose Martha and Billy to go downstairs and collect the milk.

As soon as they were down the stairs they hurried along to the chapel to carry out the first part of their plan.

They put their ears to the door and heard the sound of the nuns in prayer.

'Oh dear,' said Martha, 'we'll have to come back later.' Billy's face fell. 'Don't worry, we promised to help and we will,' Martha told him. They walked slowly up the nursery stairs trying to work out how they would get into the chapel unseen later on. Martha had just put her hand out to open the nursery door when Billy shouted, 'We forgot the milk!' They turned and ran down the stairs to the kitchen.

Cook took one look at Billy and wondered what on earth the child had been up to. She was enormously tickled by the look on his face. She had no children of her own but she knew a guilty face when she saw one. Billy's face was getting more and more red, and he almost ran when she gave him the milk. 'How amusing,' she chuckled.

It was teatime before the children approached Nancy once more. She had been distracted all afternoon, looking after Josephine. 'Cook has asked if we can help in the kitchen, Aunty Nancy.'

'Oh, very well,' she said, with no hesitation. 'Off you go.'

They went down the stairs, paused outside the kitchen, then tiptoed to the chapel. They put their ears to the door. Silence. Martha pushed the door and they all crept quietly inside. They stood like statues at the back of the chapel, hardly daring to move. Then they turned to Martha.

'Look over there,' she said.

'What are we looking at Martha?'

'Over there in the crib. Just like I told you. Lots and lots of straw.'

'You are clever, Martha.'

Martha felt very important indeed.

'You first, Martha,' the children whispered.

'Why?'

'You're the oldest.'

'Go on,' whispered Billy.

It was very dark in the chapel, except for the dim light that shone on the altar and a few candles that flickered in the semi-darkness. The Cross of Our Lord looked down on them. The children looked up guiltily and then quickly each of them made the sign of the cross.

'Do we need to genuflect?' Tommy asked. Once more they all looked at Martha who nodded. In the dim light at the back of the chapel the children began bobbing up and down making the sign of the cross at the same time. It may very well have been a trick of the light, but had anyone been looking closely it definitely looked as though Our Lord, looking down at them from above the altar, may well have been smiling.

'Come on, then,' Martha said, bravely taking a step forward. They tiptoed down the aisle to the crib and stood completely still.

'Hurry up,' Billy whispered.

'How do we carry it?' Tommy asked.

Martha thought for a moment, then looked at the

boys. 'You all fill your trouser pockets with as much straw as you can get into them.' They did exactly that.

'It's not enough,' said Billy.

Suddenly they all froze. They had heard footsteps.

'Someone's coming,' Tommy said, panicking.

'You go to the stable and we'll follow,' Martha told them.

Tommy, Billy and Norman ran to the side door of the chapel, crept out, then ran.

Martha and Mary ducked down behind the pew, their hearts thumping, and prayed for whoever it was to go away. Finally, after what seemed like an age, they stood up and went back to the crib. Martha's heart was racing and Mary's hands were shaking. Martha raised her eyes to the cross above the altar, then jumped when she heard more footsteps. She looked at the straw, then at Mary, then back to Our Lord. 'Sorry, God,' they said, then stuffed as much straw into their knicker legs as they could and ran out of the chapel without looking back.

Oliver was thrilled to see the children and they made a great fuss of him while trying to keep him quiet. Billy was worried that someone would hear him or that Aunty Nancy would come looking for them.

Oliver barked excitedly. 'Quiet, Oliver,' Billy kept saying, but the puppy only stopped when the children began to feed him. They made a bed of straw and sat stroking him. 'If he goes to sleep he might not bark so much,' Billy said.

'Maybe we should sing to him – that's how Aunty Nancy gets us to sleep,' suggested Tommy.

'Would it work with a puppy?' Billy asked.

'We could try I suppose,' Martha said.

They all agreed to try.

That Christmas, under a moonlit sky, a puppy lay in a stable and, ever so quietly, the children of Nazareth House Orphanage began to sing. Little Billy Miller finally found his voice and joined in with 'Away in a Manger' as the puppy closed his eyes and slept.

If Nancy could have heard him she would have been very pleased indeed.

Cook's Secret

It had been another busy day in the kitchen and Cook was standing at the sink washing up. The helpers had gone home and she was looking forward to putting her feet up. A sudden movement in the garden caught her eye. She stopped what she was doing and leaned forward to peer out of the window. Why on earth are the children walking around outside without their coats on? she wondered. It's freezing out there. She watched them running towards the house and saw the look on their faces as they passed the window. Cook chuckled to herself. Well, now, she thought, guilty faces. What's going on?

Deciding that a breath of fresh air would do her the world of good, she went over to her cupboard, put on her winter coat and wellington boots, then stepped outside. It was cold but Cook loved being out, before returning to the cosy warmth of her kitchen. Her feet crunched on the snow as she stumped along the driveway. I'll go to the gates and back, she thought.

She waved at old Mr Bell, who was standing at his cottage doorway. 'Hello,' she called and walked over to him. She often took him a basket of cakes, bread and her special biscuits. Mr Bell was always very pleased to see her coming towards him but today there was nothing in her hands. Disappointment was clear on his face. Cook laughed. 'I'll be over later with something for your supper – I've got a nice bit of ham and some crusty bread.' Mr Bell brightened.

Cook continued to talk as Mr Bell never felt the need for conversation. 'I'm just out for a wander. I had a feeling little Billy might be up to something, no idea what. Poor wee mite. Hardly spoken a word since he arrived. Nancy's tried everything, and I've never yet known her not get through to a child. Of course, he speaks now and again but not much. Nancy's worried, though.'

Mr Bell smiled. He knew exactly what little Billy was up to. He had let the puppy out on Boxing Day for a run-around in the morning and had seen Billy find him. It had warmed his heart to watch the child playing with the puppy.

'I'll pop over a bit later,' Cook said.

'You might want to take a look over there,' Mr Bell said, then closed his door.

I wonder what he meant by that, Cook thought. He'd pointed to the old stables where she'd seen the children hanging about earlier. In the end there was no need for her to continue guessing what Mr Bell had meant because she heard barking. She hurried towards the sound, and as soon as she pulled open the stable door Oliver jumped up at her, barking for all he was worth. For the first time in her entire life, Cook was speechless.

'Heavens above,' she said, then again, 'Heavens above.' Oliver jumped up at her again. 'Down!' Cook exclaimed sharply. She didn't want his dirty paws all over her clean clothes. Nevertheless, Oliver was wagging his tail. 'Goodness, you're causing a draught. You hungry then?' He began barking again. 'Well, quieten down and I'll bring you some food, but please be quiet. No wonder the children were acting strange.' Cook roared with laughter, thinking of Nancy. 'Oh my, wait till she finds out. I do hope I'm around when she does. It'll make my Christmas.'

Cook chuckled all the way back to the kitchen. The little animal would have to be returned to whoever owned it, of course, but then she remembered the guilty looks on the children's faces. I wonder what's going on, she thought, as she made herself a cup of tea. Suddenly the light dawned, and she slapped her hands down on the kitchen table. 'Surely not,' she said, to the empty kitchen. She remembered Nancy saying that Billy had been smiling more in the last day or so and thought again of the strange behaviour she had seen through the window. 'Well I never,' she said. 'I bet that little scamp found the puppy and hid him away. No wonder he seemed happier – and Nancy has no idea.' Cook roared with laughter once more, then suddenly stopped. Oh my, she thought, wiping her eyes, I wonder if the poor little pup is hungry. 'Nobody ever goes hungry on my patch,' she said to herself as she began opening cupboards to see what she could find. She wondered if she should tell someone but she knew that if she did the puppy would be taken away. Poor Billy, she thought.

Cook looked out of the window towards the stable block. No, she couldn't risk telling anyone. There were some old crates at the back of the kitchen and she was sure there were some old blankets in Nancy's treasure trove in the attic. Of course, nobody was allowed up there except Nancy. God forbid anyone should touch her stuff. When Nancy had returned home after the war and found that the nuns had meddled in the attic, it had been the talk of Nazareth House for years. But now it had to be done.

Cook stepped out into the corridor and looked around. If Nancy could have seen her she would have most definitely been extremely amused. Cook's face was flushed and she could not have looked guiltier. She paused for a moment with her hand on the banister, then went up the nursery stairs. There had never been any need for her to come up them before and she wondered what she would say if she was caught. Cook paused. She couldn't do it. Then she saw in her mind those big brown eyes, a waggily tail and a bark that said I'm hungry and just a little cold. Cook then took a deep breath. 'I can go where I like in this house,' she told herself bravely, and continued up the stairs.

When she reached the door that led into the nursery she glanced at it, then hurried up the narrow steps that led to the attic. In no time at all she found the blankets she needed and almost ran back to the kitchen. She was out of breath and had to take a moment to calm herself. She picked up the basket of food she had packed for the puppy – if anyone saw her they would think she was going to Mr Bell – pushed the blankets into a crate and set off.

As soon as she was outside the garden door she breathed a sigh of relief. She turned the corner, bumped straight into Nancy and screamed.

'Cook, for goodness' sake, what is the matter with you?' Nancy said.

'Well, I might ask you the same thing, Nancy.'

'No need to bite my head off. I just came out for a breath of fresh air. I was going to pop in and see you for a cuppa afterwards.'

'Yes, well, some of us are busy today,' Cook said, her face beetroot red and her heart pounding. Nancy giggled, then set off. Cook was puffing and panting, looking for all the world like she was up to no good at all. Must be something in the air Nancy thought as she made her way back to the nursery.

Cook hurried over to the stable as quickly as she could, looking around her all the time to make sure nobody was watching her. When Cook went into the stable, Oliver jumped up at her as soon as she was through the door. 'Down! Bad boy! Didn't your mum teach you any manners?' He was soon calmed, though, by all the treats in the basket. She had also brought a cooking pan for

Oliver, which she would leave in the corner filled with water. When she spotted little Billy's coat, hat and dressing-gown, her eyes filled with tears. Oh what nonsense, she thought, wiping her tears.

Cook stayed with the puppy for an hour, by which time she was absolutely freezing cold. She gave him a cuddle, then made him comfortable in the crate covered with the blankets she had brought. 'No good looking at me with those big brown eyes,' she told him. 'I have cakes to bake for tomorrow, but I'll be back,' she promised.

Cook returned to the kitchen and sent word upstairs for Billy and Martha to come down to the kitchen to collect some cake for Nancy's supper. Any pretence would do. Soon the pair knocked on the door and came in. Cook's heart melted. 'I've kept the puppy warm,' was all she said. Never had she seen more grateful looks on two little faces.

Billy's eyes filled with tears. 'Please don't tell,' he whispered.

'Oh, goodness me, away with you all,' she said laughing. 'I won't tell,' she said, 'and I'll help all I can. Now get along.' She handed them the cake for Nancy. She wanted to get back to her baking, but continued to chuckle to herself. A puppy, and Nancy had no clue whatsoever. Cook couldn't remember when she had last found anything so funny.

Nancy had watched the children on and off all day while trying to settle Josephine. She thought it was strange that the children were not as excited as they usually were when a new child arrived. They hadn't asked any questions at all. Something was going on. They were up to no good, certainly, yet they were behaving perfectly. Nancy sighed. Maybe they were just trying to think up ways of helping, bless them. Oh well, she thought, time will tell.

By evening Billy was worried, as they all were. Cook had said she would help but had made no mention of going back to feed Oliver tonight. They should have asked. It was almost bedtime now and they had no idea whether he had been fed or not. They would have to tell the adults, Martha said.

'No,' said Billy, near to tears. 'You promised, all of you.'

Martha was chosen to tell Aunty Nancy that Cook had asked for them to go and help again, as she was behind with her baking. They had forgotten all about it, they told her.

Nancy looked them all in the eye. 'Oh, she did, did she?'

'Yes,' the children insisted, 'she really did, Aunty Nancy.'

'Wait there a moment,' she told them, and hurried downstairs to the kitchen, where Cook was almost done for the day.

'Popped in for a cuppa, Nancy?'

'Well, not exactly. Did you ask the children to come and help you? It is getting rather late.'

'Ooh, yes please, Nancy, there's lots of clearing up to do. The children's help would be much appreciated,'

Cook said, with her back turned. She couldn't possibly look at Nancy and lie. Heavens above, that would be unthinkable.

Nancy was puzzled but made her way back upstairs. Some time later, she allowed Billy, Martha, Norman, Tommy and Mary to go and help Cook. They ran downstairs and made straight for the kitchen. The door was open and they could hear the strangest sound.

'What's that?' whispered Billy.

The children listened, then Norman giggled. 'It's Cook snoring,' he said.

They crept slowly into the kitchen and sniffed. Oh, the smell of newly baked cakes and biscuits. Their eyes were all drawn to the larder where Cook kept all her baking. The door was ajar and there sat the tin of Cook's special cakes.

'We can't,' said Martha. But the thought of the hungry puppy was playing on their minds. Cook suddenly snored loudly and Billy dashed forward, reached up and grabbed the tin of cakes. They ran along the corridor to the door leading to the garden, not stopping until they reached the stable.

Oliver leaped at Billy the moment he saw him. He bounded round the stable, his tail wagging furiously. 'Oh, we have to keep him,' Martha said.

'Cook said she'd help us,' Billy reminded her.

'Not when she finds out about the cakes,' replied Martha.

The children crushed cake for Oliver and played

with him. Then Oliver curled up in the straw and the children placed the blankets over him. They closed the stable door before they went back to the nursery.

Later they all climbed into bed with no fuss. Nobody wanted a story and they all pretended to be asleep immediately. 'What good children,' Sister Mary Joseph said.

'I'm not so sure,' Nancy replied. She hadn't missed the sight of wet socks and shoes, a complete mystery unless Cook had asked the children to help clear up while dancing around in the snow. Nancy turned to Sister Mary Joseph. 'Something is up, mark my words.'

Away in a Manger

It was the morning of 28 December, the day of the nativity play. Honestly, thought Nancy, what a ridiculous fuss everyone was making. Every helper available had been drafted in to clean and polish the chapel and ensure that every step, banister and floorboard throughout the house was gleaming. Rags had been saved for weeks to put into the girls' hair to make the most perfect ringlets. The laundry staff had been working endlessly, cleaning and pressing clothes to ensure every child was perfectly turned out. The waxing machine had been gliding over the parlour hallway for hours, and Nancy was frazzled. Cook making a fuss today of all days wasn't helping.

As she took her first step onto the newly polished floor her feet almost went from under her and she screamed as she grabbed onto the banister to stop herself from ending up on her behind.

Mother Superior came out of her room to see what the noise was about and saw Nancy sliding about at the bottom of the stairs. 'What is the matter, Nancy?' she asked.

Nancy straightened her clothes. 'Nothing, Mother,' she replied, 'but I suggest you warn the lady mayor that the parlour has been turned into a skating rink. She should wear ice skates unless she wants to end up flashing next week's washing in front of all the dignitaries.'

'Oh dear,' Mother said, looking around her with a worried expression on her face.

Nancy stepped carefully across the floor to Mother's room, asking if she had taken the big tin of cakes from the kitchen.

'Cakes, Nancy?' said Mother, with a surprised look on her face. 'Is that what all the commotion was about earlier? I could hear Cook shouting.' She sighed. 'I fear it's going to be one of those challenging days and I wanted everything to be so organised. It's a very special occasion after all.'

'Mother, it's the lady mayor and the dignitaries, not the royal family. Please can we all just calm down? They come every year to watch the children in the nativity play, which, by now, they know by heart.'

'I suppose that's true.'

'Then, Mother, they will all troop into the parlour smiling endlessly, have tea and go home. That's it. So, unless the lady mayor decides to skid across the parlour, do a triple Salchow, double toe loop ending with a spectacular triple axel when she enters, all will be exactly the same as every other year.'

'Oh dear,' said Mother again.

'Now, about those cakes, did you by any chance take them for the lady mayor?'

'Indeed not, Nancy. Cook will bring them through on her best tray, with the china plates, matching teapot, cups and saucers as always. They will then be placed on the table in the mirror room.'

'Not this year, I fear. Mother, the cakes have disappeared.'

'That explains the commotion from the kitchen I heard earlier.'

'We've all been blamed in turn, Mother, and Cook is furious.'

'I don't suppose she could have made a mistake?' Mother asked hopefully.

'Well now, I wonder, would you like to ask her that, Mother?'

Mother Superior shuddered and made the sign of the cross.

'Quite,' said Nancy.

'Oh dear, what are we to do?' Mother Superior lifted her rosary beads and smiled at Nancy. 'We shall pray that the cakes turn up and Cook keeps calm. Now let us pray together.'

'There's not enough prayers in the world,' Nancy replied, then threw her hands up to Heaven. 'Dear God, please may I have a tin of cakes.' There was a pause. 'Sorry, Mother, there are no cakes in Heaven today. They're all out.'

'Dear Lord, is there any chance you could keep Cook calm? No? Oh, I see. Sorry, Mother, that's one miracle too many. Any more ideas?'

Mother was shocked. 'Really, Nancy, that was quite irreverent.'

'Well then I shall leave it to you to speak to Cook. I have a nursery full of overexcited children because Dolly has told them all some daft story about the magic chain the lady mayor wears around her neck.'

Mother had to suppress a smile. Young Dolly, Nancy's helper in the nursery, was loved by all and Mother knew Nancy had a soft spot for her.

They heard a door slam somewhere down the corridor and marching footsteps. Mother looked with pleading eyes at Nancy. 'All yours, Mother,' Nancy said, as she escaped upstairs to the nursery. She took the steps two at a time and had just reached the door when she heard an almighty scream from below.

When she got downstairs again, she discovered that Cook had slipped and was lying in a heap on the parlour floor.

Pandemonium ensued. The nuns rushed out of their rooms, Nancy was shouting at them, telling them the floor was slippery. Mother was kneeling beside Cook, who was shouting at them all to leave her alone as she hastily straightened her clothes. The nuns were taking tiny tentative steps, their arms out to their sides to keep their balance. Cook looked up in despair at Nancy. 'What in all that is holy are they doing?' she called out.

'Erm, the floor is a bit slippery, Cook.'

'Slippery, a bit slippery? Nancy that's an understatement. What on earth is going on?'

Nancy hurried down the stairs.

She grabbed a chair, carried it over to Cook and they all helped her to sit down. Poor Cook was puffing and panting. 'A cup of tea, that's what you need, Cook,' Mother said, gently patting her shoulder.

Cook looked up at her and the angry look returned. 'What I need, Mother, is my cakes. They were placed in the special cake tin, in my larder, and now they're gone. Completely disappeared.'

'Oh dear,' said Mother, for about the tenth time that morning.

'Well,' said Cook, looking around her, 'where are they, then?'

There was complete silence in the parlour: nobody moved, nobody spoke. It was almost as though they were all frozen in time. Mother stole at glance at Nancy, who had a smile tickling the corners of her mouth. 'Useless,' shouted Cook. 'You're all absolutely useless!' She jumped up, then screamed as pain shot up her leg. The next half-hour was spent getting her back to the kitchen, putting her foot up on a stool and promising to call Dr Graham. A wet towel was wrapped around her ankle and she was given a cup of tea.

When everything had calmed down, Nancy looked around the kitchen. 'Oh, Cook!' she said. 'Look, Mother.' All around the kitchen there were trays of the most beautiful cakes each one looking more tantalisingly tasty than the next. They were decorated in different colours. Mother walked over to look at them more closely. 'Cook, you've surpassed yourself.'

'Well, there's no special cakes,' replied Cook, who was now more tearful than angry.

Nancy took her hand. 'But these are very special, Cook. When the lady mayor sees these, she'll be thrilled. You're so clever.'

Cook was mollified. 'Well, they are rather good, even if I say so myself.'

Crisis averted, thought Nancy.

'I've sent for a couple of the girls to help you until we can get Dr Graham to see to that ankle, and no arguments,' Mother told her.

'And now, Mother, what are we going to do about the hallway?' They looked at Nancy. 'I was asking you, Sisters,' she said. 'This is your domain, your problem.'

'I'm not sure there is anything we can do,' said Sister Ann.

'Nor me,' added Sister Lucy.

Nancy was becoming annoyed. 'Well, Sisters, you had better think of something very quickly, unless you want to see the colour of the lady mayor's knickers.'

'Nancy!' exclaimed Mother. 'Please, that is quite enough.'

Sister Mary and Sister Lucy bent their heads and tried hard not to let Mother see their shoulders shaking.

Once again, the room fell silent. Everyone continued to look at Nancy, their eyes pleading.

'Oh, for goodness' sake,' Nancy said, exasperated. 'Let me think.'

Everyone waited silently.

'Has every room been polished with the machine?' she asked.

'Oh, no,' Sister Lucy chipped in. 'The mirror room wasn't. There was no need because of the large rug.'

'Rug, Sister?'

'Well, it practically covers the whole room.'

Nancy smiled at them all and waited.

Mother was the first to understand Nancy's thinking. 'We couldn't possibly move it,' she said. 'It weighs a ton.'

'Very well, Mother. I'll wait for you all to come up with a better idea.'

Nobody could.

Nancy looked up at the clock on the wall. 'Time's ticking.'

'How do we do it?' said Mother, who was beginning to panic. The lady mayor was due in less than an hour.

Within ten minutes Nancy had grabbed a group of children from the junior department and between them all, with help from the nuns, they heaved the carpet into the parlour, slipping and sliding as they went. Eventually, after a lot of huffing and puffing, the enormous rug was in place and the children were sent away to get ready for the big occasion.

'Try it out, Nancy,' the nuns said. 'Go outside and come in through the door and see if it's all right.'

'I'll pretend I didn't hear that, Sisters. I am now going upstairs to finally get the children ready, which I should have done an hour ago. I'll leave you to bob in and out of the door to your hearts' content. Now, if you will excuse me.' Nancy went up the stairs for the second time. Only once did she look back: they were walking through the door pretending to be the lady mayor. Nancy burst out laughing and found it hard to stop.

She hurried into the dormitory and there they all were, her little angels. The shepherds stood with their crooks and the angels sparkled and shone. Mary and Joseph brought a lump to her throat. It had all been done while she was away. 'Sister Mary Joseph, Dolly, what miracles you've worked here,' she told them. 'You have no idea how much this means to me.'

Dolly and Sister Mary Joseph were beaming from ear to ear. 'They've all been good as gold,' they said. 'Honestly, everything went to plan perfectly.'

Nancy looked at them all. Everything *looked* perfect, but there was something odd ... Whatever it was, it could wait. Dolly ran over to Nancy, grinning. 'Of course, we had a very special helper, Nancy.'

'Did you? Who was that then?'

'God. We prayed to Him to help everything work perfectly and He came along and worked His miracle,' she said grinning.

'So that's why He couldn't look for the cakes!' she said.

'Cakes?'

'Never mind, you don't want to know. Come along, everyone, well done.'

*

Nazareth House was once more serene and the sisters awaited the cars that would bring the guests to their home. The bell rang and Mother carefully made her way across the carpet to welcome them. Sister Ann and Sister Lucy stood either side of the lady mayor, their hands placed under each of her elbows. The lady mayor had been here many times before and thought there was something different this morning but couldn't quite place what it was. Also they usually stood chatting in the parlour but today she felt herself very gently being guided straight to the door into the corridor leading to the chapel, where the children were lined up before the large oak doors. 'How beautiful,' she said, impressed once more at how much effort went in to these occasions.

Martha came forward and curtsied, then gave her a little posy. She was so nervous she was shaking, and Nancy moved forward to take her hand. 'Thank you,' said the lady mayor. She looked at the children. 'You all look splendid, and we're all looking forward very much to your nativity play. Well done, children.'

Nancy breathed a sigh of relief. Now I can relax, she thought. She glanced round at all of the children and her shoulders sagged. Martha, Mary, Tommy, Norman and Billy were all looking anxious, and Billy had tears in his eyes. They were fidgeting and Mary was pulling nervously at the tinsel around her waist. They all kept looking at Martha. Nancy closed her eyes for a moment. Dear God, what now?

Sister Ann and Sister Lucy moved forward and opened the doors.

Mother Superior stood beside the lady mayor and they began to walk into the chapel.

The organ was playing as the children processed down the aisle behind the guests.

Suddenly Nancy realized something was wrong. Mother and the lady mayor had stopped halfway down the aisle. There was a pause before they continued to the pew at the front. Then Nancy saw it. Her heart skipped a beat. I'm seeing things, she thought. Mother glanced at her but Nancy was rooted to the spot, shocked to the core. There on the altar stood the nativity stable without any straw. The bits that were left were scattered over the chancel steps.

Mother turned again to Nancy, who shook her head. Quietly she led the children up to the altar and put them in their places. Every child was behaving perfectly. Thank goodness for small mercies, she thought. She nodded to signal the children's first carol. Five of them were looking at the floor. Bless them, they must be a bit scared, she thought. 'Come along, children,' she said. 'Ready now.'

One by one the children lifted their heads and looked straight ahead. Nancy's heart missed a beat. Oh, dear God in Heaven, now I know what it was upstairs. She looked at each of the little faces gazing at her and raised her eyebrows in question.

Nancy knew a guilty face when she saw one and right

now, standing in front of her on the steps of Nazareth House Chapel stood five extremely guilty faces.

Nancy raised her eyes to the Cross of Our Lord behind the children. Everyone was waiting for them to sing, but Nancy was standing on the altar steps staring straight ahead in disbelief. She had averted the crisis of watching the Lady Mayor skimming across the parlour showing her knickers to all and sundry, heaved a great big carpet across the floor, looked after Cook, who, it seems, had sprained her ankle, the specially made cakes had disappeared and now this. She closed her eyes, opened them again, glanced at Mother Superior, then looked once more upon the Cross of Our Lord.

'I give up,' she said.

Trouble Brewing

It was just a feeling that's all, thought Nancy as she walked around her room making sure everything was put away and tidy. What a strange day, Nancy thought, as she sat down on the edge of her bed and looked at her holy pictures. 'There's trouble brewing, make no mistake.' The children had been acting extremely . . . extremely . . . what? She couldn't come up with the word for it.

She went over the events of the last few days. There had been the shock of finding the straw missing from the nativity crib. Nobody seemed to know anything about it but straw didn't vanish into thin air. They hunted high and low but it had never been found. Then the children had suddenly become angels at bedtime and gone to sleep straight away, not badgering her for stories and songs. Tonight they had been yawning just after five so Nancy had started the baths early and they were all fast asleep by six thirty. Little Billy's head was down all the time and he was still saying very little. And tonight when Nancy had tucked him in and whispered goodnight, she'd caught that guilty look. What on earth did he have to be guilty about? 'Trouble brewing,' she whispered once again to nobody at all.

Then there was Cook, Heaven only knew what on earth she was up to. Hysterical, complaining that there was a whole tin of cakes stolen, making everyone search high and low for them. Then, when Nancy had popped in for their usual cuppa earlier today, Cook couldn't look her in the eye. Another guilty face. Goodness only knew what all that was about. Three of the children's dressing-gowns had gone missing and couldn't be found anywhere. I give up, thought Nancy; I am too tired to care about missing straw, cakes or dressing-gowns. I shall simply pray that tomorrow all will become clear and I can shake this feeling of impending doom off me.

Nancy got undressed and knelt down beside her bed. 'Hello, Lord, trouble's brewing here. Any chance you could give me a helping hand? It's no good telling me all is well because you know I can smell trouble a mile off. This nonsense has been going on for quite long enough now thank you.'

She stood up and walked over to her window, which looked out onto the roof of the chapel and the bell. She opened the curtains so that she could look at the night sky. The bell was swaying, and the wind seemed to be gathering speed. A storm brewing, she thought. She stood for a few moments looking at the stars, thinking about Billy, then shivered. She drew the curtains, then went across the room and climbed into bed. She pulled the bedclothes around her and closed her eyes. As she drifted off to sleep, she thought how glad she was that tomorrow was her day off ... All she needed was a good night's sleep and all would be well. Nancy could never have guessed what the night would bring but it would certainly not be a good night's sleep.

She was woken by a loud crash of thunder and looked at her bedside clock: just after midnight. She lay for a moment, listening to hailstones lashing against her window. Nancy actually found it quite soothing to listen to, especially as she was curled up in a cosy warm bed. She turned on her side to watch it and her eyes began once more to close. Suddenly there was a flash of lightning which lit the room, followed by another rumble of thunder. Oh dear, she thought, if this goes on it will wake the children. She heard someone running down the corridor. Sister Mary Joseph and Dolly: they would be checking that the children weren't frightened. Nancy couldn't for one moment imagine what she would do without them both. Quite honestly, apart from the help, they were a constant source of amusement. She remembered the day young Dolly had arrived, an angry and extremely upset young girl who'd had her hopes of becoming a nurse dashed. Nancy had taken her under her wing and in no time at all she was loved not only by the staff but the children too. She could make the most ordinary story sound magical and would get the children overexcited with her funny ways but Nancy's heart warmed every time she looked at her. Dolly would be hurrying to the children, making the storm all seem like a game, as she always did.

There was another almighty crash of thunder and lightning lit the entire sky. Nancy got up, 'Well, that's me wide awake now,' she told her holy pictures and hurriedly began putting on her slippers and dressing-gown, then set off to help with the children. First, though, she went to the window to look out at the storm. She saw another flash of light – which had nothing to do with the storm. Nancy was completely confused. 'What in Heaven's name is that?'

She left her room and went into the dining room where the big window looked out onto the driveway and the grounds. There it was again. Nancy pressed her nose to the window but it was still difficult to see as the hailstones were now lashing down again. In the darkness of the room, she stood trying to focus and see what on earth it was. 'Why, Heavens above, it's a torch!' she said, feeling totally confused. 'Somebody is out in the storm with a torch! Why, for goodness sake why – and who is it?' Had something blown down? Was it Mr Bell? If so, he was going to get soaked.

There was nothing else for it: Nancy was going to have to get help. Then it happened. There was another flash of lightning that lit up the entire sky and grounds and Nancy saw who it was. She opened her mouth to cry out but couldn't. The loud clash of thunder brought her to her senses. 'Cook!' Nancy said. 'What in God's name?'

Nancy ran back to her room and grabbed her rain-coat, boots and rain hat. She hurried over to to the bottom drawer and grabbed her big torch. This is going to be fun, she thought, as she went down the stairs. She paused as she unlocked the garden door. When she opened it, it was almost wrenched out of her hand as the wind got behind it. Nancy grabbed the handle and forced the door shut. Her head bent against the hail-stones and gale, she made her way towards the old stables behind the wood where she had seen Cook with the torch. There was something wrong, Nancy just knew it, but what? The wind suddenly howled and Nancy was almost thrown off balance. 'Tell you what, Cook,' she shouted into the wind, 'you had better have a very good reason for being out here and soaking me half to death.' She leaned forward and made her way through the storm, getting blown backwards every few steps. She paused for a moment, wondering where on earth Cook could possibly be. Suddenly she saw it, dancing torch light under the door of one of the old stables. It was never used. It had been built in 1816 to the left of the wood, along with the circular driveway for horses and carriages. Nancy battled on through the storm then suddenly stopped. Oh my, she thought, am I interrupting something? Oh dear, what am I to do? Howevever there was no need for Nancy to do any-thing because at that moment the stable door opened and the next flash of lightning showed Nancy and Cook looking at each other in total bewilderment.

Suddenly Cook hurried forward and grabbed Nancy's hand. They began shouting at each other to be heard over the noise of the storm.

'What are you doing out here in this weather?'

'Well, I could ask you the same question!'

'Erm, well, I just, erm.'

'Is it something private, Cook?' Nancy shouted.

Unfortunately, at that moment there was another clash of thunder and Cook couldn't hear over the roar of the storm. 'Pardon, Nancy.'

'I said is it . . .'

'Nancy, this is ridiculous.'

'You're telling me, Cook.'

Cook grabbed Nancy's arm and dragged her towards the stable. 'It's a secret,' she shouted and suddenly Nancy blushed, not knowing what on earth she was going to find. Never in all her days would she, or could she, have possibly guessed what she was about to see. Cook pushed open the stable door and they stood there huddled together as Cook shone the torch into the stable. There in the corner, snuggled up in the nativity stable hay, surrounded by children's dressing gowns and cake crumbs, lay a little puppy in a crate.

Oliver looked up at Nancy and barked.

'Sweet, isn't he?' said Cook.

Nancy said nothing at all. For the second time that night she stood completely still with her mouth hanging open.

Oliver looked up at her, his tail wagging under the

blankets. He tried to come over to her, then must have realized how cold it was and snuggled back into his dressing gowns and blankets waiting to be told what a very clever boy he was. He barked again.

'Quiet,' said Nancy, finding her voice. 'Someone will hear you.'

'Oh, no, they won't,' Cook said. 'He's been here for days and nobody's heard a thing.'

'Excuse me?'

'I said he has . . .'

'Yes, I heard what you said. Days, Cook? How many exactly?'

'Well, as far as I know, old Mr Bell found him wandering around the wood on Christmas Day evening and took him in. He let him out for a run on Boxing Day morning, which was when little Billy found him. He hid him in here. I saw the children from the kitchen window taking turns to go the stable and wondered what on earth they were up to. I went out to check when there was nobody around and found the puppy.' Cook looked Nancy in the eye. 'Anyway, you're the one who wanted little Billy to be happy and start talking, so I wasn't going to tell on him. Oh Nancy,' Cook said, 'I've been coming out to feed the pup and make sure he's warm.'

Nancy sighed and shook her head. 'Whatever will we do? The puppy can't stay here. It needs to be properly fed and looked after.' Nancy wrinkled up her nose.

Cook roared with laughter. 'It's just doggy smell, Nancy.'

'Well, it can't stay here and that's that,' she replied.

They stood in silence listening to the storm and Nancy walked across to the puppy, knelt down and stroked him. He jumped up, trying to lick her. 'Goodness, you're a lively one,' she said. 'I know a million things about children, Cook, but nothing about dogs.'

Cook looked at her sadly. 'He's called Oliver.'

'Oh, I see you can talk to dogs now, can you, Cook?'

'Very funny, Nancy,' she replied. 'Look this what I know. Mr Bell heard Billy chatting to Oliver on Boxing Day morning, saying his daddy had read him a story about an orphan boy called Oliver Twist, and as the puppy had no home that's what he named him. He said they could be orphans and best friends together.'

'Then why in Heaven's name,' said Nancy, 'didn't Billy take the puppy back to the caretaker's cottage.'

'Because, Nancy, little Billy found Oliver in the woods; he had no idea that Mr Bell knew anything about him. He was totally unaware that Mr Bell had seen them together, let alone heard them. You know what Mr Bell is like, he doesn't get involved, and when he saw Billy hide Oliver in the stable he assumed the puppy would eventually either come back to his cottage or find his way home.'

'Oh, Cook, whatever will we do?'

'Do you think we should take him back to Mr Bell's cottage?'

They paused for a moment and looked towards the cottage but all the lights were off and there was no smoke coming from the chimney. 'Well, I'm not knocking him up out of bed,' Nancy said.

'Look, I've given Oliver some water and good wholesome food, along with some extra blankets,' Cook said. 'He'll be safe from the storm in here tonight, and we can decide what to do tomorrow. Now we have to go inside and warm up, Nancy, or we'll get pneumonia and that won't help anyone.'

Nancy and Cook opened the stable door and Oliver scampered around outside for a couple of minutes, then hurried back inside. They dried him, gave him some water, then snuggled him up in the big blankets Cook had brought. The storm was beginning to die down now and Oliver lay curled up and content. He looked up at Nancy. 'Don't look at me like that,' she said, then smiled. 'Be back tomorrow little one.'

Nancy and Cook, arm in arm, returned to the warmth of the kitchen, where Cook insisted there would be a good strong cup of tea waiting for Nancy when she had changed into some dry clothes.

A few minutes later, Nancy was sitting in one of the comfortable chairs at either side of the still-hot range. Cook carried over two hot steaming mugs of tea, then sat down opposite her. There was a comfortable silence until suddenly Nancy looked at Cook.

'What is it now, for Heaven's sake, Nancy?'

'Cook, where did you get those blankets?'

'Cake, cake, I forgot the cake! Woooh, silly me. Where is my head tonight?' Cook said, ignoring her.

'Cook?'

'You know fine well I got them from your secret stash in the attic, Nancy Harmer. Now drink your tea and eat your cake.'

The two friends sat together as their feet warmed by the oven.

'A puppy, Cook! I never would have believed it.'

'Well, it was you that was forever on bended knee, praying for a miracle.'

'Dear God, Cook, I didn't mean a dog.'

'Well then, Nancy Harmer, you should be more specific when you pray.' Cook roared with laughter at her own joke.

Nancy sighed. 'I knew there was trouble brewing,' she said.

What to Do, What to Do?

Nancy hardly slept for the rest of the night. Every time the wind strengthened she got up and looked out towards the stables. She turned to her holy pictures. 'A dog,' she said. 'Really? Is that your answer? A puppy that needs feeding, taking for walks? It's not like I have anything better to do, is it? I've looked after hundreds of children and I know exactly what to do with them, what to say, how to help them. I fail once and you send me a puppy. Well, thank you for that. Now I have a child that won't talk to me but spends his time talking to stars in the sky, one that is refusing to walk and wants to go to Heaven and you send me a puppy. Well, that solves all my problems doesn't it?'

Nancy was feeling just a little bit angry not to mention out of her depth. It wasn't just that the puppy needed looking after. It was what Cook had said about little Billy. His little eyes were lit up like none of them had ever seen, apparently, so how would he feel when the puppy was taken away? Because it must belong to somebody, although how it had got here in the first place God only knew. 'Yes,' she said, to her holy pictures. 'You know what's going on, don't you? Well, if this is your idea of a miracle then I am completely bemused and you will have to explain this yourself. Am I to understand that this puppy will solve all our problems?'

Nancy sighed. She would have to tell everyone about the puppy, and break the news to Billy when it was taken away. Cook should have told her sooner, yet Nancy knew her friend's heart had been in the right place. Nancy's anger was suddenly replaced by a sinking feeling inside. How in God's name will I tell Mother? Sister Mary Joseph on the other hand will be highly amused, no doubt. Oh Billy, Nancy thought, what on earth am I going to do?

Nancy got up and went along the corridor into the children's bedroom. She sat on the little chair next to Billy's bed and patted his shoulder. 'Don't pretend you're asleep,' she whispered. He turned over and gazed into her eyes. 'I hear you found a puppy, young man.'

'I'm sorry,' he said, 'it was all my fault. Martha – I mean, some of the children helped me. I'm sorry,' he said again, looking frightened.

'Well,' said Nancy, wiping his tears away with the edge of her apron, 'shall I tell you something?' He nodded. 'You must have made some wonderful friends and for them to help you like that they must think you are very special indeed.' There it was, thought Nancy, the sparkle in his eyes. 'When you're frightened or upset, it's always your best friends that help. You're lucky, Billy, to have such good friends, and I think you've been very brave and extremely clever.'

Billy sat up in bed. 'We've been so worried, Aunty Nancy,' he said. As Nancy sat holding his hand, he told her about taking the cakes and the straw and Nancy had to hold her apron up more than once to stifle the laughter threatening to burst out. It was quite a speech and, most importantly, he hadn't mentioned the stars in the sky once. Little Billy's heart was healing, and Nancy was about to break it again. Well, she couldn't have that; something had to be done. Nancy settled Billy down and tucked him in. 'Somewhere there'll be an answer to this,' she told him. 'You leave it with me and I'll sort it out if you'll go back to sleep. I need a strong cup of tea – this is a problem of epic proportions,' she told him, smiling. Little Billy didn't understand what that meant but he was comforted. Aunty Nancy was really rather wonderful.

'Do you promise, Aunty Nancy?' he whispered.

'I promise, Billy,' she replied.

The next morning, Nancy went downstairs to see Cook who called out, 'Slept well?'

'Don't be funny,' Nancy replied. 'I need to know what to do about Oliver,' she said.

'I've made him a nice breakfast.' Cook handed her a bowl. 'Now, away with you. I have a houseful of people to feed and you're under my feet.'

Nancy looked at Cook who was smirking. 'You are just loving this, aren't you?' Cook roared with laughter and Nancy left to make her way over to the stable, where Oliver was delighted to see her. She watched him gobble his breakfast, then went to the door and looked outside. 'We have to get you out of here,' she said. 'You need a good run around, to do your, erm, well, your business,' she said, and let the puppy out. Oliver bounded over to the wood and she watched as he ran around the trees and scampered through the snow. Every now and again he would return to Nancy and, standing on his back legs with his front paws on her knees, stare up at her, wagging his tail. 'What is it, boy?'

Oliver barked.

'Quieten down,' said Nancy. 'We have to figure out what to do with you.' She set off around the wood, Oliver trotting beside her. 'What to do, what to do, oh my goodness, what am I going to do? It's my day off, Oliver. I'm supposed to be having a lovely lie-in and going to see my friend. I hadn't planned on walking around the wood half freezing myself this time in the morning, thank you.'

Oliver sniffed and looked up at Nancy. 'Never mind looking at me with those big puppy dog eyes. It doesn't help.' Oliver kept looking over to his left and back at Nancy again. 'What can you see, pet?' she said stroking his head. Suddenly she realised what he was looking at. 'Of course, clever boy,' she said. Together they hurried towards the smoke which was now billowing out from old Mr Bell's chimney. She went straight to the cottage and knocked and Oliver barked. 'Ssssh, be quiet,' she said. Nancy waited then knocked again. Still there was no answer. She was beginning to shiver uncontrollably and Oliver began once more to bark. She knocked again and, at last, heard a bolt being pulled back and the door opened.

'Found the puppy then, have you?' he said.

Nancy looked stunned. 'Dear God, am I the only person in the world who didn't know about him?'

Mr Bell gave a low chuckle. 'Been watching the goings-on, I have,' he told Nancy. 'Seen Cook running back and forwards. Kept hoping the basket in her hand was for me.'

'Look,' Nancy said, 'I'd rather not die of pneumonia on your doorstep so will you take him until I can sort something out?'

Mr Bell opened the door wider to let the puppy in, then closed it.

'I'll take that as a yes,' muttered Nancy. Then, satisfied for now, she hurried back to the comfort of her room, where she changed into warmer clothes and hurried along to the kitchenette for a hot cup of tea.

Nancy sat quietly listening to the familiar sounds of the house around her. People were getting up and going about their business. She looked at the kitchen clock. Well, another crisis averted and all before seven in the morning. She would tell Dolly where Oliver was and who would let the children and staff know all about it. The rest could be sorted when she got home later. Nancy heaved a sigh of relief. She returned to her room and heard the children walk past on their way to breakfast. She put on her best hat and coat then left to get the trolley bus to visit her friend Tilly, feeling very pleased with herself. What tales she had to tell her friend. Tilly, she knew, would be highly amused.

After breakfast, Billy told the other children that Aunty Nancy had found Oliver and they were extremely relieved to hear they weren't all in deep trouble. 'She wasn't cross at all and she said she'd think of something. She promised.'

'Well,' said Martha, 'if Aunty Nancy promised, everything will be all right.'

'If everyone knows about him, we can just ask to go and see him,' Billy said, 'and we can ask Cook for food for him.'

The children were all very excited indeed. When Sister Mary Joseph came into the playroom they all ran over to her.

'Sister, can we go and see the puppy?'

'He'll be hungry now, Sister.'

'Oh Sister, he is ever so lovely.'

'We need to ask Cook for food for him.'

Sister Mary Joseph listened to the children's cries and wondered, not for the first time, why Nancy was always away when these things happened. She had absolutely no idea what they were talking about. 'Puppy, what puppy? Children, is this a game?'

'No, Sister, the puppy in the stable that came at Christmas.'

Sister Mary Joseph was completely confused. 'I am sorry, children, there is no puppy in a stable.'

'There is, there is, we can show you, Sister, really we can.'

When Caroline, one of the helpers, came along, Sister Mary Joseph asked her to help put the children's hats and coats on. Maybe if they saw the empty stable, that would solve the problem. It was very strange indeed.

Five very excitable children almost dragged Sister Mary Joseph down the stairs, along the corridor and out of the door leading to the stable. 'Hurry up, Sister,' they called, then let go of her hand and ran to the stable, pulling open the door. When Sister caught up with the children they were standing silently inside the stable. Suddenly Billy ran over and began to dig through the straw, throwing the blankets and dressing gowns all over before turning to the children and a very shocked Sister Mary Joseph. Little Billy Miller sat amongst the straw in the empty stable and began to sob. 'She lied,' he cried, 'Aunty Nancy lied.'

The Tallest Christmas
Tree in the World

Billy thought his heart would burst open and his throat hurt badly with unshed tears. He was too angry to cry. He didn't believe anybody any more. Aunty Nancy had promised she'd sort Oliver out but she hadn't after all. Oliver had gone. They had taken him away and he would never see him again. Billy remembered how good it had felt to play with him. It had made Billy feel all happy inside, like when he played trains. He'd told the puppy all about Mummy and Daddy being stars in the sky and how he had been the driver on the Ragdoll Express. It was easier to talk to Oliver than anyone else: he understood and would wag his tail furiously, making Billy laugh.

Billy Miller might be only five years old but he was nearly six and Daddy had said that when he was six he would be a big boy and they would go to the train station together and ride on the steam train. Billy could forget about that now. The Ragdoll Express was fun, but it wasn't real. It was just pretend. Mummy had told him that pretend things were fun but not real. There was no steam or hissing sounds like a real train made. Daddy had bought Billy books about trains and they had read them over and over again. Billy had no idea where they were now. It didn't matter anyway: without Daddy it was no fun – and he didn't want to be here any more, where people made promises they didn't keep.

There was a pain inside him that was getting stronger and stronger, a grief that would not leave him, and young Billy Miller began to sob, his small shoulders shaking. Until, finally, in anger he screamed at the injustice of what the world had done to him. They would come looking for him soon, but he wouldn't be here. He was going to run away and never come back. They had been playing hide and seek that afternoon before it got too dark to play out, but Billy was fed up with playing games. He walked through the wood, kicking the snow in anger. His face was red with the cold but he didn't care in the least. He stepped out of the wood and found himself at the large iron gates. If he was going to do it, it would have to be done now. He could hear his name being called. He looked around but there was nobody about.

He made up his mind. He ran out of the gates onto Sandyford Road and kept running until he was out of breath. He stopped for a moment and looked around. It was only a few days after Christmas but there were lots of people on the streets.

Jesmond was a busy area, full of houses and corner shops, and many trolley buses ran along Sandyford Road to the centre of Newcastle upon Tyne. Children were playing in the snow wherever he looked. Billy stood against a wall and watched a young child being pulled on a sledge by his father. How wonderful that looked, he thought. He continued to watch them, day-dreaming about how it would feel to be pulled around on a sledge. The door opened behind them and a lady came out carrying hot drinks. Billy closed his eyes and imagined the taste of whatever was in those mugs she was carrying. It would be hot cocoa or something else just as wonderful, he just knew it. Bet they've got a dog as well, he thought and he kicked the snow angrily. He watched the little boy get picked up and swung around before being carried indoors. There were pretty lights on the Christmas tree in the window and he watched them twinkling until the lady closed the curtains. It wasn't fair, it just wasn't fair.

Suddenly, Billy noticed how cold he was. There was nothing for it: he would have to go back. He didn't care if he was told off. His feet felt like lead as he trudged through the snow. It was getting dark now so the lights of the bus coming down the street blinded him for a moment. Then he saw a group of people standing at the stop and ran across the road.

'Only going as far as Central Station,' the conductor called to them as they hurried onto the bus.

Billy paused only for a second before ducking through the crowd and jumping on, hurrying to the front, hoping and praying the conductor wouldn't notice him.

As luck would have it, all the conductor was concerned about was finishing his shift and getting home. He had three days' holiday when he was finished this shift, and a good hearty meal was waiting for him, then he was off to the pub with friends for a pint or two. He was thinking about that now and taking no notice whatsoever of the little lad at the front of the bus. It was full anyway and the boy could have belonged to any of the people on the packed bus. He wandered up and down, shouting, 'tickets, please,' out of duty but without any real sense of purpose. Only fifteen more minutes and he would be finished.

Billy was remembering last year, when Mummy and Daddy had taken him to Newcastle's Central Station to hear the carol singers. He'd thought it all sounded extremely boring until they told him he would be able to see and hear the steam trains. There would also be a big surprise for him when they got there, he had been told. Billy had hardly slept the night before, wondering what on earth it could be. Billy could see it all now. Mummy had scolded him when he woke her up at five a.m. but Daddy had just laughed and pulled him into bed with them. Together they had ridden on the trolley bus to the station, the biggest building Billy had ever seen, and hundreds of people were milling about. Everyone was smiling. 'That's because it's Christmas,' Mummy had told him, 'and Christmas is magic.'

Daddy had lifted him onto his shoulders and held his hands. 'Close your eyes, son,' he shouted. 'I've got a surprise for you.'

Billy had shut his eyes tightly.

'Keep them shut now, Billy.'

'Yes, Daddy.'

'Promise, Billy.'

'I promise.'

'All aboard,' shouted Daddy, and ran into the station with Billy bouncing on his shoulders.

Billy could hear people singing and trains in the distance. Then he heard something else. It was much nearer. Toot-toot. Chuff-chuff-chuff. A whistle blew.

'Open your eyes, son,' Daddy said.

Never in all his life would little Billy Miller forget the sight in front of him. He looked up and up and up for what seemed like miles until he saw the bright shining star at the top of the tallest Christmas tree in the world. And at the foot of the tree a miniature train was puffing its way around its track. Billy was lifted down and Daddy took him closer to watch the train circle the enormous tree. Every year a fir tree grown in Bergen, Norway, was sent to Newcastle as a symbol of friendship between the two countries, and this year it was standing in the station. It was a great tradition to come along and see it. Once it was decorated it was a wondrous sight to behold and the people of Newcastle flocked in their thousands to see it.

Billy was enchanted. He had to be dragged away. The family had gone to a nearby café and had hot cocoa to warm themselves. Billy remembered what he had asked next.

'Daddy?'

'Yes, son?'

'Can we come again next year?'

'We'll come every year, son.'

'Promise, Daddy.'

'Promise, son.'

Daddy had broken his promise too.

Now Billy rubbed the window with his sleeve so he could see outside. The bus was cold but the windows were steaming up. His eyelids were drooping and he was frightened he would fall asleep so he made himself look out of the window, but it was dark and almost impossible to see anything. He would have been frightened if he hadn't been so sad and numb.

He jumped when he heard the conductor shout, 'Newcastle Central Station next stop.' When the bus stopped, he climbed off with all the other people. He stayed very close to a man with a young boy and pretended he was with them as they got off.

A policeman was standing on the corner of the street. Billy ducked quickly into a shop doorway and waited. His heart was thumping and now he was beginning to feel very frightened indeed. Suddenly Billy's little world became a very scary place to be. Bravely, he peeped out and saw the policeman had gone . . .

Suddenly a man grabbed him and Billy screamed. The man was swaying from side to side and had a bottle in his hand. Billy stamped on his foot and ran as fast as he could along the street, then across the road to the station entrance before stopping to catch his breath. He was nearly there – he remembered it now. Across the road he saw the café he had been to with Mummy and Daddy. He wondered if the huge tree would be there.

He closed his eyes and wished. Aunty Nancy said if you believed hard enough wishes could come true. With all his heart he prayed that the tree with the train would be there. Eventually he opened his eyes and whispered over and over to himself, 'Let it be there, let it be there.' He slowly made his way through the enormous portico and into the station.

There it was. Just like last time. Exactly the same. The tree was so tall it almost reached the ceiling of the station and at the very top there was a shiny star. Toot-toot. The miniature train was circling the tree, and Billy was mesmerised. The sound of the little train and the hissing of the steam trains at the platforms soothed him. He was beyond freezing now, but he didn't care in the least. He sat down, cross-legged, and watched the train as it went round and round and round.

Where's Billy?

Nancy had enjoyed her day off and was smiling as she made her way through the gates. She was looking forward to a good natter and a cup of tea in her room with Dolly, who would have told Billy where Oliver was. She wondered how Billy had taken the news about the puppy being able to stay. That, of course, was the easy bit: she was still dreading having to tell Mother Superior about him. In her head she had gone over and over how she would tell Mother about the puppy in the caretaker's cottage. This had all gone on long enough now, but Nancy hoped and prayed the puppy could stay as long as old Mr Bell was happy to keep it. She would speak to Mother tonight.

Billy would have been extremely relieved to know where Oliver was. He would have been excited, too, she imagined. Nancy could hardly believe the children had managed to keep the puppy secret; honestly, Nancy had never known such a thing to happen. It had been impossible to be angry with them. Poor little mites, she thought. A puppy indeed – as if she hadn't enough to worry about – and yet those eyes that looked at her. Nancy too had felt Oliver's charm. She would call on old Mr Bell tomorrow, with Billy and a few of the others. They could take Oliver for a run in the woods. The fresh air would do them the world of good. It had been kind of Mr Bell to give him refuge. Nancy just hoped he would let Oliver stay. It was your idea to send him here, God, she thought, smiling, so please make sure we're allowed to keep him. Now for a couple hours' feet up and a strong brew.

Nancy was startled by shouts from the bottom of the driveway. She looked towards the front door, which was wide was open. Sister Mary Joseph was hurrying towards her. 'Nancy, come quickly!' Any thoughts of a nice relaxing evening faded as she saw the fear on Sister Mary Joseph's face.

'Calm yourself, Sister. What on earth has got you into such a state?"

'Billy! Oh, Nancy, it's Billy.'

'Billy? Why, what's wrong? Did Dolly tell him about Oliver?'

'Oliver?'

'The puppy, Sister.'

'Puppy?'

'Oh, please tell me. Didn't Dolly tell you about him staying at Mr Bell's cottage?'

'Thank God! But why is Billy there?'

'Not Billy, Oliver. Oliver is at Mr Bell's cottage.'

'Who's Oliver? And where is Billy?'

Nancy took a deep breath. 'Can we start again, Sister, before I lose patience altogether?'

'It's Billy, Nancy.'

'Right,' Nancy sighed. 'Today, before leaving for my day off, I left Oliver, the puppy Billy found, with Mr Bell, who is happy to look after him. I asked Dolly to let Billy know.'

'Dolly's mother is poorly so she was told to go home and help with the family. Oh, Nancy, he's gone.'

'Gone?'

'Yes, gone. Nancy, we have searched and searched the house and grounds.'

'Oh dear, well, maybe he ran home after all.'

'Ran home?'

'Yes, Sister, Oliver, maybe he went home.'

Suddenly, Nancy heard barking coming from the caretaker's cottage and her heart froze.

'Sister, who exactly is gone?'

'It's little Billy, Nancy. Little Billy has disappeared. He's gone.'

The Pretendy Train

Nancy almost ran down the rest of the drive and her heart was pounding when she saw the police car at the front door, Mother Superior standing beside it. 'Honestly, Mother, I have just one day off,' she said.

'The children are extremely upset, Nancy.'

'As well they might be, Mother,' Nancy replied. 'I'm not over happy myself.'

There was a cough and a young policeman stepped forward. 'My name is PC Joseph Dodds and if you wouldn't mind,' he said, interrupting them, 'I need to take some details from you.'

Nancy turned to look at him and said, 'Firstly, young man, it's extremely rude to get somebody's attention by coughing and, secondly, I mind very much indeed. I have a nursery full of young children who are extremely upset by all of this so you'll have to excuse me.' She hurried off, leaving the young man red-faced, his pencil and notebook held mid-air.

Mother turned to the policeman and said, 'We find it best to let her make the decisions. It makes for a quieter life altogether. Come along and have some tea, and I'll see what I can do.'

*

Upstairs the children gathered around Nancy. It took some time to calm them all down. The helpers were sent off to make some warm milk for them, and Nancy took them into the playroom.

'Aunty Nancy will know exactly what to do', said Martha, and the children all turned to look at Nancy and waited.

'Would you like to play, children?' Nancy asked.

The children didn't want to play or sing. Then came the tears and Nancy took them to the television room. 'Put the TV on,' she said to the helpers, 'and sit with them while I think what to do.'

'Maybe they could play trains, Nancy. It seems to be their favourite game at the moment,' a helper suggested.

Thomas said, 'It's Billy's train and he's the driver. We can't play trains without Billy.'

'Anyway,' said Martha, 'Billy's fed up of pretendy trains. He wants to go and see the real ones.'

Nancy was standing with her eyes closed and the children watched as she muttered to herself. 'Trains? Real ones?' Suddenly she opened her eyes and looked at Martha. 'What else did he say, Martha, can you remember?'

'Well, Auntie Nancy, last year he went to the big station with the real trains and it had a pretendy train as well.'

'Pretendy train, darling?'

'Yes, and it went round and round the tree.'

Nancy's heart sank; this was making no sense at all. Had he made it all up?

Then all eyes turned to Thomas, who was murmuring, 'Round and round and round the pretendy train goes.'

'Where is the pretendy train?' Nancy asked. 'Can you remember?'

'Oh, yes, Aunty Nancy. Round the big tree that goes up to the roof.'

Nancy took a deep breath. This was making no sense. 'Anything else, my darlings?'

'I've told you already, Aunty Nancy,' said Thomas. 'Round the big tree in the station where the real trains are.'

'Yes,' added Martha, 'and you can hear the steam hissing on the real big trains. Billy told us all about it.'

Little heads were nodding in agreement as Nancy finally began to understand. Surely not, it couldn't possibly be? He is only five years old, well, almost six; he would never manage it . . . Dear God, where would he be now? Nancy ignored the noises all around as she closed her eyes and tried to figure out how it could be done. He would either be completely lost and could be anywhere, cold and frightened, or somehow he had jumped on the trolley bus to the Central Station, but then surely to God someone would have seen him.

Downstairs in the nuns' parlour Mother Superior was asking the young policeman to sit down for a slice of Cook's special cake with his tea. He licked his lips when it was placed in front of him. 'I don't mind if I do,' he said. 'Just until I can get the details I need, of course.'

'Naturally,' said Mother, and raised her eyes to Heaven. She would go and get Nancy, she told him. As it happened there was no need. At that moment, the door was thrown open and Nancy burst into the room, just as PC Dodds lifted the cake to his lips.

'What on earth do you think you're doing? There is no time for that. Come along, no time to waste, she said.' PC Dodds was dragged out of the parlour. 'That is your car outside, I presume, Nancy said, not needing an answer. She jumped in and told him to drive to Newcastle Central Station.

PC Dodds opened his mouth to say something, then closed it. They were halfway up the drive when Nancy screamed, 'Stop!' and the poor man got the fright of his life. She jumped out of the car and he watched her run across to an old cottage, emerging seconds later with a puppy wrapped inside her coat. She climbed back into the car, saying, 'Hurry up, come along then. Hurry, please hurry.'

PC Dodds thought about remonstrating but in the end he did as he was told. Most people did where Nancy was concerned.

It seemed to take for ever to get there but eventually they pulled up outside the station and Nancy jumped out and ran towards the Christmas tree with PC Dodds, hoping and praying with every step that Billy would be there. Along with everybody else who lived in Newcastle, she knew about the special Christmas tree at the Central Station. Nancy and PC Dodds stopped and looked around. There was a carol service going on and many people were standing by the tree listening to the singers.

'Where is he?' she said to Oliver, whose tail was wagging furiously. If Billy wasn't here, then he really was lost, and the thought terrified her. 'Dear God, Billy, where are you?'

Suddenly Oliver barked, leaped out of her arms and tore off towards the tree. Some of the people moved aside, wondering what on earth was happening, and it was then Nancy saw him. Her legs almost gave way as she saw him sitting there. 'The pretendy train,' she whispered. Clearly Billy had heard the commotion and turned just as Oliver jumped into his arms and licked his face.

PC Dodds moved towards Billy but Nancy stopped him. 'I think not,' she said. 'Any telling off will be done by me.' She walked towards Billy, who looked up at her, his eyes full of tears. She reached for his hand, which was freezing cold. They looked at each other as the choir began to sing once more, and Nancy lifted him into her arms and wrapped her coat around him and Oliver.

PC Dodds stepped forward. 'I need to make a report,' he said.

'I need a bigger coat but I'm not complaining,' Nancy replied. 'Come on,' she said, feeling a little sorry for PC

Dodds. 'Take us home and you can have the tea and cake you were promised.'

They settled into the car and Nancy clasped Billy tightly to her, trying to warm him up. She saw her reflection in the car window. Look at the state of me, she thought, sitting in a police car with a frozen child and a puppy wrapped in my coat. She tapped Billy's shoulder. 'Oh, by the way, just one thing to remember, Billy,' she said. 'I never break a promise.'

Billy smiled, closed his eyes and slept.

Confessions

Well, that was the easy bit, thought Nancy. Now to explain it all to Mother. She had no idea how to broach the subject but it could no longer be kept a secret. Mother had to know. Fortunately, as long as Mr Bell allowed the puppy to stay at the cottage there shouldn't be a problem. She made her way to the parlour, muttering and mumbling under her breath, hoping that Mother wouldn't be too cross with her.

'What else was I supposed to do, Mother?' she would say. 'After all, it seems God sent the puppy. It wasn't my idea.' No, Mother wouldn't be like that at all. Nancy continued to mutter to herself as she made her way down the parlour stairs.

Sister Angela came out of her room and approached Nancy. Mother had gone to bed early, feeling a little under the weather. She had actually been in her room resting all day and had only got up when Billy had been reported missing. Mother, Nancy was told, was hoping to be at Mass tomorrow morning to hear the children singing. From next week, Mother knew, Nancy would be starting to teach them hymns for the Easter service. Nancy liked to be prepared well in advance. There would be no confessions tonight, it seemed, and with a heavy heart Nancy made her way back up to the nursery and went into her room.

Sister Mary Joseph popped in with a pot of tea and told her that Billy was chatting away happily.

'And Josephine?' asked Nancy.

'Still refusing to walk. The doctor's calling in on Monday to see her.'

'I've let her down with all this fuss about the puppy,' Nancy said. 'Josephine is a sweet little thing and I'm beyond sad to hear her say all she wants is to go to Heaven to see Mummy and Daddy. Have you ever heard anything so heartbreaking?'

They sat for a while in silence, sipping their tea, neither one of them knowing what to say. It was quite simply two friends together and, after a comfortable time had passed, Sister Mary Joseph reached out for Nancy's hand. 'What are we going to do?' she asked.

'I have no idea, Sister,' Nancy replied. 'I usually know exactly what to do but I've failed. I almost failed little Billy and now this. Oh, Lord, we go from one problem to another at the moment.'

They fell into silence once more. Nancy and Sister Mary Joseph heard barking in the distance and walked to the window to look out into the night. They could see old Mr Bell's torch light bobbing between the trees and heard Oliver barking happily. 'I'll take the children to see Oliver tomorrow,' Nancy said. 'They'll love that.'

*

Nancy decided on an early night and crept into bed, only pausing when she heard Oliver barking happily again in the wood. She glanced over at her holy pictures and shook her head. 'A puppy indeed,' she said, smiling, before reaching out to switch off her bedside lamp.

The next morning Nancy told the children they would be taking Oliver out for a run after Mass. The resulting uproar made her wish she had left telling them until after breakfast. She had hoped that Mother would not make the service, but was told she was feeling much better and would be there. I'll tell her after Mass, she thought. I can pray for forgiveness during the service before I go and get a telling-off. The children knew their carols by heart and this would be the last time they would sing them this year.

Well, regardless of what I have to do after Mass, I am not going to let anything spoil the thrill of seeing little Billy standing at the altar singing, thought Nancy. The children were eventually calmed down and made their way downstairs.

The priest began and it was a lovely service. Nancy kept glancing at Mother from time to time, but she never looked over once. At the end of Mass the children all took their place at the altar and Sister Angela played the introduction to 'Hark! The Herald Angels Sing'. The carol was only halfway through when Nancy heard it. Sister Mary Joseph turned to her. It was quite faint but they could hear Oliver barking. The children's faces told them they had heard it too. Nancy stared at them and lifted her hand. 'Louder,' she mouthed. When Mother turned her head, Nancy was sitting once more with her hands in her lap, the picture of innocence.

Oliver began to bark once more. This time Nancy quickly raised her hands again, mouthing, 'Louder, louder.' The children began to shout 'Hark the Herald Angels' so loudly that Father looked over to Mother who looked over to Sister Mary Joseph. When the carol was over, Sister Mary Joseph and Nancy sat like statues, hardly daring to breathe. Please God, please God, Nancy was praying, not until I have the chance to explain myself, please. Her wish was granted: all had fallen silent.

They all stood up and she hurried the children down from the altar into a line and walked behind them as they made their way out of the chapel. Nancy kept her head down, but just as she reached the front pew Mother reached out and touched Nancy's arm. 'You know, Nancy, I'm almost sure I heard a dog barking.'

'Did you, Mother, did you really?' said Nancy and almost fell over the children as she pushed them in front of her to get out of the chapel as quickly as she possibly could. Mother raised questioning eyebrows at Sister Mary Joseph whose face was by now beetroot red.

When everyone except Mother had left, the chapel fell silent. The rosary beads in her fingers were lifted to her lips and she kissed them, then sat on the pew to wait. She had known for days that something was going on. She was disappointed that Nancy had not felt able to come to her with it. Mother had called into the kitchen before Mass. She had seen Cook going regularly to the wood, which was quite out of character. In the end Cook had muttered and mumbled until at last the whole story had tumbled out. Whatever Mother had expected, it had not been that.

It wasn't long before Mother heard the door open and footsteps down the aisle. She heard Nancy walk to the altar and watched her make the sign of the cross, then come to sit beside her.

'Come to confess, Nancy?'

'Confess, Mother?'

'Yes – you know, when you have done wrong and you wish to unburden your soul.'

'Yes, thank you, Mother. I know what confession is.'

'Well then, Nancy?'

'Oh, Mother, you already know, don't you?'

'I think this is not a conversation for the chapel. Shall we go?' Mother stood up and together they made their way up the aisle.

'Are you angry with me, Mother?' Nancy said with a catch in her voice.

'Only saddened that you couldn't tell me, Nancy.'

'Oh, Mother, I'm sure it was God sent us the puppy. What do you think?'

'I think,' said Mother, 'I need a very strong cup of tea.'

Happiness Bubble

Little Billy Miller had no idea how to explain exactly how he was feeling but it was really rather wonderful indeed. It was a kind of strange feeling, like a little bubble inside that made him want to laugh.

He had been running around in the wood for over an hour now and Oliver showed no signs of slowing down one little bit. Yet every now and again Oliver would stop and check that Billy was there following him and wag his tail furiously every time Billy spoke to him. Billy was too young to understand what was happening; all he knew was that the horrible heavy feeling inside that made him want to cry over and over again was fading away. He could open his mouth and shout out now without feeling like something was stopping him. Of course, he still looked up to the stars in the sky, but he believed what Aunty Nancy had told him about 'for-ever magic' because Aunty Nancy always told the truth.

Today Oliver had almost knocked him over when he bounded out of the cottage towards him. Mr Bell told him that Oliver knew he was coming even before he got there. 'Doesn't do that with anyone else,' he had said. Billy felt very important indeed. When he thought about it, he got that bubbly feeling again and it always made him smile.

It had all started the first time he saw Oliver in the wood on Boxing Day. That was the first time he had felt the bubble. It had got stronger and stronger and now Billy could feel it just by thinking of Oliver.

Later Mr Bell had called over, saying he had a cup of hot chocolate for him and Oliver had gone bounding over, nearly knocking him over as he ran in the door to grab his place in front of the fire. Billy laughed and laughed and the bubble got bigger and bigger.

Now Billy sat in front of the fire and Oliver curled up beside him, listening to the crackling sounds and watching the flames.

There was a knock on the door. It was Aunty Nancy, telling him it was time to go back to the house for tea. Oliver stood up and climbed onto Billy's knee as if to say please don't go. Billy thought the bubble was getting so big it would surely burst and he put his arms around Oliver and cuddled him.

Nancy came over and patted Oliver, who looked at her with sad eyes. 'Never mind looking at me like that, Billy has to eat, you know. I will bring him back in the morning, I promise,' Nancy told him.

Nancy found it hard to believe the love that Billy and Oliver had now. Somehow this young child and the dog had forged this incredible bond from the moment they'd met. Nancy thought it was one of the most beautiful things she had ever seen.

Billy was beside Nancy holding her hand then suddenly he looked up at her, smiling. 'Aunty Nancy.'

'Yes, Billy?'

'I have been feeling strange.'

'Oh Heavens, Billy, are you feeling unwell.'

'No, Aunty Nancy, I feel bubbly.'

'Bubbly?'

'I get bubbly in my tummy when I see Oliver and it make me smile. At first it was just one bubbly feeling but now it feels like lots of bubbles. Sometimes it even makes me laugh out loud.'

A sob escaped Nancy and she had to gulp hard.

'I like my bubbles, Aunty Nancy. What are they?'

Nancy stopped for a moment and then took both the young child's hands. 'Well, Billy, it's called the Happiness Bubble and we get them when we love someone, and when we are loved in return, it bursts into lots of little happiness bubbles. You, my darling, have a tummy full of happiness bubbles because you are kind, loving and one of the bravest children I have ever met.'

Nancy turned away quickly so that Billy wouldn't see the tears in her eyes and together they walked back to the house.

Billy smiled. Happiness bubbles. He liked that very much indeed.

New Year's Eve

It was always about the children, Nancy thought. Maybe it was because she knew how it felt to lose a mother. When hers had died she had tried hard to remember her voice. There had been no New Year celebrations like there were today. It had been quiet in their house, even though she had two brothers and two sisters. The only sound was of weeping and Nancy remembered it now. Her own tears had been held in check – somehow she couldn't cry. She remembered rocking her baby sister, Mary, to comfort her. She had often dreamed of having her own baby when she grew up. She used to take the children sitting or lying down in their prams in the back lane for a walk. 'Look at her,' the neighbours would say. 'She's a proper little mother and just a little one herself.' Everyone knew Nancy loved children. Patience of a saint, they said, yet she had a stubborn streak: if she made up her mind about something she couldn't be moved.

Tonight Nancy was thinking of herself as a child, her grief, fears and loneliness. She knew how the little ones placed in her arms were feeling and drew on that to help them. When she held them and wiped their tears with the corner of her apron she was telling them,

I understand. I'm here. I'll help you through this until you can smile again. Nancy was thirty-three and, at the moment, a mother to thirty-four children. They came and went – some were adopted – but the children she had at the moment had been there for quite some time. Normally Billy would have gone downstairs by now, as would Josephine – Nancy only had them with her until they were five. However, the junior department was full, so she had kept those two and Martha too. She was such a great help with the little ones. Next week Billy would go to school with the children downstairs. She still hadn't been told what was going to happen with Josephine.

Every year there were more and more babies. Nancy was saddened each time she heard about a young girl whose baby had been taken from her. What were the words they used to describe those mothers? Fallen, disgraced and other things Nancy refused to think about. Nobody dared say those words in front of her, they would get the sharp end of her tongue if they did. They were young girls who had made a mistake and the poor souls would pay for it for the rest of their lives. That was punishment enough, she thought. Not that Nancy knew or would ever know how it felt to hold her own child in her arms. She had dreamed about it, of course, and would then brush the thought away. Nancy Harmer was grateful for the life she had been given. Yet still those thoughts would pop into her head when she least expected it. Goodness me, Nancy thought, what is it about New Year's Eve? I'm getting ridiculous.

She walked over to the window and closed the curtains, then went to sit at her small table, where she poured herself a cup of tea. Sister Mary Joseph and Dolly would be along soon to share supper with her. There would be no time for daydreaming then, Nancy thought. Dolly would be full of chatter, telling them about things at home, and they would all have a good laugh. You could never fail to laugh with Dolly around.

All in all, it had been a good year. The Ragdoll Express had been a great success, Billy was now chattering away endlessly and Josephine had begun to smile more. She was settling into life at the orphanage, yet the loss of her parents caused her great pain. Why wouldn't it? thought Nancy. They would talk again tonight about how they might help her. Oliver had been a saviour for Billy so maybe he could help Josephine too. Nancy giggled to herself. If anyone had told me that a puppy would arrive at Christmas and solve our problems, I would have told them to go away and stop being so utterly ridiculous. She had never known what it was to own a dog and never really understood people who talked endlessly about their little darlings like they were children. Yet that moment when she picked Oliver up and he turned his face up to look at her, something inside Nancy melted. Oh those eyes, those big brown eyes, you could drown in them. What a little darling he is, she thought. Nancy burst out laughing. 'Look, I'm doing it now,' she told her holy pictures. 'Whatever next.'

There was a knock on the door and Sister Mary Joseph came in with Dolly bouncing behind her, talking as she walked in the room. 'What are you laughing at, Nancy?' they asked.

'A puppy, of all things,' she replied. 'As if I haven't enough to do with a nursery full of children.'

'You love him just as much as we all do,' Dolly said. 'Now tell us what Mother said about Oliver.'

'Well, nothing's settled yet, but Mother said as long as Mr Bell agrees to keep Oliver in the cottage there shouldn't be a problem. However, she is going to contact the mother house to make sure it will be allowed.'

'She must have got such a shock,' Dolly said.

'Shock, my foot,' said Nancy. 'She knew perfectly well what was going on and was waiting for me to confide in her.'

'Nothing much gets past her,' agreed Sister Mary Joseph. 'Maybe tomorrow we can take all the children out with Oliver. He'll love it and so will they.' She was smiling from ear to ear.

'Come on, Sister,' Nancy said. 'Tell us why you're sitting there looking like the cat that got the cream.'

'I have news about Oliver – and you're never going to believe it.'

'Oooooh, come on then, tell us, tell us.'.

Sister Mary Joseph looked at them both, she was thoroughly enjoying this moment when she knew something they didn't. The waited. 'Sister,' Nancy said, 'if you don't tell us now, there will be no cake.'

That was threat enough. 'Well,' she said, leaning forward, 'Oliver has got a proper lead.'

'Oh, is that all?' they said, disappointed.

'Did one of you buy it?' Sister Mary Joseph asked.

'Oh, I see what you mean!' said Nancy. 'Don't tell me Mr Bell went out and bought one. Well I never!' As far as anyone knew, Mr Bell never left the grounds. He had a sister who visited once a month and brought him anything he needed. He got his food from Cook and his coal was delivered. It had been a shock even to see him walking around the wood, with Oliver scampering among the trees.

'I even saw him smile the other day,' Dolly said.

'Looks like the little chap is healing more hearts than just Billy's,' said Sister Mary Joseph.

'Maybe God *did* send him here,' said Dolly.

'Happy New Year,' they all said with a smile.

They were quite right. It was a still night and the moon shone brightly over the wood where the trees were still, with a layer of frost on their branches. Behind the wood, in the caretaker's cottage, the roaring fire in the grate spat and crackled. Old Mr Bell sat with his socks off, warming his feet. On the big old rug in front of him lay Oliver, curled up happily and content, dreaming of little Billy and how it felt to be in his arms. He missed his mummy though. He could remember vaguely the warmth of her fur and how her nose nuzzled him and tickled him. There had been another fire like this one fairly recently and he remembered a lovely lady who cuddled and kissed him. He liked her too. Like the children's, his memories were fading slightly, but then he remembered Billy and he yawned contentedly. He liked this house with the big fire and the man who constantly patted and stroked him. Yes, Oliver was quite happy to be here. As Nancy, Sister and Dolly chinked their cups together, the moon shone down on the caretaker's cottage. For the second time that year old Mr Bell was smiling.

Fun and Frolics

Nancy was kept busy after New Year. She made what seemed like hundreds of trips up and down the stairs to her treasure trove in the attic. Every piece of wrapping paper was saved and folded, then placed under heavy boxes to flatten it. Glitter was scraped off the Christmas cards and placed in a tin for next year's decorations. All the beds were stripped, the floors cleaned and polished.

Downstairs in the kitchen extra help was brought in to scrub it from top to bottom until every pan and every surface gleamed. Nobody came near the kitchen while this was going on. They didn't dare disturb Cook's cleaning days.

As the weeks went by the snow disappeared, and by mid February it was still cold but dry and crisp. Josephine was taken once a week to the local hospital for check-ups and physiotherapy. She was coming along nicely, they told Nancy, but she still refused to walk. Yet Nancy thought she seemed much happier. She would sit on the floor in the playroom with the other children, but outside she would stay wrapped up in her wheelchair, watching them play and run around the wood with Oliver. Nancy was teaching Josephine to read and write and had discovered she was clever, with a bright, inquisitive mind. There was talk about special help for her at school but nothing had been arranged yet.

The garden door was beneath Nancy's window. One afternoon she heard a frantic knocking. She looked out, and there stood Mr Bell with Oliver. She called down, 'Is something wrong?'

'Is Billy there?' he said. 'Thought he might like to come with us.'

Nancy was thrilled and hurried off to find Billy, then watched him and Mr Bell walking up and down the driveway while Oliver ran in and out of the wood, always coming back to check they were still there. Nancy smiled, it was a happy sight. What joy the little chap had brought to the orphanage, she thought. She couldn't imagine life without him now. Every day the children knocked at the cottage and Mr Bell let Oliver out. Sometimes he went with them and Nancy watched him change. He smiled more, and she had even heard him laugh at Oliver's antics. Oliver had brought more than fun to the orphanage: he had brought a sense of peace, he was healing hearts. I never knew dogs could do that, she thought. How absolutely wonderful it is to watch. I don't understand how it works but maybe it doesn't matter. It is enough to know it does work and this beautiful creature is doing God's work. He has his own little character, just like the children, Nancy thought, remembering yesterday.

*

That afternoon when Nancy was outside with the children, Oliver had gone to Josephine and grabbed her glove, which was attached to a string that ran up one sleeve, across her back inside her coat and down the other. (All the children's gloves were attached to them in this way.) Oliver had the glove in his mouth and had begun to pull while Josephine and the children shrieked with laughter until Josephine almost toppled out of the chair.

Nancy ran over and shouted for Oliver to stop. He stood perfectly still, almost like a statue. Not a muscle moving, no wagging tail. The children all watched and waited, and it was only when they started to laugh that he began running about again. Five minutes later he walked towards Josephine, put a paw on a wheel of her chair and stood perfectly still. 'Look, Aunty Nancy!' the children shouted. 'He's playing statues again.'

Nancy walked across to him and put her hands on her hips. 'Oliver, darling, just beacause you are standing perfectly still it doesn't mean I can't see you or know what you're up to.' He edged his head nearer to Josephine. 'No,' Nancy said. Once more he stayed perfectly still. Nancy was highly amused. Oliver slowly turned his head and then put his head on one side, looking up with those beautiful puppy eyes . . .

Suddenly he grabbed the glove and ran. Josephine was screaming and there was pandemonium as the children tried to grab the dog. Josephine's arm was stretched to its limit – and suddenly she was out of the chair, stumbling towards Oliver. As she fell, Nancy caught her.

The children stood still, shocked into silence. Oliver lay down with his head on his paws. He had been a very naughty boy. He was in trouble if Aunty Nancy's eyes were anything to go by. He whimpered.

Billy went to him and knelt beside him. 'It's all right, boy,' he said, hugging him.

But the children weren't looking at Oliver or Billy. All eyes were on Aunty Nancy and Josephine, who was still standing up. 'Are you all right, Josephine?' Nancy asked, holding her steady.

Josephine burst out laughing. 'Oh, Aunty Nancy, that was the best fun I've ever had.'

The children began to crowd round Josephine and Oliver began to dance round them, bounding up and down until he nearly knocked Josephine over and she had to sit back in her chair. Nancy reached out and picked Oliver up. He looked up at her with his big puppy dog eyes that always worked. Yes she was smiling now. He was very good indeed at this. Oliver waited. 'Well, Oliver,' she said, 'that was certainly one way of getting her out of the chair. Do you think we could find a safer way next time?' Oliver barked in reply.

'Well done, good boy. Now off you go and play,' Nancy told him and he leapt out of her arms.

Nancy walked around watching the children play thinking how happy they looked. They wheeled Josephine around and today she was laughing and shouting along with the rest of them. Their little faces were red and flushed with the cold and Nancy could see their breath, yet as she looked around, every child was smiling happily. Wish I had a camera, thought Nancy; this would be the most perfect picture ever. Still, with or without a camera, I will never forget this sight as long as I live. As Nancy gathered the children together, telling them it was time to get washed for lunch, they were all pleading to come back out again later. 'Tomorrow,' Nancy said, 'I promise, tomorrow.' Mr Bell took Oliver back and waved to them, calling goodbye. It really was quite wonderful to see him smiling, Nancy thought.

After lunch the children went into the playroom and some of the younger ones fell asleep on cushions after their busy morning outside. Nancy set up the ironing board as she watched them. The hospital had been right. Josephine could stand unaided. A bit wobbly, perhaps, but she could certainly do it. Oliver had shown them that. More encouragement was needed.

Later that afternoon, after her mammoth ironing session, she passed Mr Bell's cottage and heard hammering. What on earth was going on? She walked over and knocked on the door. Immediately, Oliver was barking.

'Who is it?'

'It's me, Mr Bell. Are you all right?'

'Busy,' he shouted, and the hammering continued once more.

'Oh, well, that's that then,' thought Nancy.

Nancy set off back down the driveway. Cook waved at her from the window and Nancy waved back. What a good life this is, she thought, and what a wonderful day it's been.

Now, I wonder what Mr Bell is up to . . .

A New Start

Jennifer never knew when the feeling would resurface. Sometimes it just took her by surprise. Today it had been a song on the wireless that made her cry. She never told Michael how much she cried. He was working hard to make his way in the world, he had told her yesterday, then swung her up into his strong arms. Jennifer had laughed and pretended to be happy. She had wanted to say, 'Why? What's the point? It's not like we have a family to feed,' which would have been terribly unfair. Michael was her family and she loved him with all her heart. But, she thought, he should be a father, with a young child bouncing on his knee. She began to cry again as she imagined him with a child on his shoulders.

Michael worked shifts so she was expected to stay at home, make sure there was always a hot meal on the table no matter what time of day or night he came home. Was this it for the rest of her life? Cooking, washing, cleaning: was that really all the future held for her? Last week he had told her he had been promoted, which would mean more money for them. Going up in the world, he had said excitedly. They already had enough to pay the bills, buy food or go out if they wished. Recently he had treated her to a new handbag and a pretty scarf, and there would be a trip to the hairdresser next week when he got his bonus. Why do we need more money, with no child? she thought.

Last week she had met Julia from the office where she used to work when she was shopping and they had gone for a coffee in the local café. 'I want to come back to work,' Jennifer told her. 'I'm going crazy at home.'

'Will Michael let you?' Julia asked.

'I don't know that I care,' Jennifer replied. 'I'm sick and tired of people telling me what to do.'

'What about . . . well, you know?'

'Nothing's happening, and maybe nothing ever will. I lost my baby and everyone just says I should get over it.' Jennifer's hand was shaking and once more the tears were in her eyes – they almost never went away. 'It was my baby, Julia, and I loved it from the moment I knew I was pregnant. It was a boy, I know it. I imagined how he would sit on my knee when I told him stories, how he would sit on Michael's shoulders. I could smell him, feel him in my arms, and then he was gone. Believe me, Julia, if I could get over it I would, but I'm in that house on my own, cleaning and polishing, looking at the clock, checking what time the meal needs to be prepared and I'm fed up. I need to do something so I am not constantly thinking about it all.'

'Go on, then,' Julia said. 'We need someone in the office who knows what to do. I've been promoted to junior manager so I could put your name forward. The last two youngsters we got in haven't a clue. They do as little as possible, then take their pay packets at the end of the week. It would be rather wonderful to have you back. Leave it with me.'

Jenny thought for a moment. 'Thank you. I'll discuss it with Michael tonight.'

Jennifer had a spring in her step when she called at the butcher's on her way home. Would Michael be angry? She hoped not. She'd make a lovely dinner for him tonight. Fortunately he'd be home at five today and they would have the evening together. Perfect, Jennifer thought. She was nervous, though, and spent the afternoon going over the speech she planned to make to Michael. She almost let the potatoes boil dry, then burned her finger on the matches lighting the gas, her hand was shaking so much.

Once the dinner was prepared she lit the fire. Michael liked nothing more than walking through the door to a roaring fire and the smell of dinner cooking. He would kiss her, then go upstairs to wash and change. Jennifer would switch the big light off and leave the lamp on. They would have dinner, and after she had cleared up, she would tell Michael her plans. This was a good idea, yet as the day went on Jennifer felt less and less sure of herself.

Michael was whistling as he walked through the door. 'Something smells nice,' he called. 'I'm going straight upstairs to wash.'

Jennifer served dinner and put the lamp on. Michael didn't miss the flush in her cheeks as he kissed her. 'You're looking mighty pretty and dinner smells wonderful.'

'Tuck in then,' she said.

Michael chatted while she pushed the food around her plate.

'Not hungry?' Michael asked.

Jennifer told him that she had met Julia and had had so much cake it had ruined her appetite. After dinner he sat in front of the fire and called to her to join him. 'Leave the washing-up,' he said.

'Michael Harrison, who do you think I am, leaving dishes in the sink?' She laughed before plunging her hands into the hot water. Truth be told, she had left the dishes lots of times, and they sometimes washed up together later in the evening, but tonight Jennifer was putting off the planned conversation. Could she do it? Would he be hurt or angry? Well, there was only one way to find out. She was vigorously wiping the surfaces after putting all the dishes away when Michael laid his hand on her shoulder and she jumped. 'Are you trying to frighten the life out of me?' she said, with a false laugh.

Michael kissed her cheek, then took the cloth out of her hand and led her to the chair by the fire.

'Jenny, are you going to tell me what all this is about?'

She flushed. Michael knew her better than she'd realised. She opened her mouth to speak but couldn't find the words.

'Is it the baby again?' Michael asked. 'Tell me, Jenny, please. I can't help if you don't tell me what's wrong.'

When Jennifer looked at him, her eyes full of tears, Michael thought his heart would break. He too had felt the loss. Jennifer was right when she said nobody understood. He hadn't told a soul how much pain he had felt when their baby was taken from them. But it was what their loss had done to Jennifer that hurt him most. 'Nature's way of saying something was wrong,' people said. How in God's name was that supposed to make you feel better? he thought angrily. It didn't help in the least when people spouted their ridiculous sayings. It had been their child from day one. My poor Jenny.

Michael held out his arms. 'Come on now,' he said jokingly. 'Surely it can't be me, your handsome husband, you're upset with? I mean, just look at what a catch I am,' he said, spinning round.

Jennifer burst out laughing. 'Idiot,' she said, as Michael wrapped his arms round her.

They stood in each other's arms, perfectly happy in the moment. Then Jennifer spoke quickly: 'I want to go back to work,' she said. She told him about the job at her old firm, then stepped back and waited.

Michael grabbed her hand. 'Is that what this is all about? You want to go back to work? So what's stopping you?'

Jennifer sighed. 'Everyone. You work shifts. They said my job is to look after you, making sure I'm always here when you come home from work. I cook, clean and think about the baby morning, noon and night. I need more, Michael. I have to get out of here.'

Michael sat in the large armchair by the fire and pulled Jennifer onto his knee. They sat there enjoying the heat of the fire as Jennifer curled up on his knee. She loved it when Michael stroked her hair like he was doing now. She had said her piece, and now it was a waiting game. Michael liked to think things over. He stared into the fire, his arms around her.

He didn't want Jennifer to return to work. He liked things just as they were. He wouldn't want to come home to an empty house. But wasn't that what his wife was having to put up with? A constantly empty house when he was at work. Especially with all the hours he had been working lately. He was being selfish. And who had the right to tell them how to run their lives? Well, whoever they were, they could tut and whisper all they liked. If his Jenny wanted to go back to work, they could run their complaints past him and he'd tell them straight. 'I'll make us some tea,' Jennifer murmured.

'Never mind tea.' Michael lifted her off his lap, stood up and grabbed her round the waist. 'Get the hard stuff out! We're celebrating.'

'We are?' Jennifer said, and took out the sherry glasses.

'They'd be fools not to take you on so here's to your success,' Michael said, and Jennifer threw her arms around his neck.

'I'll prepare all your meals,' she said, the words tumbling out of her mouth. 'I'll always have something ready for you before I leave for work and when you come in from the night shift. I can also –'

'Whoa!' Michael said. 'I am capable of warming up food, you know. I think I can almost manage to switch the gas on and light the cooker.' He hadn't seen that sparkle in his wife's eyes for months. If a job cheered her up, they'd make it work between them. She had got pregnant once. Maybe if she wasn't thinking about it all the time she would again. This work thing could be just what she needed. If not, there were tests they could have. So far Jennifer hadn't wanted to go down that route, terrified their failure might be her fault. There was adoption, of course – everyone knew about the babies that were being taken from single mothers. Michael shuddered. He couldn't imagine how awful that must be for the girls and their little ones. They had talked about it once when they'd passed the local orphanage on Sandyford Road. 'Poor lambs,' Jennifer had said.

That night as Jennifer crawled into bed she had a grin on her face that wouldn't go away away and an excitement in her heart that she hadn't felt in a long time. I wonder where the puppy went, she thought. I do hope he's all right. 'Oh well, a new start,' she whispered to herself before switching off the light.

*

The poor little lambs, as Jennifer had called them, were fast asleep, dreaming of running around in the garden with Oliver tomorrow. They were loved as well as cared for. Nancy had a heart that stretched in a million different ways with the capacity to love every single child in her care.

Only a mile separated the two homes and there was no way of knowing how their lives would soon be intertwined in the most incredible way. God worked in mysterious ways, Mother Superior was heard to say often. Indeed he does, and sometimes it was really rather wonderful indeed.

The Thingy

Finally, spring was on its way: crocuses and snowdrops were in bloom, and bluebells would soon fill the wood with colour. Winter already seemed long gone, and although it was not particularly warm, the sun was shining. The hammering in Mr Bell's cottage had gone on for weeks now, and still nobody knew what it was about. Except Oliver, who was in on the secret.

It was 1 April, and when Billy came home from school he burst through the door and asked if he could take Oliver out. 'Hello to you too,' Nancy said, laughing. She was thinking how much the children had grown in the last few months. Billy had shot up and would be needing some new shorts soon. Oliver, too, was bigger, not to mention a source of constant fun. Nancy wondered what they would do without him. He was part of them now and the children loved him. They all did.

With spring in the air Nancy was happy, despite a little sadness. Josephine was still having regular physiotherapy but she wouldn't walk. She loved to be in the garden with Oliver scampering around her and often got out of the chair to sit on the grass with him lying beside her. Somehow Nancy had to find a way to get through to her. The little girl's reading, writing and arithmetic were excellent, and Nancy was a great teacher, but Josephine needed to be at school. They had talked about her mummy and daddy being in Heaven and the children had told her about the stars in the sky, yet still something was stopping her walking.

Josephine missed her parents so much and would for a long time to come. Nancy understood that. She had had a few difficult conversations with Josephine and had told her she couldn't go to Heaven yet because God wasn't ready for her. 'Why did He take my mummy and daddy if He wasn't ready for me?' Josephine had asked.

Why indeed? thought Nancy. Still, she told Josephine that she was getting much better and stronger every day. 'What if I try to walk and it doesn't work?' she said, looking down at the callipers on her legs.

'Well,' Nancy said, standing her up, 'there's only one way to find out, darling. What do you think?'

Josephine had asked if she could try tomorrow, and Nancy had had to be content with that. Then there had been three days of solid rain, and the children had been confined to the playroom, watching Oliver in the grounds with Mr Bell.

Billy was taken over to see him every day, and was allowed to stay for an hour in the morning and another in the afternoon. Nancy ruffled his hair and said, 'Don't you get bored? Mr Bell isn't exactly a chatterbox.'

'He talks to me all the time,' said Billy; 'we talk about lots of things.' Nancy could not have been more surprised.

Finally the weekend brought some dry weather and Nancy had two new helpers to give her a hand. 'Take them outside, and let them play in the garden whilst I tackle the ironing,' she said. Nancy had set the ironing board up in the playroom where she could hear the children and watch them playing out of the big window with the bars on.

There was no sweeter music to Nancy's ears than listening to the children play. The hours whizzed by that afternoon and Nancy eventually bent down to switch off the iron. She wandered over to the window. She watched for a few minutes before realising something very strange, and pressed her nose up against the window. 'Well I never,' she said out loud, 'I don't believe it.' Josephine's chair was empty. Nancy's heart jumped for joy. 'Oh thank you, thank you Lord,' she said, furiously looking around the garden to see where Josephine was. The children were all there, some playing with old tyres, others sitting around the huge oak tree and playing chasing games, yet still she couldn't see Josephine. Nancy could see some of the children were playing mummies and daddies; it was one of their favourite games. The helpers had taken a big old pram out and the children were walking around the garden with it. All was exactly as it should be, but where was Josephine?

Both helpers were in the garden so they couldn't have taken her anywhere.

Nancy began to worry and hurriedly put the iron and ironing board away before hurrying down the stairs that led to the garden. The children saw her as soon as she entered the garden and came running over, asking her to play with them.

'Where's Josephine?' Nancy asked them. When they looked puzzled, she asked again. 'Children, where is Josephine?'

'She's playing over there,' Martha said.

Nancy turned to where they were pointing. 'I can't see her, children. I can't see Josephine.'

'She's playing mummies and daddies and she's the baby,' they told her before running off to play.

Suddenly light dawned. Babies! Nancy burst out laughing, then ran over to the children pushing the pram and there was Josephine bundled up inside, thoroughly enjoying being pushed around. 'Hello, Aunty Nancy! Do you want to play with us?'

'How in God's creation did you get in there, Josephine?' she asked.

The children smiled. 'We all helped, didn't we?'

Josephine nodded with a grin.

'You'll have trouble with your back as well as your legs if you stay squashed in that,' Nancy said, lifting her out.

There were disappointed cries until suddenly there

was the sound of barking and Mr Bell arrived in the garden with Oliver. The children all ran to them. 'Hello, Oliver!' they shouted.

Josephine was sitting on the grass, watching.

'What's that you've got, Mr Bell?' Norman wanted to know.

The children gathered around him, oohing and aahing and saying, 'What is it?' and 'Can I have a try?'

'Mr Bell, what's it called?' shouted Martha again.

He scratched his head. 'Don't actually know,' he replied.

'Oh well, in that case it's a thingy then,' said Martha.

'A thingy?' the children queried.

'Yes, it's what you call things with no name,' Martha told them.

Nancy hurried over to see what all the fuss was about. 'Let me through, children,' she said. 'Come along now.'

They all stood to one side and Nancy gasped. 'Is this what I think it is?' she said, although nobody had ever seen such a thing before. In fact, nothing of its type had ever existed until now. The children fell silent as they all stood round it.

'Aunty Nancy, it's a thingy,' they told her, giggling.

'Really, children? And what does the thingy do?' she asked them. They all looked at each other but nobody knew what it did, so they all continued to stare at it.

The thingy stood there in all its glory, waiting. There was a big piece of board with wheels attached at each corner, then what looked like an old piece of piping bent into an 'n' shape like a handle. To the front of the thingy was a harness. Nancy slowly began to realise what it was – a walking frame. Mr Bell picked the thingy up as though it was as light as a feather, yet it looked extremely sturdy. He made his way over to Josephine and the children all followed, huddled around him with Oliver at their heels. He placed it in front of Josephine.

Everyone stood quietly and watched. Something very special was about to take place. Oliver went to stand beside Josephine and licked her hand. He ran to the thingy, then back to Josephine, then back once more to the thingy, wagging his tail furiously. 'He wants you to follow him, Josephine,' Billy told her.

Now the children were shouting, 'Come on, Josephine, do it! Please stand up and have a go. It's for you, your very own special thingy. You have to try it!' Josephine grinned and all the children helped her to stand up.

Nancy couldn't have spoken or moved even if she tried. This moment was going to be one of those incredibly precious moments that you want to remember and relive over and over and over again for the rest of your life. She watched silently, almost holding her breath, although her arms were ready to catch the child if she fell. Josephine was holding on to the side of her chair. She let go with her left hand. Oliver wagged his tail. Josephine let go with her right hand and stood unaided. Oliver barked. She put her hands onto the handle of the thingy. At a word from Mr Bell, Oliver knew exactly what to do – Mr Bell had been training him. Oliver knew not to jump up at people any more, he sat down when told to do so, and he had practised pulling this thing for days. He ran to the front where he was placed in the harness.

'Won't hurt him. It's well balanced,' Mr Bell told them all. Oliver was standing still, waiting for orders. 'Ready now,' said Mr Bell.

Everyone waited. Even the breeze dropped. The mighty oak held its branches still and every single person in the garden stood silently. It could quite easily have looked just like a picture postcard. 'Slowly now, Oliver, good boy,' encouraged Mr Bell.

Ever so slowly, Oliver moved forward and Josephine took a step, holding on tightly to the thingy.

'Well done, Josephine!' the children were shouting. 'Go on, do it again.'

Oliver moved again and Josephine took a few more steps, then a few more, as the children encouraged her, shouting her name and clapping.

That day, Josephine learned to walk again in the gardens of Nazareth House, with the help of Oliver and the thingy. Never had Nancy seen a bigger smile on a child's face. When she was finally eased back into her wheelchair, Nancy was watching her and the strangest thing happened. Josephine Jones was sitting perfectly still yet somehow her plaits seemed to be quivering all on their own.

'Ah, that's better,' said Nancy. 'A happy child. Heaven, I am afraid, will have to wait.'

Smart Shoes and Swinging Handbags

Jennifer had been told she could return to her old job after Easter and was very excited indeed. For days before she was due to start she had been cleaning and tidying, washing and ironing. She had bought extra work clothes to ensure Michael had a clean set each day. She had spent hours going through his shift patterns and working out what meals would be best so that there was always something for him to come home to. Just as she had expected, people had tutted and said nasty things, like, 'Fancy your man having to come home to an empty house with no hot meal on the table!' and 'A disgrace, that's what it is'. Michael just laughed and told her to ignore them all. He had already warned his parents not to say anything, and when his mother had offered to come over with hot food on those mornings he came home after a night shift, he had put his foot down.

Jennifer had worried for days about what to wear for work and had eventually settled on a pale blue skirt and cardigan with smart black shoes. She was to take her place in the typing pool but would also have extra duties, helping her friend Julia as needed. 'Stop worrying so much,' Julia had said. 'You've done the job before and you can do it again. There've been a few changes but nothing major. I'll be away on holiday for your first week so just one thing. The girl you're replacing is leaving this week and she's pregnant. I want you in a week early so she can go through with you where she's leaving off. Can you handle that?'

'Of course,' Jennifer had said, with a bravado she did not feel.

That morning, Michael had left for work at six and, although she wasn't due to start until nine, Jennifer was up at five, with breakfast ready and sandwiches for his lunch, and tonight she would be home before him so would have dinner on the table by six. Michael kissed her, wished her luck and left.

Jennifer sat alone at the table, her heart pounding. Surely this was the worst idea ever. What if the girls didn't like her, or she didn't fit in? What if she'd forgotten how to type? Don't be ridiculous, she told herself. By the end of the week she would be settled into a routine that would suit her and Michael. She would make this work.

Here we go, then, she said to herself, as she closed the front door and set off along Sandyford Road. It was only two bus stops or a twenty-minute walk so she decided to walk. It was such a lovely morning, and for the first time in ages she felt truly alive. Excitement bubbled inside her and she swung her handbag as she walked along.

A young girl walking in the opposite direction

stopped just as she reached the gates of Nazareth House and leaned forward to soothe the toddler in the pram she was pushing.

Jennifer's heart skipped a beat. What a perfect picture. How lucky that girl is, she thought, and tears stung her eyes. Why didn't I take the bus? Yet all around her everywhere there were going to be mothers walking their children in prams. It simply wasn't fair.

I wish I was her, she thought.

Gertie had noticed the girl with the swinging handbag and had had to lean forward into the pram to hide her tears. She had refused point-blank to let anyone come with her today. She had infuriated the family and the children's officer by insisting she, the child's mother, would be the last person to hold the little one before she handed her over. 'It's for the best,' her mother had said. Gertie had brought disgrace to their door and shame on the whole family. It could have been avoided if she had given the baby up for adoption immediately instead of continuing to believe Jack would come back and marry her. Hard, cruel words.

Gertie had never stopped hoping that Jack would marry her, so she had been sent to live with an aunt in Castle Eden, a small village in Durham. It was only twenty-four miles away but nobody knew them there. 'Let's see how serious he is,' her mother had told her, before sending Gertie on her way. 'If he turns up with a ring, let me know.'

Aunt Edie lived in a small farmhouse with Uncle Robert. They would try to talk some sense into her and arrange to have the child adopted, they promised. Gertie would see sense, surely. Conversations went on around her while everyone decided they knew what was best. All Gertie had to do was come to her senses and see they were right.

Gertie had been too angry to cry, and when she arrived at the farmhouse she was shown to the bedroom that was to be hers until the baby was born. There was no need for anyone to know she was there, and Aunt Edie would ensure she had everything she needed. She had no need to leave the house, Gertie was told. She had looked out of the window and seen the fields for miles around, feeling like a prisoner. Jack would come to get her. These small-minded people would have to back down when she had a ring on her finger.

Jack had promised to tell his parents about the baby and assured Gertie that then they would get married. He had kept his promise, but the next day he was sent to Scotland, where his family had said there were lots of jobs going. They didn't want their boy tied down to a girl of that sort. Jack wasn't strong enough to fight back and did as he was told. Sitting on the train, he had felt guilty, yet not guilty enough to stay and defy his family. 'Sorry, Gertie,' he whispered.

Gertie prayed for Jack to find her until the day her daughter was born. Then she knew he wasn't going to come for her and finally she lost hope and cried as her heart broke. It hadn't been all bad. She had become very close to her aunt and uncle, who had never had children of their own, and she hadn't missed the tears in her aunt's eyes when she held the baby in her arms. Against the wishes of the family, Aunt Edie had told her she could stay for a while longer. Gertie's family were furious and stopped speaking to them all. Gertie prayed it would stay that way and she would be allowed to remain there and bring up little Alison. It had been a hard two years because there always seemed to be so much to do. To pay for her keep she cooked, cleaned and helped on the small farm as well as looking after the baby. It was hard work and Gertie loved every single moment of it.

Two days before Alison's second birthday, Aunt Edie had had a stroke and suddenly it was all over. She wasn't expected to recover, and if she did, she would need full-time nursing care. The farmhouse would have to be sold and her uncle was moving in with family until something could be sorted out. Gertie was not welcome.

There was nowhere to go except home. All the way back a million thoughts had run around in her head. Surely they wouldn't dream of separating her from Alison now? It would be too cruel. They would fall in love with Alison the moment they saw her. The thought of losing her child was beyond terrifying. Gertie's legs were shaking when she knocked on the door of the home she hadn't seen for over two years. She held on tightly to Alison, who was chattering non-stop.

When the door opened, Gertie said, 'Hello, Mum,' in a shaky voice, then realised this was not her mother or any of her family.

'Do come in,' the ladies said.

Where was her mother? Where were the rest of the family? She was told to stop asking questions and sit down. Gertie knew instinctively who these people were. They were children's officers. Nobody would ever get to know Alison.

It was explained that the child was to be taken to Nazareth House in Jesmond to be put up for adoption. Alison would be placed in the nursery department until suitable parents were found. If Gertie did not agree to this, she was to leave with the child and not come back. That, naturally, would be a selfish act on her part when there were good people waiting to give the child a proper home. Something Gertie could not do. Alison was asleep in Gertie's arms and she held her close as her tears dropped onto the little cheeks. If it was to be, she would do it herself, she told them angrily.

There was a pram in the corner of the room that belonged to her sister's child. Obviously they were all somewhere close by, waiting for the children's officer to leave with Alison. Somewhere out there behind net curtains, Gertie knew they were watching and she felt angrier than she had ever felt before. She stood up, walked across the room and placed Alison in the pram. The officers made to move towards her but backed away immediately when Gertie screamed at them not to take another step towards her. She was shaking from head to foot but managed to push the pram out of the door and run down the street. More than one set of net curtains twitched as people tutted and gossiped.

Gertie reached the gates of Nazareth House and wondered if she could do this. Alison began to cry; she was hungry, and Gertie had no money to feed her. There was absolutely no other option. Somehow Gertie had to make one foot move in front of the other and step onto the driveway that led to Nazareth House Orphanage, where Alison would become somebody else's daughter. 'No, no, no,' cried Gertie, as she walked down the driveway. 'She will still be my daughter and I will always be a mother. Always.' She thought about the girl with the smart shoes and the swinging handbag.

'I wish I was her,' she said.

Gertie was right. She would always be a mother, even though her child would be brought up by others. Like many others at that time, she was surrounded by injustice and prejudice.

The hearts of a childless couple would be filled with joy, thanks to Gertie, who would spend the rest of her life suffering grief so raw it would never quite leave her.

Mr Bell's Day Out

A trip to the seaside was always looked forward to with great excitement, which was why Nancy tried to keep it from the children for as long as she could before telling them. Dolly, though, was almost as much of a child as they were and kept hinting about the treat so the children guessed. 'I give up, Dolly Marshall,' Nancy said. 'You are utterly hopeless at keeping secrets.'

She had to smile when Dolly said, 'I can't believe we're all going together on a train just for us. Ooh, it's like being royalty, isn't it, Sister Mary Joseph?'

'It is indeed.'

'Oh, don't you start,' Nancy said, but with a smile. 'Make yourselves useful, if at all possible, and go and find the box with all the buckets and spades in it.'

'Will they need washing, Nancy?' Dolly asked.

Nancy put her hands on her hips, raised an eyebrow and looked questioningly at them both.

'Washed before they were put away, weren't they?' Dolly said, laughing.

'Naturally,' Nancy replied. 'Now go away while I sort out everything that needs to be done or it'll be autumn before we leave.'

Once again the people in the north-east had shown

their generosity and the local railway company was putting on a train from the local station in Heaton to take the children to Tynemouth beach. A whole carriage to themselves and helpers on board if needed.

Nancy had suffered many trips to the beach, trying to manage twenty or more children on and off a packed train, all with buckets and spades, carrying a mountain of sandwiches and at least two flasks of hot water to make tea when they got there. She had been saving to make sure Dolly, Sister Mary Joseph and herself had a deckchair each. It would be a lovely treat for them. There were no worries about the weather: it had been a glorious July so far and the sun was set to shine. Everything was perfect in every way except one: Oliver was not allowed to come along. No matter how much the children pleaded he was absolutely categorically not allowed to come. Nancy had twenty children to cope with and enough bags of sandwiches to feed the whole of Tynemouth to carry, not to mention flasks, tins of cake, towels and Heaven knows what else. Nancy liked to be prepared.

It would have been so much more fun, thought Billy, if Oliver was with them, but Aunty Nancy was having none of it.

Josephine was doing well, thanks to Oliver, who always walked beside her when she wasn't using the thingy. Nancy knew she felt safe when he was there. The dog was around nine months old, they thought, and deserved a day at the beach just as much as the children but it was hard enough trying to keep an eye on all the little ones without looking after a boisterous Oliver as well. No, it simply couldn't be done. The youngest children were staying behind, and today Nancy was taking the over-threes.

The children all had bathing costumes or trunks on under their clothes. They would get wet and dry out before coming home. Nancy did not have the resources to bring underwear for everyone. The children wouldn't care: they would be covered in sand from head to foot, and Nancy would spend days getting rid of it from the bathroom.

The children trooped downstairs with their buckets and spades, trying not to smack each other on the head with them. The noise was deafening and Nancy had to shout to be heard. Once downstairs, they were put into pairs. 'It's like the Ragdoll Express,' they all shouted.

'Can I be at the front?' called Billy.

'You can be the driver,' Nancy said, 'as long as we get out of here before its time to come home.'

Billy ran to the front. Sister Mary Joseph was at the back with Josephine in the wheelchair. Josephine was doing exceptionally well, walking a little further every day, but the station was too far for her. Dolly was in the middle and Nancy at the front.

'Go on then, blow the whistle, Nancy,' shouted Sister Mary Joseph, waving her hands.

'Honestly, I don't know who is worse,' Nancy muttered, 'the children or the adults. Off we go, children. It's a long walk, mind, so be good.' She glanced towards

Mr Bell's cottage. Somehow she'd thought he might come to wave the children off. Things had changed a great deal all round since Oliver had arrived. Shame about today, but the children's safety came first and she would need those eyes in the back of her head for sure when they got to the beach.

Mother Superior was watching them from the window, and felt a catch in her throat as she saw them walking up the driveway in twos, Nancy at the front. She was remembering the day, many years ago, when her heart had frozen as she watched the children walk in twos behind Nancy up the driveway, pretending to be following the Pied Piper. War had been declared and they were being evacuated to Carlisle. Nancy had turned the whole thing into an adventure for them. It had been one of the saddest sights Mother had ever seen, and she had seen many. Today, she could hear their excited voices, and watched as young Tommy swung round and smacked Martha with his bucket. Mother laughed. Oh, how much better this was – just how things should be.

It had been quite an interesting few months. If anyone had told her a puppy would come to live at the orphanage and the children would manage to keep it hidden, she would have told them not to be ridiculous. Yet here he was, as much part of the orphanage as everybody else. Dogs were sent by God, too, and this one seemed to have arrived just in time. It was Oliver who had helped little Billy to open up and had then helped Josephine to gain in strength by walking more and more each day. Mr Bell, who as far as Mother knew very rarely left his cottage, was now often to be seen in the grounds, smiling, if you could believe it. God-given miracles, she whispered. She waited until the last child had walked through the gates then made her way along the corridor to the chapel to pray for their safe return.

'Not much further,' Nancy kept calling to the children, as they trudged to the railway station. They were only halfway there and some of the smaller ones were asking to be carried, which was not possible as Nancy, Sister Mary Joseph and Dolly were weighed down like pack horses.

'I'm sweltering,' complained Sister Mary Joseph.

'Sister,' called Nancy, 'you're here to help, not complain. Anyway, there'll be a lovely cup of tea when we get there, and I have a real treat for you.'

It took just over half an hour to get to Heaton Station and Nancy was beginning to worry they would be late for the train. Nancy was always on time and never late. By the time she came huffing and puffing into the station she was bright red in the face and panting. The children all scrambled onto the train and grabbed the nearest seat, so glad to be sitting down at last. Oh well, be thankful for small mercies, at least they weren't jumping up and down excitedly on the seats, which was what she had expected. Nancy collapsed into a seat beside them. The stationmaster blew his whistle and Nancy looked round for Billy. Look at him, she thought, forgetting totally about how hot and tired she was.

'It's a real train, Aunty Nancy,' he told her, his eyes sparkling.

'It is, darling,' she said.

There was a screech, then a chuff-chuff *hisssssss* as the train began to move and all the children shouted, 'Hooray.'

'Wish Oliver could have come too, Aunty Nancy,' said Billy, looking sad.

'I'll tell you what,' Nancy said, 'maybe we can let you meet the train driver when we get there.'

'Ooh, yes! I'd like that!' Billy rushed away from her to join the other children as they piled on top of each other to look out of the window.

Nancy watched them. 'Isn't life just perfect sometimes?' she said.

The children began to sing but twenty minutes into the journey some fell asleep. Having been up early, then making the long walk with all the luggage, and with the rhythmic sound of the train, Nancy herself was struggling to keep awake. Her eyes must have drooped for a moment because she got the shock of her life when she heard Billy scream. 'Look!' he was screaming at the top of his voice. The train was drawing to a halt and the children had gathered at the window. Nancy jumped up. 'Look, Aunty Nancy! Look over there!'

Nancy leaned forward and peered out of the

window. 'Goodness me! Never in the whole wide world. I can hardly believe my eyes!' she said, her mouth hanging open.

'Isn't it absolutely wonderful!' Billy said. There on the platform as the train chuffed into the station and the steam cleared stood old Mr Bell and Oliver, whose tail was wagging furiously. He was trying his best to break free from the lead around his neck. 'Settle now,' Mr Bell was saying.

The children piled off the train and ran over to him. Nancy looked at Mr Bell, feeling choked, as though tears would spring into her eyes at any moment.

'Day out,' he said, looking embarrassed.

'And why not?' said Nancy.

Sister Mary Joseph and Dolly were lining up the children in pairs. 'You go up front with Oliver and lead the children,' Nancy said to Mr Bell, and wondered why he seemed to be shuffling from foot to foot. Oh, she thought. He hasn't been before and doesn't know the way. 'Dolly will walk with you.'

Mr Bell, Oliver and Billy stood at the front with Dolly, Sister Mary Joseph was in the middle and Nancy at the back with Josephine in her wheelchair.

'Isn't this just the most marvellous surprise!' shouted an excitable Sister Mary Joseph. 'Praise the Lord, Nancy! Please God, we'll have the most wonderful day.'

'Mm,' replied Nancy. 'Please God, I've got enough money for another deckchair.'

Never Before a Lipstick So Red

Jennifer had forgotten how good it was to be at work. The talk was all about the latest songs on the wireless, who had bought what to wear, where the next dance was to be held, boyfriends, and so it went on. The canteen where they all sat for lunch was a hive of activity. Jennifer did more listening than talking. Her life had shrunk since she'd got married and given up work, but she wouldn't have changed it for the world. She loved Michael so much. This week, though, she hadn't thought about losing the baby nearly as much or gone over and over what life would be like now if she had become a mother. It had definitely been the right decision to come back to work. The money meant she could go out and buy some pretty new clothes without Michael having to pay. And maybe she could buy some things for fun, like the lipstick the girls were all talking about. It was called New Viv and was in six shades of red, one as bright as a fire engine. 'And it stays on no matter what,' Monica had said.

'Not after five minutes with Jonny Wilson,' replied Janice. They all roared with laughter.

Oh, it was all so innocent and so much fun. Jennifer wanted the New Viv lipstick, and there was a dress with a

matching coat she could never have imagined asking
Michael for, not after the latest expense. Michael had told
her last week that they were to have a television set. 'Cheer
you up when you're at home on your own in the evenings,'
he'd said. They could easily afford the rental each week and
if ever they couldn't, well, it simply went back to the shop.
What fun, thought Jennifer. Her thoughts turned again to
the lipstick. Well, if she couldn't have a baby, she would
have some fun. Michael's shift gave him the weekend off at
the end of the month just after she got paid. This time it
would be her treat. I'll get dressed up and we'll go out. I
can't have been much fun to live with this last year, she
thought sadly. Oh well, that's going to change now.

Lunch break was over and she returned to work happily. When they got back to the office, a bouquet and
presents were waiting for Barbara, the girl who was
leaving. There were many hugs, congratulations and
promises to bring the baby in to see them when it was
all over. The matinee coats and baby blankets were in a
beautiful shade of cream to ensure they would be
acceptable for boy or girl. Naturally, there was a rattle
and a big card, which they had all signed.

Jennifer stood back and watched, her heart beating
fast. I can do this, she was telling herself, over and over
again.

'It's your fault, Monica,' Barbara said, laughing. 'It's
that chair! It's fated. The last three girls who've sat on it
have got pregnant.'

'Oooooh it's bewitched,' they all laughed.

'Hey, the new girl's married,' another said.

'Don't know long you'll be here, then!' Monica said, good-humouredly pushing Jennifer into the chair.

Julia, who was on holiday but had popped into the office say goodbye, stood frozen to the spot, not knowing how to stop this.

Barbara grabbed an empty box and shook it. 'Start the collection now, shall I?'

Jennifer grabbed her bag and ran, not even stopping to collect her coat. She was down the stairs and out into the street before anyone could catch her and ran all the way home. Once inside, she collapsed onto the floor, burst into tears and sobbed. She punched the cushions, screaming, 'I want my baby!'

A little while later, the lady from next door knocked when she heard the sobs subside, but Jennifer was curled up on the sofa having cried herself to sleep. The knocking woke her but she didn't answer the door.

She got up and began to make dinner for Michael. She freshened up and changed her clothes. When Michael came in at six, she gave him a peck on the lips and told him not to be long, dinner was almost ready. She gave him no chance to ask about her day as she continued to chat.

Michael hadn't missed his wife's red eyes and his heart broke. What on earth had happened? She would tell him in time if she wanted to, he thought. They had dinner and Jennifer washed up, then came to into the living room. 'Want to watch some TV? We're the envy of the street,' he said, as he got up and switched on the set. Jennifer curled up on his lap and looked at the screen.

The lady on the TV smiled at them. 'Never before a lipstick so red . . . in six vibrant colours,' she said. Jennifer burst into tears.

Burned Breakfast and New Ideas

Michael had been watching Jennifer for days, unsure what to say in case he said the wrong thing. Goodness only knew what had happened at work. He thought back to the moment they had found out she was pregnant. He remembered how radiant she had looked, and how the little spots of colour in her cheeks had made her even prettier than before.

'My beautiful Jenny,' he sighed.

Losing the baby had changed everything and she had looked pale and dreadful for weeks. She had been constantly crying, and asking questions Michael couldn't answer. He had absolutely no idea what to say to her. The family and friends all made it worse with their silly remarks about it being Mother Nature's way and suchlike. The truth was that both sets of parents were devastated for themselves as well as for Jennifer and Michael.

My poor Jenny, he thought.

Something had happened at work, yet in all these months she had never told him what it was and he had never asked. She would tell him eventually, he supposed. Lately, he had come up with an idea but still not broached the subject. There was still no reason to think she wouldn't get pregnant again, yet as the months went by nothing happened and Michael had asked if she thought it might be time to get tests done. Jenny had become distraught. 'It can't be you, can it?' she said. 'So it has to be me, and I don't need a complete stranger poking and prodding and asking me private questions that will embarrass the life out of me. What if they tell us it's me? What then? At least now we have hope that maybe one day it will happen for us. If I try to forget about it, maybe it will.' He hadn't known what to say. Then she had taken his hands. 'Think about this,' she'd said. 'You've always wanted to be a daddy, running around with a child on your shoulders, playing daft games, and remember when we talked about the first Christmas together?' It had been the most wonderful afternoon and that night they had sat by the firelight making plans, then suddenly it was all over. It was almost like coldness had descended upon them. Nothing was fun any more; life took on a serious note. After a few weeks Jenny went about cooking, cleaning, smiling all as usual but there was something missing. Some undercurrent that said all is well on the surface but underneath the grief and pain still waited to reappear at the most inopportune moments. Then she turned to him and said, 'So remembering that day, Michael, dig deep into your heart and tell me the truth. Would you want to stay with me, knowing I couldn't ever give you a child? Would you, Michael?'

My poor sweet Jenny.

He hadn't handled the question too well. He was suddenly extremely angry and had stormed out of the room. Afterwards, they hadn't talked for days, or at least only to be polite. 'What would you like for your lunch today?'; 'Shall I put more coal on the fire?'; 'Are you warm enough?' It had been an awful few days – they had never fallen out like that before. Michael was relieved to go to work and forget about it for a while. He was a grafter, they all said, and was working towards the job he had always wanted, and he was going to get it, whether or not they said he was still a bit young. Michael had family on the railways, who would put a word in, but he wanted it on his own merit . . . He was always tired at the end of a shift, especially the late ones, and usually couldn't wait to get home but his footsteps seemed to drag all of a sudden, knowing there would be an atmosphere at home. Even when he was on shift at two a.m., Jenny would be in the kitchen with a hot meal in the oven ready to serve up. Before falling out, they would go and sit by the fire together and chat about their day. Then Jenny would clear up in the kitchen, kiss him goodnight and go up to bed.

On Michael's first weekend off after the falling-out, he had woken to a bright sunny morning. He had jumped out of bed, gone downstairs and walked purposefully into the kitchen. There, he grabbed Jenny by the shoulders and swung her round to face him.

'Michael, I just need to –'

'Never mind that. Let's sort this out here and now.'

Jenny opened her mouth to speak but closed it when she looked into Michael's angry eyes. They stood staring at each other, until Michael's eyes softened. She threw herself into his arms and they held each other tightly. 'I'm so sorry I was angry,' he said, 'but I can't imagine why you'd think I could love you less because you couldn't give me a child. I've loved you from the moment I set eyes on you and that will never change. If we have a child, it will be wonderful.'

'And if we don't?' said Jenny.

'Then I'll love you even more to make up for it,' he said, tilting her chin upwards so he could kiss away her tears. 'We have a whole lifetime, Jenny, and who knows what the future holds in store for us? If there are further challenges and heartbreak ahead, we can face them together. If we're together, we can survive anything.'

'Michael, can I just –'

'I've not quite finished. I love you, Mrs Harrison. Now, don't you go forgetting that. What was it you wanted to say?'

'Michael?'

'Yes?'

'The breakfast's burned.'

Today, Michael was smiling, remembering that morning. Who cared if the breakfast was burned? They were back to normal. He just wished Jenny could trust him with whatever had happened at work. Was his idea ridiculous? Would it cause trouble if he broached it?

He couldn't bear to go through all that upset again. He wasn't even sure it was something he wanted, but the more he thought about it, the better an idea it seemed. If only Jenny had thought of it, it would have been so much better.

Michael held off saying anything, then suddenly realised what the answer was. He would just drop hints to see if she thought of it for herself. Yes, he decided. That's exactly what I'll do.

Over the next few weeks, when Michael's shifts were such that he was home in the evenings, he suggested going for a walk. Jennifer liked the idea, and now she looked forward to their evening outings, although they always seemed to take the same route. Along Osborne Road, turning onto Sandyford Road, passing the orphanage and back again. Although Michael also looked forward to their walks, there had been no sign of her noticing the way his mind was working.

Tonight, I'll say something, Michael decided, as they left the house, holding hands as always. It was a beautiful warm evening and they strolled slowly past the gates of Nazareth House Orphanage. He stopped. 'I often wonder about the children there,' he said. 'Don't you think it's sad?'

Jenny suddenly remembered the young girl standing at the gates with the pram some months ago, and her eyes clouded over.

Michael began to panic. He started to move away but Jennifer remained where she was. 'I saw a young girl here with a child in a pram at these gates,' she told him, 'and I was so jealous. It was my first day at work. Oh, Michael, at that moment I just wanted to be her.'

'Darling,' Michael said, 'this is an orphanage. She may have been taking her child to be adopted.' Fate was playing into his hands at last.

'Oh, no! How awful. Poor soul.'

'It's happening all around us, Jenny. My mother told me about the girl at the end of our street being sent away and not allowed to come home until she'd had the baby.'

'What happened to her?'

'Well, all I know is she's home now.'

'And the baby?'

'Without the baby. It was put up for adoption.'

Michael was almost holding his breath, afraid his wife would become upset again. He waited. Suddenly, Jennifer smiled, then linked her arm through his. 'I think I'd like to go home now. I'm tired tonight,' she said, but Michael saw she was smiling. They chatted happily on the way home, although once or twice she seemed a little distracted and he had to repeat himself.

As they had walked away from the orphanage, Jenny had glanced back over her shoulder.

I wonder . . . she thought.

Reminiscences

Has it really been a year? thought Nancy as she settled down in her room and put her feet up for a while. It was late evening and all was going to plan this Christmas. 'No last-minute catastrophes, Lord, please,' she said, with a smile. If somebody had told her this time last year that they would adopt a puppy who would help a young child to talk and another to walk, she would have told them to stop bothering her with ridiculous notions. Yet that was what had happened and Oliver had brought joy to everyone, especially Billy, they were inseparable. It had been the perfect solution for Oliver to live with Mr Bell – yet it was clear whom he belonged to. It had been a coincidence, Mr Bell had thought, the first time Oliver had run to the door, scratching and barking to go out. When he'd got up and looked outside, he couldn't see anything. 'Silly boy,' he said, about to close the door when Billy arrived.

'Did you know I was coming?' Billy had said, kneeling down for Oliver to lick his face. Now, according to Mr Bell, it happened often so he always knew Billy was on the way well before he arrived.

And Josephine was doing wonderfully well now and there was no longer talk of going to Heaven. Somehow

Oliver had crept into her heart in a way nobody else could and helped her not only to walk but to want to walk. She was even trying to run and that was the main thing. Nancy smiled again remembering last week when the children were all laughing, saying her plaits were shaking all on their own, and Josephine got so excited she attempted a cartwheel. Fortunately the children caught her in time and they all ended up in a heap on the ground. Their squeals of laughter had brought a lump to Nancy's throat. Billy was forever running round shouting and skipping through the woods with Oliver at his side, his eyes bright, and Nancy absolutely loved the sound of his voice chattering non-stop when he came back, telling her all about his adventures with Oliver.

They had turned into happy, healthy, talkative, energetic children who no longer spent hours staring at the stars or praying to go to Heaven, she thought. Eventually Nancy had found a train set for Billy, but the children's favourite game was still to line up the chairs, blow the whistle and go adventuring on the Ragdoll Express. Nancy loved listening to them make up stories of where they were travelling to and what they could see. Imagination is a wonderful thing, she thought, not for the first time. 'Yes, it's been a good year,' she told her holy pictures, then went to look out of the window. Smoke was pouring out of Mr Bell's chimney. 'Goodnight, and God bless you both,' she said.

She sat on the chair by her table and poured herself

a cup of tea. She raised her cup to her holy pictures. 'And wishing all of us an extremely peaceful, uneventful Happy Christmas this year, thank you very much indeed,' she said.

A Christmas Prayer

Nancy wasn't the only one looking back on the year. Just a couple of miles away, Jennifer sat in front of the fire thinking how fast it had gone, even though not much had happened. She had talked to Michael about getting another puppy but still couldn't decide whether or not it was a good idea. They had tried everything possible to find their puppy. Michael had walked for miles, putting up posters but the harsh weather had ruined most of them. They had checked with the RSPCA, asked all of the neighbours but to no avail. Jennifer had prayed that the puppy, which must now be a full-grown dog, was safe somewhere.

She had never returned to work and, no matter how hard she tried, she couldn't put aside the heartache of not falling pregnant. Everyone around her seemed to be talking about Santa and how excited their children were. Jennifer was losing hope that they would ever sit around the Christmas tree with their own child. This time of year made everything harder and both families tried not to mention children in front of her. She knew it hurt Michael, too, that they had no child. She had wondered often about the children at the orphanage but something held her back, she just didn't know what it was. The wireless was playing 'Silent Night' sung by a children's choir, and Jennifer felt tears welling in her eyes. Oh, it's all so unfair, she thought. I would be a lovely mummy. They had a lovely home to offer a child, and Michael even had his dream job now.

Jennifer wished she had gone back to work, it would have distracted her and eventually things might have got better. This next year would be different, she vowed. I can't go on living a half-life. She had made such an effort lately to seem happy and not let Michael see how she really felt. She shivered and got up to put some more coal on the fire, then checked that all the presents were wrapped and under the tree. They had been invited to both Michael's and her parents' homes for Christmas Day but Jennifer had insisted on celebrating at home by themselves. 'I can't take the sympathetic looks and how everyone tries to pretend they wouldn't rather see us arriving with a grandchild. I can't do it, Michael. We can go for lunch on Boxing Day and you can have one whisky too many with your father. Then we can go to Mum's for tea. Normal stuff, just not on Christmas Day. I won't be miserable, I promise, but please, let's just stay home.'

Michael, of course, had agreed. Anything for his Jenny, but he was disappointed.

He hurried off to work early one morning and as he walked into the station he made his way over to the Christmas tree that stretched almost all the way to the ceiling. The crowds had visited in their thousands to see the tree this year, especially the children. Children, he thought as a stab of pain touched him. He was the man of the house, supposed to keep things going, stiff upper lip and all that utter rubbish. The pain of losing his child had hurt more than he had shared with anyone, then on top of that he had given up counting how many times he caught his wife crying this year. He walked towards the tree where there was a little nativity scene that had been made by children from a local school. He knelt down at the shiny Star of Bethlehem standing on top of the stable. Well, it is Christmas, he smiled, supposed to be a time of miracles, so here goes. Michael closed his eyes and wondered, Do I make a wish or pray? Maybe prayers were wishes anyway. 'Here goes,' he said. Silently, on his knees, he prayed to God for a Christmas miracle, then stood up and watched the train running round and round the tree. God always heard your prayers, he had been told. Michael closed his eyes once more and prayed to God it was true before hurrying away to start his day at work.

The star of Bethlehem twinkled as it caught the lights of the Christmas tree. Had God heard Michael's prayers?

The Photo on the Mantelpiece

A fire was blazing in the hearth and old Mr Bell sat beside it in the big old fireside chair. It was old and tattered but he loved it. His sister, when she came to visit, often said she would bring him a new one. Eventually he had to tell her that if she did it would get left outside. He was perfectly happy with the one he had. Oliver liked to curl up on it during the day and often they sat on it together. Tonight, as the flames danced and the coal crackled, Mr Bell stared at the photograph on the mantelpiece.

The pain would ease, they'd told him, but after thirty-eight years it hadn't done any such thing. Of course, he didn't think about them every day, like he had done at first, yet there were days when the pain would engulf him, as raw as it had been all those years ago. 'My fault,' he told himself, 'my fault.'

He had lived his life with a guilt that was not his to feel, another victim of a pointless war in which innocent people had died, destroying the lives of those left behind. How brave he had thought he was, when he went off to war. On those nights when the nightmares returned he could still hear the guns, smell the gunfire, and would jolt awake, sweating and crying. He never told anyone how much he had cried in the early days. Men didn't cry: they stood tall, chin up, and braved the world, shouldered the challenges that were thrown at them. Somehow his shoulders hadn't been strong enough. And the death and destruction he had witnessed at war were nothing compared to what he'd had to face when he'd come home.

It was only thoughts of Hilda and little Margaret that had got him through the war. What tales he would have to tell when he got home, and he would work hard, harder than he had ever worked in his life, to provide for them. The photograph he carried of little Margaret was the only one they had, a present from Hilda's uncle, the only member of her family who had a camera. Hilda and James Bell didn't have such luxuries, but he was sure one day they would.

This last year there had been a slight easing of his soul. Young Billy and Oliver had seen to that, and he smiled. Those walks in the woods had brought him a comfort he could never have expected, and he remembered the day Billy had told him about the stars in the sky. Afterwards they had sat together on a huge log in the wood and looked up at the sky, Oliver sitting happily beside them. He had begun to cry silently, and the little lad had just sat beside him and held his hand. There had been no need for words and in thirty-eight years it was the first time a comfort began to settle over him.

After Oliver had been with him a few months he

broke his silence. He had never told a living soul how he felt or why he had chosen to come here and help the children. It was his penance to do for other children something he had never done for his own.

Oliver had begun to follow Mr Bell everywhere. If he got up, so did Oliver, and the dog's eyes gazed at him with understanding. 'What's up, boy?' he had said one day, patting him. Oliver had looked at the photograph on the mantelpiece. 'Want me to tell you all about it?' he asked, as Oliver came and sat at his feet. So Mr Bell told Oliver, who seemed to understand perfectly and his tail hadn't wagged once throughout the whole story. It had been strange and yet comforting that night to tell his story to Oliver.

Tonight Mr Bell slid a little further down in the chair as his head drooped. He was no longer in the cottage where he lived today. He was back at the small house he shared with his mother, sister, wife and daughter. He could hear his wife shouting at him and his young daughter crying. 'Volunteers!' she screamed at him. 'It's volunteers they're asking for. You don't have to go, James! What about little Margaret? Only thinking of yourself, James Bell.'

He had never seen her so angry and had tried to take her in his arms. 'Let's not fight.'

'I won't fight if you don't try playing the hero,' she said angrily.

'I saw the poster again today, Hilda. I looked straight at it. It was our country talking to me. You know the poster I mean. You've seen it too. "We Want You," it says.'

'We want you too!' she shouted. 'Remember us? Your wife and child? We damn well want you too.' At this point she'd burst into hysterical tears.

He waited until she had calmed down. 'I've already done it, Hilda,' he told her quietly. 'If we all stayed at home because we had a wife and family there wouldn't be anyone to fight for the country.'

Much later that day, she had looked at him with red eyes and said, with a catch in her voice, 'Go on, James, go and be a hero and cover yourself in military glory but you'd better get your backside back here by Christmas. I am telling you now, and woe betide you if you're not.'

That evening they had sat together in front of the fire and held each other tightly.

Now Mr Bell wiped away the tears that were once more falling. He could still remember the little damp patch on his shirt from Hilda's tears.

James Bell had taken his place alongside his fellow volunteers. Some of those boys looked like children. 'If he's eighteen I'll eat my hat,' he'd said to the man at his side. Head held high, he marched forward with the rest. It would be a heroic adventure. 'I'll be home for Christmas,' they all shouted, waving to their families as they left.

Thousands of them did not return home for Christmas. In fact, they never came home at all. James Bell was one of the lucky ones, they told him. Injured and broken, he came home to an empty house. On 1 April 1916 there had been a surprise attack by the German Navy off the north-east coast. His wife and daughter had been killed. The day they were married he had promised Hilda he would take care of her for ever. When Margaret came along, with the prettiest blue eyes he had ever seen, he had sworn to keep her safe always. Well, he had broken that promise. Not only had he not protected them but he had left them to die alone. Somehow, he believed that had he been at home, he would have saved them. The burden of guilt was a heavy one and each year the load seemed to get heavier.

Then, all those years later, along had come little Billy and Oliver. It had helped. And when Josephine said she wanted to go to Heaven, Mr Bell was the only who understood. He had remembered standing outside his empty house, screaming for God to take him too. It was his eldest brother, John, who told him about the job of caretaker at Nazareth House Orphanage, which had recently opened. 'Apply for it,' he had said. 'You know, our James, you can fix, mend or build anything. You'll be a Godsend to them.' And so he had been. John had married and gone to live in Australia, where he had died many years before. Over the years when people asked how long Old Mr Bell had been there, nobody could actually remember, For ever, I think, they would say, laughing.

Mr Bell continued to dream and doze as the fire blazed.

*

Oliver lay in his basket by the fire. Suddenly, he lifted his head. The tone of that snore wasn't right. Nothing any human would detect, but Oliver was cleverer than humans. He got up, went to Mr Bell and nudged his arm. No response. Oliver barked, then grabbed Mr Bell's sleeve with his teeth and shook it, but the hand dropped down the side of the chair.

Oliver bounded to the door and jumped at the door latch. No luck at first, so he tried again and again until suddenly the door clicked open. He tore outside and raced through the woods to the door in the garden that led up to the nursery.

Nancy was dozing in her chair beside the window when she heard barking. She flung up her window. 'Oh my goodness it's freezing, Oliver, what in God's name are you doing down there? It's far too late to see Billy, they are all in bed. Go home now, good boy.'

Oliver continued to bark, refusing to go.

'Oh Heavens, thought Nancy, so much for a peaceful night. She closed the window, grabbed her coat and hurried downstairs before Oliver woke the whole place up. 'So much for no drama at Christmas,' she muttered to herself. 'God forbid we should have an uneventful one.'

Oliver was at her side as soon as she was through the door. 'Go home, Oliver,' she said again, but Oliver went on barking.

Sister Mary Joseph came hurrying up behind her,

having heard the constant barking. 'What are you doing out there, Nancy? Is that Oliver?'

'It is indeed, Sister, and he won't stop barking.'

Oliver looked at them, then trotted ahead, stopped and gazed back at them.

Nancy and Sister Mary Joseph took a few steps forward and Oliver repeated the process.

'He wants us to follow him, Nancy,' said a bemused Sister Mary Joseph.

'Well, if you want to go dancing through the woods with Oliver like a Christmas fairy at this time of night, please be my guest, Sister.'

Sister Mary Joseph laughed. 'Nancy, you are funny. Oh, look, he is doing it again.'

Please, Oliver's eyes were saying, please listen to me.

Sister Mary Joseph had stopped laughing and she looked at Nancy. 'Something's wrong.'

Together they broke into a run, following Oliver to the cottage. They went inside and Nancy ran over to Mr Bell's chair. 'Mr Bell, can you hear me? Are you ill?' There was no response. 'Sister, go and wake Mother and ask her to ring for an ambulance.'

Sister Mary Joseph hurried off, and Nancy knelt beside Mr Bell as Oliver stood beside his chair, whining. 'What a clever dog,' said Nancy, 'do you know how clever you have been? Clever, clever boy,' she told him.

Before the ambulance drivers put the old man in the ambulance, they asked Nancy his name and age. 'His name is, er, Mr Bell. I don't know his Christian name or how old he is,' she said. She took the caretaker's hand. 'How old are you, pet?' she asked him. 'When's your birthday?'

His eyelids fluttered. 'Don't know,' he whispered. 'It's never mattered.'

When the ambulance had left, Nancy picked up Oliver, held him closely and wept bitterly. 'Doesn't know or care when his birthday is. Oh dear God, that has got to be one of the saddest things I've ever heard in my entire life.'

There was a knock on the door. Mother Superior called out Nancy's name and found her sobbing with Oliver in her arms. 'Come along,' she said gently. 'I'll make some tea.'

'I'm not leaving Oliver. Mr Bell might have died if it hadn't been for this clever dog.'

Mother sighed. 'Unfortunately, Nancy, Oliver is not allowed into the convent. I'm so sorry.'

'Then I'll stay here, Mother,' Nancy replied.

'I'm not sure that's a good idea,' said Mother, looking worried.

At that moment Dolly ran into the cottage – she'd heard the ambulance pulling away – and flung her arms around Nancy.

'Mother, I have Dolly now so everything will be fine.'

Mother knew there was no point in arguing with Nancy. She wished her well and said if there was anything further she needed to let her know. 'A peaceful Christmas for once would be nice, Mother, you know, one with no calamities, dramas and catastrophes. That would be much appreciated.'

Mother took Nancy's hand. 'The Lord sends us these challenges, Nancy, and we must face them bravely.'

'Yes,' Nancy said, with a flash of anger in her eyes, 'and that's all very well, but when you pop into the chapel for prayers tonight, is there any chance you could ask Him to spread these challenges out over the year, Mother, and not save them all for Christmas? Just a thought.'

Mother's heart was warmed. Nancy was such a wonderful soul, and she herself often wondered at the challenges she'd had to face. 'We will have a Mass for Mr Bell tomorrow,' was all she said.

'That will be lovely, Mother,' Nancy said, smiling now. She loved Mother very much.

After Mother Superior had left, Dolly and Nancy stared at each other.

'Nancy?'

'Yes, Dolly?'

'You're not really going to stay here, are you?'

'Not on your life. We'll give it five minutes. Gather the basket and blankets.'

Oliver was warned not to bark, and they crept out of the cottage and through the woods, then made a run for the garden door. They hurried up the stairs, terrified they would be caught. Never had Nancy looked so guilty. In Nancy's room, they settled Oliver, and Dolly went back to her own bedroom.

For the next ten minutes, Oliver sat like a very good boy, listening to all the house rules. He whimpered and settled down. He wasn't sure he liked the sound of this at all but then Nancy told him again what a clever boy he had been and he wagged his tail happily. Nancy cleared up her tea things then looked once more at her holy pictures and shook her head. 'Not even talking to you tonight,' she said and switched off the light.

Downstairs, Mother Superior had been standing at the window for some time. Her rosary beads were clicking between her fingers and a smile was tickling the corners of her mouth. She knew quite well that Nancy would never have stayed in the caretaker's cottage, and the sight of her and Dolly creeping out of the wood had amused her, despite the seriousness of the occasion.

She turned away from the window and made the sign of the cross. 'Oh well, Lord,' she said, 'what I pretend not to see is my business.' She made her way to chapel.

Pretty Blue Ribbons

Nancy was hoping they would hear from the hospital soon. Mother had promised to let her know as soon as she heard anything. Nancy had not slept at all well, Heavens that puppy could snore. More than once Oliver had got up and walked over to stand by Nancy's bed. 'Not a chance,' she told him pointing to his basket and his head would droop as he made his way back to it. He tried curling up and looking at Nancy with his big puppy dog eyes. 'No good looking at me like that,' she told him. 'It doesn't work.' Oliver whimpered and Nancy turned over in bed, closed her eyes and waited for sleep. And waited and waited. This is ridiculous, she thought, turning over in bed, then shrieking. Oliver was standing right beside her. 'Goodness me, you're going to give me a heart attack,' she told him. 'Back in your basket and no barking.' Oliver did as he was told and Nancy had to laugh. She got up and walked over to him and knelt beside him. 'Fancy a midnight snack?' she asked.

Oliver barked and wagged his tail. Nancy made her away along to the kitchen to make a cup of tea and get some biscuits for Oliver. She couldn't sleep anyway; she was worrying about Mr Bell. Fancy not knowing your birthday, she thought. It upset her a great deal.

What had he said? 'It doesn't matter.' Well, it mattered to Nancy. Whether he liked fuss or not, when he came home Mr Bell was going to have a birthday party, no matter when his actual birthday was. She would ask Cook to bake a cake. One of her very special cakes. Cook loved being asked to bake something special. Of course, Nancy would have to listen to the speech about rationing and how nobody would tell Cook what she could or couldn't have. Honestly, nobody ever knew how Cook managed to work her wonders with food rationing, and although rationing had ended five months before, Cook still liked to complain and no one was brave enough to challenge her.

By mid morning Nancy was feeling the effects of having been up half the night. It normally didn't bother her. There had been many nights when she had sat up with a sick child or spent the dark hours wiping tears. She decided that a good run-around outside would do them all the world of good. Oliver had been taken to Mr Bell's cottage this morning and given his breakfast, then told to be a good boy and wait for someone to come back for his walk. She and the children went first to the cottage to collect the dog, then played in the grounds with him for a couple of hours. By then Nancy was feeling revived by the fresh air.

Sister Mary Joseph had just arrived to take the children in for lunch when Nancy saw someone approaching Mr Bell's cottage. Who's that? she wondered, and went across to introduce herself.

'I'm Norah,' the lady replied, staring at Oliver with disapproval.

'Norah?' Nancy queried.

'James's sister.'

Nancy was still puzzled.

'I've come to collect some belongings for my brother,' she said, and walked past Nancy into the cottage.

I didn't know he had a sister, thought Nancy, and followed the lady into the cottage. 'Behave now, Oliver, no jumping up,' she whispered to him, 'I have a feeling she wouldn't like it. 'Any news?' she asked.

'Not much at the moment,' Norah replied. 'I've just come to get the things he needs. Would you like to help me?'

'Of course, I would love to help,' Nancy said, smiling.

Oliver ran to the fireplace and stared at it, then at Nancy, as if to say, 'No roaring coal fire, what's going on here?' They all shivered. It was cold in the cottage, which had an air of loneliness and emptiness. 'Would you like tea, Nancy?' Norah asked.

'Marvellous idea,' she replied. 'I'm going to see if I can get this fire going, keep the place warm.'

Norah and Nancy sat at either side of the fireplace and enjoyed a good strong cup of tea in a comfortable silence, as the fire crackled and warmed them. Norah Bell was not one to talk about her private affairs; it simply wasn't done. Life was easier, she thought, when you put up a wall and kept people out. She never knew what made her do it but somehow, sitting here, looking at the lady opposite with the bluest eyes she had ever seen, she felt something she had not felt in many years. There was a kindness and understanding in her that made Norah feel a warmth inside that had nothing to do with the cup of tea in her hand. It wasn't only children who felt Nancy's magic.

Nancy was looking at the photograph of the young child on the mantelpiece and Norah's eyes stung with tears that had been held back for more years than she could remember. 'May I ask who the child is, Norah?' Nancy said.

Norah stared at the photograph for some time. 'She was so pretty, a sweet little girl, a joy to her parents and the whole family. Times were tough in 1916. I was twenty and James was twenty-seven. Our father had died when we were both young children and it was my job to help at home. We had little family, so when James got married it was a wonderful occasion. Mother and I loved Hilda, and even before they married she was very much part of the family. When their child, Margaret, came along we all felt as though the whole family had been blessed. It may have been a huge struggle but it was one we would all face together.'

'Oh, Norah,' Nancy said, leaning forward. 'I didn't even know he was married, let alone had a child. What happened?'

Norah stared into the fire for a few moments before she could continue. 'Hilda and James lived with Mother and me, so we watched Margaret grow into a little girl. Mother and I used to fret about Hilda, Margaret and

James moving out. The thought of not having them with us was so painful. I wish now that they had lived anywhere else. Mother and I were out the day the house was shelled. When we heard the noise we prayed with all our hearts for them to have been saved but it wasn't to be. One moment they were here and the next they were gone. The worst thing, Nancy, the very worst: it was Margaret's birthday, and we had gone out to buy her some handkerchiefs with little flowers on. We had saved and saved all year, and we knew she would love them. We had even managed to buy some blue ribbons for her hair. Blue was her favourite colour.

'It didn't matter then how little money you had. You could beg, steal and borrow, as Mother used to say. James could make anything out of nothing. You could give him a piece of wood and he would look at it then suddenly there would be something rather wonderful in front of you. If it needed fixing he could fix it, if it needed making he could make it. Before he went away to war he had been hammering and sawing in the back lane for weeks, shooing us away if we dared to look. Margaret had wanted a doll's pram but, no matter how hard we saved, there would never have been enough money for that. When he showed us what he had made, Mother cried. It was a box on legs with wheels at the ends and an old pram handle. He had painted it and written Margaret's name on the side. Oh, Nancy, Margaret would have loved it. When I see children now with their dolls and prams it still hurts.'

'I'm so sorry,' Nancy said. 'I never knew any of this.'
Norah shivered.

'Would you like more tea?' Nancy asked, but Norah
shook her head and continued to talk. She seemed unable to stop now that she had started.

'She died on her fifth birthday and the little lamb
never saw her pretty handkerchiefs or the blue ribbons,
and the pram was destroyed in the blast.' Norah's tears
were silent as they trickled down her cheeks to land on
her coat.'

Oliver whimpered and looked at Nancy. Her face
was dry but the pain in her eyes was clear to see as she
continued to stare at the photograph of little Margaret,
who never got to wear her pretty blue ribbons.

'James never forgave himself. He was convinced if he
had been there they wouldn't have died. "I put King and
country before my own family," he used to say. He was
broken when he came home and wanted to die. Mother
and I should have helped him but our grief was so heavy
that we, too, struggled to get through each day. I don't
know how we managed to carry on. Day by day the war
raged and we didn't care a jot. It was like we were all frozen
inside. When it was over and everyone was celebrating,
we all sat around our kitchen table drinking tea. We were
imagining what we would be doing if Hilda and Margaret had been there too. Somehow we had to put this
family back together again, start caring about each other,
if we were to survive. Each one of us had almost turned
in upon themselves in their own grief.

'Then, suddenly, Mother died and James was so angry. "Why couldn't it have been me?" he said.

'"Not your time, our James," I told him, but he was ever so angry, Nancy. He smoked and drank like he was trying to destroy his body and I hadn't a clue how to help him. To be honest, I was a bit angry myself. He wasn't the only one who loved Hilda and little Margaret. We were all suffering. "My fault, my fault," he would mutter in his sleep.'

'How did he end up here?' Nancy asked.

'Well,' replied Norah, 'he had odd jobs but we were struggling more than ever before. People rallied round and helped but I was just at the point of feeling like giving up myself when James came home and said he had a job. I was thrilled until he said he was leaving home. It was a caretaker's job at this orphanage. I couldn't have been more surprised because he was going to be surrounded by children. Up till then he would turn his head away when he saw parents and children together, yet here he was taking a job surrounded by little ones. He promised he would look after me and send me money every month and that was it; he never was a man of many words. The morning he left, I couldn't stop crying. I had gone from living in a house full of laughter and love to living by myself. I have never felt so lonely in my life. James and I weren't ones for displays of emotion but I felt like hugging him the morning he left. He was my brother and I loved him. I had watched him suffering yet that morning he seemed to be at peace somehow.

I was about to close the door when he came back and kissed my cheek. "I've got to make up for it, you see," he said. "Help the little children that have nobody. I didn't help my Margaret but I will do anything in my power to help these little ones." And with that he was gone. In all these years, Nancy, he never forgave himself, but doing what he could here helped him enormously, I know it did.'

Norah coughed. 'Listen to me, blethering on end-lessly,' she said. 'I'll just get his few things together and I'll be off back to the hospital with them.'

Nancy wasn't sure her legs would allow her to stand, she seemed to be stuck to the chair. Pull yourself together, woman, she thought as she managed to get up out of the chair and walk to the kitchen to clear up.

About half an hour later Norah called that she would be leaving now. Her manner had changed. It was as though their chat around the fireplace had never hap-pened. Truth be told, Norah Bell was embarrassed and hoped Nancy wouldn't be going around telling every-one her business. Whatever was I thinking, she thought. I do not want everyone thinking I'm soft. She straight-ened her back and added, 'I'll be back tomorrow to make sure the place is spick and span.'

Nancy opened her mouth to speak and closed it again. What an infernal cheek, she thought. There was a sudden coldness in the room.

Norah said she would let Mother Superior know of any change in her brother's condition and left.

Moments later, Nancy ran up the driveway after her, Oliver at her heels. 'Norah, wait!' She was out of breath when she caught up with Norah at the gate.

'Whatever is it?' Norah asked.

'His birthday! When is your brother's birthday? I want to do something special. Please tell me.'

'He's refused to celebrate his birthday since that dreadful day.'

'Tell me anyway. Please, Norah.' Nancy waited. Her eyes were pleading and she whispered, 'Please tell me, Norah.'

'Very well. My brother will be sixty-six on Christmas Eve,' she said, then turned abruptly and walked away.

In the quiet cottage, Nancy stood staring once more at the photograph on the mantelpiece. It was then the tears finally began to fall and she closed her eyes and swayed slightly. Oliver immediately ran to her side and jumped up. I'm here for you, he was saying, let me help you. Nancy opened her eyes and smiled at him. 'Good boy you are,' she said. Nancy knelt in front of the fire and Oliver placed his head on her lap.

James Bell. Nancy hadn't known his story. She had never taken the time to find out and that had been so wrong of her. They should all have made an effort to find out. Did Mother Superior know? Mr Bell had nothing to feel guilty about. Nancy lifted down the photograph of Margaret and, as she did so, something else fluttered down. 'Oh!' she cried. 'Oh my.' Stuck to the back of the photograph was a silver star, like the ones the children had made at Christmas. Billy must have given it to him and told him about the stars in the sky.

There was something else. It was a small piece of paper, folded. Nancy opened it, her fingers shaking. Immediately she recognised it. Josephine had drawn it and told her it was Mummy and Daddy in Heaven, waiting for her. Over the last year since Oliver's arrival, the children had spent lots of time with Mr Bell, which had never happened before. Mr Bell had been almost reclusive, doing his fixing and mending in the cottage unless something in the house needed fixing. This year, Nancy had seen him spend much more time out of the cottage, in the grounds with the children, and he had even been smiling. He had been extremely embarrassed when Nancy caught him. 'We are allowed to smile here you know,' she said, laughing.

Nancy picked Oliver up and hugged him. 'Seems God sent you after all, boy. Do you know what you have done, little one? You have healed an old man's broken heart and helped him to smile. In thirty-eight years not another living soul has managed to put the joy into his heart as you have done. Then to cap it all, it looks like you saved his life. You helped little Billy to feel like he had a friend who understood like no one else did and you gave him his voice back. Then there's Josephine. Who knows if she would have walked if it hadn't been for you? It wasn't just the "thingy" that did it, Oliver. It was you. You made her want to walk.' Nancy's tears dropped onto Oliver's fur and he didn't mind at all. 'Oh, Oliver, I do love you,' she said.

Oliver leapt up at those words and began licking Nancy's face, forgetting he wasn't allowed to. Then he barked happily. I love you too, he was saying.

That night, Nancy crept through the woods to collect Oliver and took him back to her room. He jumped into his basket and enjoyed the treats she had left in it for him. Nancy looked out of the window and realised how she missed the usual sight of smoke billowing from the cottage chimney.

She walked over to her holy pictures and made the sign of the cross. There was no noise or movement in the room except for the slight movement of Nancy's lips as she said her prayers. Oliver watched Nancy as she walked over to put the night light on. This is when she gets into bed, he thought, and began to settle down. His ears pricked up and his tail began wagging as she walked towards him. No, surely not? He had licked her face today and not got told off, but there were more surprises to come.

'Come on, boy,' Nancy said. Oliver didn't need telling twice and almost leapt into her arms. 'Heavens, you almost knocked me over,' she said, laughing.

Oliver could hardly believe it. Was he going to be allowed to sleep at the bottom of Nancy's bed? How wonderful that would be. His tail was wagging furiously.

Oliver looked at the bed, then at Nancy, then back to the bed.

Nancy was mortified. 'Absolutely not, young man,' she said, ruffling his fur, 'but you can lie beside me all right.' Nancy moved his basket right next to her bed and as Oliver settled down for the night, Nancy's hand dangled over the bed stroking him.

'Goodnight, God bless you, Oliver,' she said.

The Treasure Box

The cottage in the wood fell silent – even the fire no longer crackled. There was still a cosy red glow from the embers, though, and the room was warm. Mr Bell's bed was perfectly made, the corners tucked in tight for the first time ever. Every surface had been polished to a high shine, and the rugs had had a good beating. There was a whiff of baking soda, vinegar and soap in the air. It was important, Norah said, to ensure all germs were removed. Chances are when Norah walked purposefully through that door, her arms packed with every cleaning product known to man, the germs would have gone running for the hills before a cloth was even unpacked.

Nancy, of course, had refused to let anybody touch Mr Bell's belongings. 'They're private,' she had said, horrified, when Norah had started opening cupboards. James Bell might be her brother, but this was Nazareth House and Nancy had no intention of letting her pry into his private life, sister or no sister.

'I was looking for his treasure box, Nancy, if you don't mind.'

'Treasure box?' Nancy had wondered if Norah was making things up. She knew a nosy-parker when she saw one and didn't like it at all. She thought Norah must have had a sad life and felt compassion for her but that did not mean she'd allow her to root through Mr Bell's cupboards. Not in Nancy's presence anyway.

Norah had ignored her and continued to look around the room. 'He was apparently muttering in his sleep, asking for his treasure box. I have no idea what he was talking about,' she told Nancy.

'Wouldn't it be better to ask him now that he's better, rather than to continue pulling cupboards apart?' Nancy had replied.

'I did ask him,' she'd said haughtily, 'but he said he had no idea what I was talking about.'

'Then I rather think the best thing to do would be to stop looking, don't you?' Nancy had said with a stern look on her face that said I am not listening to any of this nonsense. Prying, that's all she was doing.

Now Nancy sighed. What on earth was going on? She had tried to be kind to Norah, but the woman she'd met today had been very different from the one she had talked to yesterday. Nancy decided not to mention their little talk. Norah obviously regretted taking Nancy into her confidence.

When Nancy had done all she could, she walked around each of the rooms with Oliver at her side. Another thing Norah hadn't been pleased about. 'Hard to clean with a dog around,' she'd said.

'Then we will all have to try to clean a little harder,' Nancy had replied.

Nancy sighed as she walked round the little cottage

by herself before she locked up for the night. She patted Oliver. 'Honestly I don't know what's wrong with me,' she told him. 'I usually have much more patience and understanding but you saved his life and you have more right than any single one of us to be here. Anyway, I will tell you a secret. Mr Bell is going to hate all the fuss that has been made. I have a feeling he won't be best pleased. Really, Oliver, for goodness' sake, she didn't really think I would fall for the story about the treasure box. An excuse to pry, that's all it was.' Nancy burst out laughing, 'How daft does she think I am?'

Oliver suddenly raced into Mr Bell's bedroom. 'Where are you, Oliver? Come here this moment. I'm too tired for games,' she added. Nancy found Oliver standing in front of Mr Bell's bedside table, barking and pawing at the little drawer. 'Leave that alone at once,' Nancy shouted. 'I didn't let Norah look in there and I'm certainly not letting you pull it open.' Oliver sat down in front of the dressing table and whimpered. He looked at Nancy, then back at the drawer. Nancy walked over. 'What is it then?' she said. Her fingers touched the handle on the drawer, and Oliver waited. Nancy shook her head. 'Sorry, boy, it just isn't right. Come along now.'

Outside the cottage it was a clear night and the stars were shining brightly, which meant it was freezing cold around the grounds of Nazareth House. There was already a thick layer of frost everywhere making the little wood look like an enchanted forest. The weather vane on the roof of the cottage looked down upon the pretty scene.

The moon shone down through the window and the moonbeams played round the dressing table that stood beside old Mr Bell's bed. At the back of the drawer lay a small tin box. It had lain there for thirty-eight years, untouched. Nobody knew it was there, except, of course, for James Bell.

He had never forgotten.

Wholesome Muck

'It was a heavy cold that had got onto his chest and affected his breathing,' the doctor had said.

Norah had called in to let them know it had been touch and go whether or not it would turn to pneumonia. He'd be in hospital for another couple of weeks at least but should be home for Christmas. 'I'll be popping into the cottage regularly from then on to make sure James eats properly,' she said.

'Oh, of course,' said Mother. 'That is perfectly acceptable. If there is anything further that we can do, please just ask, Norah.'

'Thank you, Mother. That's very kind,' she had said before leaving.

Mother and Nancy stood together and watched Norah walk up the driveway. 'Well, Mother,' said Nancy, 'shall we tell Cook that Norah's popping in to make sure Mr Bell eats properly?'

Mother looked appalled. 'Not unless we want to cause the onset of World War Three,' she said, smiling. 'Come to chapel,' she added.

They chatted as they walked along. 'I can hardly believe we'll be decorating for Christmas next week,'

Nancy said. 'I'll be getting the nativity figures and crib down on Friday, with a whole new tub of glue.'

Mother smiled. She had given up asking if Nancy would like a new set of figures. She knew quite well what the answer would be.

'Can it really be a year since the children crept down and stole the straw for Oliver? It's hard to believe, isn't it?' Nancy marvelled.

'It does seem to have been an eventful year, Nancy,' Mother agreed. 'Maybe this Christmas . . .'

'Oooooh, Mother, don't say it, please don't say another word. Let's not tempt providence, shall we? Every time I say all is well, He sends us another challenge.'

'Likes to keep us on our toes,' Mother said, smiling at Nancy.

'Well, my toes are getting awfully tired, Mother,' Nancy laughed.

They made their way up the aisle and knelt at the altar, then went to the candles and lit one each, silently saying their own prayers. After a little while they sat on the front pew and Nancy closed her eyes. What a difficult few days it had been. Her heart had hurt when Norah had told her Mr Bell's story. Nancy discovered that she could never refer to him as James, it felt really strange to call him that. Let him be home for Christmas, she prayed.

Nancy's prayer was answered: on 18 December Mr Bell was to be brought home. Norah had been in the cottage again, scrubbing and polishing. 'She'll wear the furniture away if she does much more,' Nancy had whispered to Sister Mary Joseph. Mr Bell wouldn't like it one little bit and Oliver didn't like the new smells at all.

A strange smell was coming from the kitchen. Nancy went in to investigate. Some sort of stew, she thought, and lifted the lid of the pan to have a look. She nearly dropped it when Norah came up behind her and asked what she was doing. 'Just looking. It smells . . . erm, lovely,' Nancy said hastily, trying hard not to wrinkle her nose.

'It's a healthy stew, full of goodness, just what he needs. Times are hard but it's the best I can do. It's got all the things in it he needs to get better. Just make sure he eats it,' she told Nancy.

Nancy said nothing; she did not hold with telling lies. She muttered something about seeing to Oliver and left the room. 'Is the dog staying?' Norah called.

Nancy stopped in her tracks. She paused for a moment, then walked back into the kitchen and for the first time Norah saw a steely look in Nancy's eyes. The look that said, 'Do not mess with me.' Nancy looked Norah in the eye. 'Yes, Norah, Oliver will be staying. Let's remember, shall we, that if it wasn't for "the dog" your brother might not be coming home tomorrow.' Then she busied herself with the fire. Anybody who knew Nancy well would see through the smile on her face and run for cover.

By late afternoon Norah had decided there was no

more to be done and thanked Nancy for all her help. Once she had gone, Nancy breathed a sigh of relief, then took Oliver for a walk in the woods. They were just about to go back inside when she heard Cook calling her. She was puffing up the driveway carrying what seemed to be half a dozen pots of food on a large tray. 'Heavens above,' Nancy shouted, hurrying down the driveway. 'Stay where you are.' Nancy reached her just in time to grab the pot balancing on the top and together they walked to the cottage. Once they were through the door, Nancy suddenly realised she would have to keep Cook out of the kitchen and led the way into the living room. 'Let's put them by the fire. It will keep them warm.'

'Don't be ridiculous, Nancy. He isn't coming home until tomorrow. Do you want to poison him?'

'Maybe we should leave them outside then. Keep them cool.'

'Nancy, have you totally taken leave of your senses? Why in all that is holy would I leave them outside? His larder is quite cold enough to keep the food fresh until tomorrow. He'll need good wholesome food as soon as he returns.'

With that, Cook marched into the kitchen and Nancy stayed where she was. Oh dear, she thought, her shoulders sagging. She waited. Yes, there it was.

'Nancy Harmer! What in God's name is this muck?'

'Now, Cook, I can explain.'

'Who left this muck, have you smelt it?'

'I have, Cook.'

'And yet it's still sitting on the stove.'

'Now, Cook, listen to me. His sister Norah brought it. She wanted to ensure he got some proper wholesome food when he came home.' Oh dear Holy God in Heaven, did I just say that? thought Nancy and waited for the onslaught.

'And what exactly, Nancy Harmer, do you imagine this is? I have been sweating all day cooking it. In case you wondered, this is proper wholesome food at its best. This rubbish over here is muck. Do you hear me? Muck.'

By this time Cook was red in the face and shouting. Nancy thought it was absolutely hilarious and burst out laughing. 'Oh, Cook, you are funny! Of course it's muck. I was going to throw it away. I knew you would have thought ahead and made something wonderful for him.'

Cook was looking mollified. She looked at the offensive pan and lifted the lid, 'Dear Lord in Heaven. I wouldn't even give it to Oliver.'

'Let's get rid of it and put your dishes in the larder, then I will make us a nice cup of tea and we can sit by the fire for a little while,' Nancy said.

'Best idea you've had all day,' Cook said, as she began getting rid of the offending muck.

A little while later, as they sat together enjoying a cuppa, Nancy told Cook Mr Bell's story. Cook had to dab the edge of her eyes many times during the story. 'I never knew,' she said, shaking her head sadly. 'So his birthday is Christmas Eve, is it? she said looking into the fire. Well, you know what we'll need, don't you?'

'Oh, Cook, could you?' Nancy said, knowing exactly what she meant.

'I can do anything I put my mind to, just like you, Nancy,' Cook said. 'We're quite a twosome, you and me.' Then she roared with laughter before asking what his favourite colour was.

Nancy shook her head. 'Favourite colour, Cook, he has been here thirty-eight years and I have only just found out what his first name is and the date of his birthday. Oh, Cook, tell me you are planning what I think you are.' Nancy watched Cook, knowing she was loving every moment of this. 'Rationing, though.'

'Don't tell me about rationing!' Here we go again, Nancy smiled. This was Cook's favourite rant even though the war had been over for years. 'If I want to make a cake it will be a spectacular one. Nobody will tell me what I can and can't have. It will be a sponge, my lightest ever. It will have buttercream icing and jam in the middle.'

'Mmmmmm, will you dust the top with icing sugar, like the last one?' Nancy licked her lips in anticipation.

'No, Nancy, I will most definitely not. I shall make proper icing and then you know what I will do?' Cook was thoroughly enjoying herself and Nancy was loving it.

'Come on then, tell me what you'll do that is so special.'

'I shall put "Happy Birthday" on the top and . . .' there was a pause for effect '. . . I shall then put his name on.'

Nancy was about to say how wonderful that was, then stopped.

'What's wrong, Nancy?'

'It sounds wonderful . . . except won't that be a bit much? "Happy Birthday, Mr Bell".'

'You told me his name's James.'

'It is, but . . .'

'"Happy Birthday, James" . . . Oh, I see what you mean. "Mr Bell" is too formal for a birthday cake but you're uncomfortable with calling him James.'

The two friends sat either side of the fire pondering this dilemma. Oliver was asleep, curled up warm and cosy.

'Nancy! I've got it.'

'How wonderful, Cook. What do you think?'

'"Happy Birthday, Welcome Home".'

'Perfect!'

'All that thinking has made me thirsty. Pop the kettle on again, Nancy.'

After more tea had been drunk they cleared up and left the food prepared for Mr Bell's return tomorrow.

'What shall I do with Norah's muck, I mean stew?' Nancy said.

'Double-bag it and burn it for all I care,' said Cook.

So the muck was double-bagged, the cottage was clean and warm and the good and proper food was all prepared for Mr Bell's return. Nancy, Cook and Oliver were making their way down the driveway when Cook stopped suddenly. 'Nancy, why is Oliver following us? He needs to go back to the cottage.'

Nancy's face turned red.

Cook slapped her on the back. 'Nooooo, the good and honest Nancy Harmer has been keeping a secret, has she? You're keeping him inside, aren't you?'

'Don't you dare tell,' Nancy said, her face getting redder by the minute.

'Oh, don't worry, I won't. Nancy Harmer with a dog in her room! I've never heard the like.' Cook had to wipe her eyes with the corners of her apron she was laughing so much.

Cook's laughter could be heard all the way down the driveway to the main house. They parted as Cook went to the kitchen and Nancy sneaked through the garden door with Oliver. As they reached the end of the corridor she heard footsteps. She ran into her room and closed the door quickly. That was close, she thought. She jumped at the sound of a knock on the door. 'Sssh,' she told Oliver.

'Nancy,' Mother called.

'Oh, Lord,' she muttered, making the sign of the cross and asking for forgiveness before she told a lie. 'Sorry, Mother,' she called back. 'Just getting changed. It's been a long, tiring day.'

There was a pause.

'Very well. Goodnight. God bless you, Nancy.'

Nancy heaved a sigh of relief. 'Goodnight. God bless, Mother.' Nancy put her ear to the door. All was quiet.

'Goodnight. God bless, Oliver,' called Mother.

There was a single bark in response.

Mother Superior smiled. Sometimes she, too, liked a little joke, and she wished with all her heart she could see Nancy's face.

'Oh, Lord,' Nancy sighed, 'she really does have eyes in the back of her head.'

Long Shiny Ringlets

Mr Bell wasn't the only person at Nazareth House who celebrated their birthday on Christmas Eve: Josephine Jones had come into the world on that day, much to the delight of her parents. It had been such a surprise to them, as she wasn't due to arrive until the beginning of January. 'Couldn't wait to share her first Christmas with us,' her father had said, smiling down at the child in his arms. Nancy always made a special tea for a birthday girl or boy, with Cook's special cakes. The children made decorations to hang in the dining room and the birthday child would sit at the table with cards from the staff and a bowl of sweets. They were also allowed to choose what they would like in the sandwiches and there were jugs of juice, instead of water or milk.

Mr Bell was at home where he belonged and the children visited him every day. Oliver was thrilled to be back in the cottage although those strange smells were not what he was used to. He looked questioningly at Mr Bell. 'Don't worry, boy,' he was told. 'We'll pretend to be out next time she turns up with her washrags.' It was very kind of Norah but she wouldn't be getting her way and taking over his life as she wanted to, Mr Bell thought. Oliver wagged his tail in agreement.

Mr Bell was ordered not to go walking in the woods and to keep warm, so Nancy and the children took Oliver out, and Cook always had delicious meals to send along. While Oliver and the children were running about, Nancy often found Billy and Josephine lingering in the cottage with Mr Bell, telling him what had been happening while he had been away. Today, Oliver was lying on the hearthrug while Josephine told Mr Bell their birthdays were on the same day and that Aunty Nancy was going to make a party for them both. Mr Bell looked at the children and shook his head. 'No,' he said.

'Oh, but you must,' pleaded Josephine and Billy together. 'It is going to be so wonderful. We have made decorations specially, please come.'

'Your birthday too, Josephine?' said Mr Bell.

'Oh yes. Mummy and Daddy used to say just because it was Christmas didn't mean I wouldn't have a very special present on my birthday. I don't suppose I will get one this year but Cook is making cakes. You must come to my party, Mr Bell, really you must.'

Josephine and Billy looked at Mr Bell who was staring into the fire. He was far away in another place and there were tears in his eyes. Josephine looked at Billy. 'What have I said?' she whispered. Mr Bell began to cover his embarrassment by shovelling coal into the fire and then he held the paper up while the fire caught. The children sat and watched him as he sat back down again. Oliver moved closer to the fire – oh, how he had missed this.

They all sat in front of the roaring fire in silence until suddenly Mr Bell coughed. The children jumped up and tucked the blanket around his knees. 'There you are,' they said, fussing about, making sure he was comfortable. Josephine knelt beside him and he leaned forward and put his hand gently on her shoulder and nodded. 'Very well, young lady, if you insist.'

'You'll come to our birthday party?' Josephine was brightening.

Mr Bell nodded, then leaned back and closed his eyes. Oliver was asleep, snoring loudly, and the children crept out closing the door behind them.

They ran over to Aunty Nancy. 'I've told him all about the birthday party.' Josephine was smiling.

'Oh,' Nancy said. 'You weren't supposed to do that. He doesn't like coming into the big house, he never has, except to mend things. I was trying to think of ways to get him to come.'

'But he *is* coming!' Josephine squeaked, excited. 'I told him it was my birthday too and he had to come and he said yes.'

'Well I never!' said Nancy. 'Well done, Josephine.'

It had been a good day, Nancy thought, as she was settling the children for the night. They had all had lots of fresh air and some of the younger ones were asleep before she had undressed them. Josephine, of course, insisted she was a big girl and didn't need any help. When all the children were lying down to sleep Nancy noticed that Josephine was still sitting up in bed and went over to sit beside her. 'What is it, darling?'

Josephine was staring out of the window. 'Do you think Mummy and Daddy have forgotten me, Aunty Nancy?' she said.

'Oh, Heavens above, no, Josephine,' she replied, sweeping the little girl out of bed and onto her knee. 'Mummies and daddies never forget us, not for one single moment.'

'Why did God not take me with them?'

Nancy thought for a moment, then carried Josephine over to the window. 'As long as we hold them in our hearts, darling, nobody can ever take them away, and as long as you can see the stars in the sky, you can believe that they're watching over you. Sometimes God chooses very special people to do very special jobs. Mind you, you have to be very, very important and extra-extra special to be chosen by God to do these jobs.' Nancy waited for her words to sink in, then carried Josephine back to sit on her bed.

'Aunty Nancy?'

'Yes, Josephine?'

'Do you think I got chosen to be special?'

'Oh, most definitely, darling.'

'So am I supposed to do something extra-extra special?'

'Well, you know, Josephine, I think you already have.'

'What have I done, Aunty Nancy?'

Nancy took Josephine's hand. 'You overcame huge challenges and many other children couldn't have done that. You taught us all what it is to be brave. When you walk into a room you bring with you a heart full of love, compassion and understanding that I have never seen from a child so young. I know you've spent many hours with Mr Bell and made him feel comforted and eased the pain in his heart that has lain there for so many years. You are so very special, Josephine, and I have a feeling that in the future everyone who crosses your path will be a better person for having known you. Your mummy and daddy would be so very proud of you, darling.'

Josephine lay down, snuggled under the bedclothes and closed her eyes. Nancy leaned over and kissed her forehead. 'Is there anything at all you'd like for your birthday?' she whispered.

There was no answer. Josephine must already be fast asleep and dreaming, Nancy thought. She stood up to leave and suddenly Josephine opened her eyes and said, 'Ringlets.'

'Pardon me?' said Nancy, puzzled.

'I would like real ringlets for my birthday,' said Josephine, and fell asleep.

Nancy didn't know whether to laugh or cry. Ringlets indeed! Well, if that was what she wanted that was what she would get. At least she'd asked for something that was possible. Nancy gave a sigh of relief.

*

The next few days were busy, with the approach of Christmas, the practices for the nativity play and the carol service. There were all the donated Christmas gifts to be sorted and wrapped too. At this time of year nobody saw Cook. The kitchen door was firmly closed on the days before Christmas Eve. The smells that drifted all along the corridors were so tantalising and the nuns hung around the kitchen door in huddles, trying to work out what was cooking.

One day Mother saw them there. 'Sisters, could you kindly remember who you are? You must retain your dignity at all times,' she said. Then the smell had wafted under her nose and she, too, was dreaming suddenly of all the lovely food that Cook was making. 'Let's move along, shall we?' she said, gliding purposefully away. 'Mmmmm,' she said when she was out of earshot.

Upstairs in the nursery Nancy was making sure she had collected enough rags to do Josephine's hair. It was the birthday party in two days' time and tomorrow evening she would put the little girl's hair into rags to make ringlets. Never had Nancy seen the children so excited about hair. It was the talk of the nursery department. The beautiful hair that reached down her back was brushed over and over. That afternoon when Nancy had asked if they wanted to be in the playroom she was told that they were far too busy: they were taking turns to brush Josephine's hair. As the afternoon turned into evening, she had to take the brush away, telling them that if they didn't stop soon Josephine would have no hair left to make ringlets.

Nancy had taken a few of the children to the cottage to collect Oliver for a walk and they had stayed for a little while. Naturally Josephine told Mr Bell about the ringlets for her birthday and Nancy had seen his eyes grow sad. She was about to change the subject when Mr Bell suddenly smiled and looked at her. Not a word was spoken but that look was telling her something. She didn't know what it was, and didn't like to ask in front of the children, but there was contentment in that look and Nancy was so thrilled. Just a year ago she hadn't known this man at all and that had been a mistake. It had taken Oliver, little Billy and Josephine to bring him the comfort he needed for his heart to heal. It was really all rather wonderful, she thought, walking back to the house.

Nancy had worked hard to ensure that everything she would normally do on Christmas Eve was done early so they could all enjoy the birthday party. There had been no new children this Christmas to throw her into yet another panic. Now just let all go to plan with the party and I will be happy and grateful, she thought. Up in the attic the Christmas socks, all with a little bell attached, were in a box ready to be hung up. Some beautiful dolls with clothes had arrived, along with a splendid spinning top, some toy cars and lots of sweets. Nancy was very pleased indeed.

Cook had made fairy cakes for the children and the cake for Mr Bell was almost finished. The tea party would start in the dining room and then they would all go to the television room to have Cook's special cake. Eating cake in the television room was such a treat that the children could hardly contain their excitement. Nancy knew the mess would take ages to clear up but she didn't care. 'Just this once,' she kept saying to herself.

On the evening before Christmas Eve, all the children were put to bed at the usual time, except for Josephine, who was allowed to stay up late to have her hair done. 'Oh, how wonderful it will be,' everyone said. 'Can you imagine long ringlets all the way down her back?' Her eyes sparkled and shone and there was a spot of colour in both of her cheeks as she sat in the chair in front of Nancy in the television room. Nancy took the first strand of hair and began winding. Josephine never moved, not once. She sat totally still while her hair was being wound round the rags. Her tummy was bubbling with excitement. Aunty Nancy had told her how special she was and Josephine Jones felt very important indeed.

Much later when Nancy took Josephine back along the corridor and put her into bed she wondered how on earth she would sleep with all those rags in her hair. Were they too tight or too loose? Please let them be perfect, she prayed.

*

There were lots of oooohs and aaaahs when the children woke the next morning and saw the rags in Josephine's hair. They had many questions for her.

'How many rags are there?' they asked.

'Hundreds, it took hours and hours,' she said importantly. 'I was up almost half the night.'

'Did it hurt?' Martha asked.

Josephine nodded. 'Yes, very much, but I stayed completely still.'

'You are brave, Josephine,' said Martha.

Nancy was listening to them, amused by it all. What fun children can be, she thought, not for the first time.

It was going to be a busy day. The nativity play was to take place in the afternoon and Josephine had been chosen to be Mary so her head could be covered with a veil. The rags would be taken out just before the party.

At eleven o'clock the children were wrapped up and sent out to play for half an hour while Nancy went to the parlour to check everything was in order and to reassure Mother Superior that all the arrangements were in place. The play was at two thirty. At three fifteen there would be Josephine's special birthday sandwiches in the dining room. At four Mr Bell was due and they would all gather in the television room where the big table would be set with tea, juice and cake.

She knocked on the door of Mother's room and went in when Mother called. Mother smiled when she saw

Nancy's flushed face and the sparkle in her eyes. This was going to be a wonderful Christmas for all of them. 'Heavens, Mother,' Nancy said, 'could we ever have believed this time last year what the year ahead would bring? Oh, Mother, it has been absolutely incredible. I can't even put into words how happy I am. The children are so happy this year.' Mother got up and brought over her beautiful china cups and saucers and poured them both a cup of tea. 'God has looked down upon us this year and greatly blessed us.'

'I bet He's had a good laugh, too, Mother.'

'Yes, I rather think I can agree with you there.'

'I think this is the first Christmas Eve when I've not been in a complete panic of some sort.'

'We shall thank God at the service for not sending us more challenges.'

'I will drink to that,' said Nancy, laughing, and they raised their cups. There was a loud knock at the front door and Nancy and Mother paused with their cups on their lips then slowly put their cups gently back down on the saucers. They looked in silence at each other and both jumped at another loud knock.

Nancy raised her eyes to Heaven. 'Oh dear Lord, Mother,' Nancy said. 'It looks like we've spoken too soon.'

The Biggest, Most Beautiful Eyes in the Whole Wide World

Michael wasn't due home until late evening and they were going to enjoy a Christmas Eve supper together in front of the fire. Jennifer was looking forward to it. She put more coal on the fire and moved the guard in front of it. Fresh air, that was what she needed this morning. She was determined not to sit around feeling sorry for herself today, Christmas Eve.

Coat on, she stepped out into the cold. It was looking like snow, but she didn't care. The new year would be better for them. Michael deserved to come home to a happy wife and she was going to do everything she could to make sure he did. 'I want to be happy, I want to be happy,' she said over and over, as she began to walk with no idea where she was going.

Jennifer wondered about God. She had always gone to church as a child but since the baby she hadn't set foot inside one. She was too angry. As she reached the end of Osborne Road she saw the lights of the church were on and stopped to look at them. She made her way along the street and paused at the door before opening it. There were only a few people inside, obviously preparing for Midnight Mass. Jennifer walked down the side aisle to where the candles were burning.

She made the sign of the cross, then knelt down and prayed. A beautiful feeling of calm came over her. She looked over at the crib, where Mary and Joseph gazed at their tiny baby boy. Jennifer didn't cry. Instead there was a warm feeling inside and she smiled.

She had no idea how long she had knelt there when she stood up to light a candle. As the flame flickered, she looked up at the cross on the altar. 'You took my baby – you even took my puppy. They tell me God works in mysterious ways that we don't always understand. Please, God, I will try to understand. I won't complain but, oh, dear God, please give me my baby. Please God, please.' Jennifer waited, then made the sign of the cross again and made her way out of the church.

She took a deep breath when she stepped out into the cold, rubbing her hands together. It was a freezing morning but there was warmth inside her and lightness in her step as she continued her walk. 'Oh, I do feel better,' she said, surprised, to herself. 'Time to move on, Jennifer Harrison. Heavens above, I'm talking to myself now,' she said out loud and then laughed.

She walked all the way along Sandyford Road, and when she was approaching the gates to Nazareth House she heard children playing. Jennifer made herself stop and listen and it actually made her smile. They sounded happy and she was glad of that. Children should be happy and excited on Christmas Eve. The first flakes of snow began to fall and she began to walk away, then suddenly stopped. What was that sound? Surely not?

The children at the orphanage wouldn't be allowed to have a dog, would they?

Jennifer's heart almost froze as she remembered bringing the puppy for a walk last year and how they'd had to drag him out when he'd seen all the trees . . . No. Oh no, it just wasn't possible. She stood still, willing her heart to stop hammering in her chest, until a lady passing asked her if she was all right. 'I'm fine,' Jennifer said, and began to hurry away. She had walked for ten minutes when she swung round and walked back to Nazareth House. This time she went to the gates and peered through. To her left she could see a cottage with smoke billowing out of the chimney and a wooded area with children running about. She went through the gates and hid behind a tree, not thinking what she would say if she was caught. She held her breath when she saw the Labrador scampering around the trees and the children running after him, squealing with laughter.

Jennifer couldn't have moved even if she'd tried to. He's mine, she thought. He's my puppy. I don't know how I know, I just do. But how did he get here? She continued to watch the children and had to smile. There was one little boy who the puppy seemed to keep returning to time and time again. 'Oliver!' he was shouting. 'Here, boy.' Oliver stood on his back legs, resting his paws on the child's shoulders and licked his face, wagging his tail frantically. Jennifer laughed. Oh how wonderful, she thought, never taking her eyes off them for a single moment. Suddenly Oliver looked towards her and jumped away from Billy. Jennifer gasped as the child ran towards her, then stopped. He seemed to be looking straight at her and she couldn't take her eyes off him. When he smiled she jumped behind the tree again. Please, no, she thought, keeping quite still.

She was saved by someone calling for the children and listened carefully until their voices had faded. Jennifer peeped out from behind the tree. The dog was still in the wood. Then the door of the cottage opened and he trotted inside. Jennifer was shivering, but she couldn't move from the spot so she stayed there, thinking. The little boy, could it be his dog? But he lived here and wouldn't be allowed a dog. Jennifer's puppy had been three months old when they'd lost him. Surely the orphanage would never have taken in a puppy. Then she thought of those big beautiful eyes. She had wanted to pick him up and run away with him. There was just something about him. Love me, those eyes said. Play with me, laugh with me.

Jennifer's heart wouldn't calm down so she had to close her eyes, take several deep breaths and count to ten. What's happening to me? She wondered. The snow that had starting falling earlier had stopped a little while ago and Jennifer had no idea when it had started again. All she knew was that her coat was soaking yet her face was burning. In later years when she looked back, she never knew what had made her step out from behind the tree that day and purposefully march down the driveway, not stopping until she reached the big oak door. She knocked once or twice and waited with an impatience she had never felt before for someone to answer.

The first person Jennifer saw was Mother Superior and the second was a lady standing behind her with a questioning look. Kind blue eyes were gazing at her and Jennifer stared past Mother Superior at the owner of those eyes. 'Whatever it is, I will understand,' the eyes said. Then the lady smiled – and the tears that Jennifer had promised she would not cry on Christmas Eve came pouring out.

Mother stepped out of the way as the lady rushed forward. There were a million thoughts running through Nancy's head. Was this one of the girls who had had their child taken from them, was she in some sort of trouble? Then common sense kicked in. 'You're freezing. Come inside, child,' she said. Mother looked at Nancy and sighed. 'I'll take her upstairs with me, Mother. She looks half frozen to death. What is your name?'

'Jennifer,' she whispered, although for a moment she wanted to laugh at being called a child.

'I'm Nancy.' Then there was an arm around her and the tears came again. Jennifer found herself being led up some stairs through a door and into a small kitchenette, where her coat and hat were removed. 'Back in a minute,' Nancy said. Jennifer sat down and listened to a kettle boiling. It was so comforting and warm here.

Nancy returned and busied herself making tea and

opening tins. 'The best cakes, I think,' she told Jennifer. She sat down opposite Jennifer and poured her some tea. 'Drink up,' she said.

Jennifer did as she was told. Somehow, she thought, everyone would do what this lady told them to do. She was kind but firm and Jennifer liked that.

Nancy waited. It was never any good hurrying people. Best they do it in their own time. This young girl had cried many tears, she suspected. *I hope she isn't the mother of one of our children, poor soul.*

Jennifer drank the tea, and when Nancy refilled her cup she drained that too. 'Better?' Nancy said.

'Better,' Jennifer replied, smiling. She looked around the pretty little kitchenette and sighed. She seemed calmer. 'Oh, Nancy, I'm married to the most wonderful man called Michael and I lost the baby we wanted so much and it almost broke my heart. I just couldn't seem to get over it, especially as another baby never came. Last year on Christmas Day, Michael surprised me with the sweetest little puppy. He was adorable, and I fell in love with him the moment I saw him. Does that sound ridiculous?'

Nancy's thoughts turned to Oliver. 'Strangely enough, I can well understand that. I know how much comfort and love they can bring and I'm glad you have him.'

Jennifer shook her head. 'I lost my puppy too. I was so excited when Michael and I took him for his first walk in the evening on Christmas Day. It was so cold.

Poor little soul, he got a bit tired so I picked him up, wrapped him in my coat and carried him all the way home. I remember feeling happier than I had in a long time.'

Jennifer's eyes were shining and she was so lost in the memory of that evening a year ago that she didn't notice Nancy's eyes were closed. Dear God, no, she prayed, don't let it be Oliver, but in her heart Nancy already knew it was. The puppy that had arrived here last year, who was now so big a part of the life of the orphanage, belonged to this young girl. She would naturally want him back. Nancy heart sank.

At twelve o'clock Nancy realised her perfectly timed plans for Christmas Eve were starting to go astray. The girl was looking much better now and her tears had dried.

'Do many people tell you their troubles, Nancy?' Jennifer asked.

'There have been one or two,' Nancy agreed.

Now Jennifer stood up, ready to leave.

It was no good, it would have to be done, Nancy thought, and asked Jennifer to sit down for one more moment. 'I have something to tell you,' she said, as she fiddled with the corner of her apron nervously. It might be my own eyes need drying after this, she thought. 'A year ago, little Billy, a child who had just arrived with us, found a puppy playing in the grounds on Boxing Day and, with some of the other children, managed to hide him in the stables so they could keep him.' Nancy smiled at the memory and Jennifer gave a little laugh. 'Oh my,' was all she managed to say but looked extremely amused. 'Billy was a troubled child and the bond between him and the puppy did more for him that anyone else here could do. Believe me, I tried everything. It was Billy who called the puppy Oliver because of the book *Oliver Twist*. Both orphans, you see.'

Jennifer's hand flew to her mouth. 'That's the saddest thing I've ever heard,' she said, 'and also one of the sweetest.' She glanced at the clock and jumped up. 'I really must go, Nancy, thank you so much. Just wait until I tell Michael.' She burst out laughing.

Nancy had no idea what to say as she led Jennifer back down the stairs. She had expected Jennifer to ask to take Oliver home and was surprised, yet extremely thankful, that she hadn't. She looked completely different from the woman who had arrived at the door that morning. Her cheeks were glowing and her eyes were shining. When Nancy opened the door, Jennifer turned to her. 'Doesn't he have the most beautiful eyes?' she said, then set off up the driveway, stopping briefly to wave.

Nancy was still standing at the doorway, completely bemused, when Mother Superior joined her.

'Nancy, is everything all right?'

Nancy reached into her apron pocket for her rosary beads with the tiny Cross of Our Lord attached. Suddenly Nancy smiled. 'Well now,' she told Him, 'I think I see where you're going with this.' She kissed the tiny cross. 'Nice idea, I like it.'

Treasure Box and Shiny Ringlets

After lunch there was the usual pandemonium, which ensued regardless of how much preparation and organisation there had been. One of the angels was crying because Norman had bent her wings. The three wise men had lost their gold, frankincense and myrrh. Nancy was informed that the statue of Joseph's head had fallen off and there was a scramble to find the glue. 'All as normal,' Nancy said, laughing. She was too distracted to care about things going wrong. Jennifer's words were playing in her head. I wonder, Nancy kept saying to herself. I wonder.

At two thirty, the children trooped into the chapel, looking angelic. There was nothing to show the chaos that had been left upstairs in the nursery. Honestly, Nancy thought, when you see the finished product you wouldn't believe all the hard work that's gone into it.

Nancy had done herself a disservice. Mother Superior was perfectly well aware of all her hard work and thanked God for her every single day.

Sister Mary Joseph and Dolly sat beside Nancy. As usual, Sister Angela was playing the organ and Nancy looked up and nodded at her. The children were all in place at the altar, and as soon as the organ began to play,

Nancy signalled for them to sing. This was the first performance of the nativity play: there would be another in a week's time for the lady mayor and the dignitaries as usual. Hopefully Mother had hidden the polish this year, Nancy thought, and had to stop herself giggling in the chapel.

As the children raised their voices in song Nancy looked at each of them. Finally her eyes rested on Billy. She had to gulp back tears. He was beaming, no tears, no sadness, no hours spent looking out of the window at the stars, although he still talked about it occasionally. Billy would never forget the Ragdoll Express, she thought. All this year it had been the children's favourite game. How many times have I dragged those chairs out of the dining room into the corridor in the last twelve months? she wondered. Billy was always the driver, and once the children had decided on their destination, the whistle would be blown and off they went.

Josephine no longer had the callipers on her legs. She still walked with a slight limp, but the sight of her trying to run around the grounds chasing Oliver was nothing less than a miracle. There had been a few of those this year. Old Mr Bell was recovering nicely and they were all looking after him. How he would cope without Oliver, if Jennifer came back for him, was Nancy's only worry. Still, the children visited him all the time now. There was no more sitting in his cottage preferring his own company.

The nativity carols went on but Nancy was miles

away. She was remembering the day she had gone with Cook to take Mr Bell some lunch and a special pudding she had made for him. As soon as they were through the door he had called, 'Hello' and said he could smell the food all the way up the driveway. Cook's face flushed red, she was extremely pleased. It should have been a wonderful moment but just then there was a knock at the door. It was Norah, come to check all was well with her brother. Polite hellos were said, and Mr Bell was staring at Nancy and Cook. Stay, please, those eyes were saying and both Nancy and Cook took a seat. 'We can stay for a little while,' Nancy said to Norah. 'We have just popped over to bring some lunch and pudding.' Norah's nose twitched.

Norah put her large bag, which contained goodness knows what, down on the floor and turned to her brother. 'Well now,' she said, 'did you enjoy my specially made stew that I left for you?'

'Your what?' said Mr Bell.

Cook jumped up, 'I, ooooh, left a pan on! I've got to go.'

Nancy followed her. 'Children to see to,' she said.

The door closed behind them. 'How rude,' said Norah and went to busy herself in the kitchen. A smile tickled the corners of James Bell's mouth; he knew exactly what Cook and Nancy would have done with the stew. Norah paused with her hands in the sink when she heard a strange sound in the living room. It was one the room had never heard before. It started with a splutter, which turned into a giggle. Then, for the first time in thirty-eight years, James Bell roared with laughter. Nancy and Cook didn't hear it as they were running as fast as they could all the way back to the house.

Dolly, digging Nancy in the ribs, dragged her back from daydreaming. The children were standing quite still, waiting for Nancy's signal to begin the next carol.

Her thoughts wandered again. There were changes in the air. I have a feeling this is going to be a very special Christmas, she thought. I wonder how it will all turn out.

There was no time for any daydreaming now. Once the play was over it was upstairs as quickly as possible for the children to get changed. There were lots of helpers to get them into their party clothes. Josephine was dressed first and brought to the television room.

'Nancy,' Dolly said, 'all the children want to watch Josephine getting her hair done.'

'Very well,' Nancy said. 'Dress them as quickly as you can and bring them along.'

Moments later the children were running down the corridor and into the room where Josephine sat on the chair by the big table in front of the window. Usually at this point, they would all be asking if the sandwiches were ready and when the birthday cake was coming, but not today. They piled in and sat on the big sofa or on the floor to watch. Josephine couldn't remember feeling so important before. All eyes were on her.

Nancy said a quick prayer, 'Please, God, let this be

perfect,' then unravelled the first rag. The ringlet fell out, perfectly formed, shining and bouncy.

'Ooh,' the children said.

Josephine said nothing, just remained perfectly calm.

Nancy continued to unravel the rags and as each shiny ringlet bounced out the children all shouted with delight: 'Ooooh,' and 'Aaaaaah.' Martha was staring at Josephine, with eyes like saucers. 'You look just like a real princess,' she said.

Finally, the last ringlet was revealed, and Nancy took Josephine's hand to lead her across to the mirror in the corner of the room.

Josephine Jones, who had once wanted to go to Heaven to see her mummy and daddy, couldn't believe her eyes. She shook her head and all the ringlets quivered. 'Do it again!' the children shouted. She did so, and the ringlets swung out around her head and shoulders. The children began clapping and Josephine thought she had never been happier.

The children all fussed around her as they made their way into the dining room. Happy children. I can ask for nothing more, Nancy thought.

The birthday sandwiches were being eaten, along with all the little treats that Cook had sent up, when Josephine called, 'Aunty Nancy, when is Mr Bell coming to the party?'

Nancy walked over to the window and couldn't see him. He must be here already, she thought.

Indeed he was. He was standing outside the large oak door, feeling ridiculous. He had one best suit, which he was wearing now. Fortunately, after all these years it still fitted him, a little on the large side but that was all right. He had brushed the jacket and laid the tie over the fireguard so that any creases would drop out. Mr Bell had no need for a suit. He didn't wear one to fix and mend and he hardly went anywhere. There was that day in the summer when he'd gone to the beach with Oliver and the children. Naturally, he'd needed to be dressed for the beach, so he'd taken his good handkerchief, tied knots in the corners and used it as a sunhat, as everyone did. Going to the beach was one thing but going into the big house was another. He had never been into the nursery's television room. He was shuffling from foot to foot. Could he go home and say he hadn't been feeling well? They would understand and make a fuss of him, but he could tolerate that in his own home.

Somehow, though, his feet wouldn't take him away from the front door. He was thinking about Billy and Josephine. It was time to stop feeling guilty and sorry for himself. Life had meaning again. He wanted to live, really live, and to give something back before it was too late.

He looked down at the treasure in his hand. He had always called it that. When he had retrieved it that morning, he'd had a job opening the drawer. He'd thought his heart would stop when he saw it again but, of course, it didn't. It had, however, been a little while before he could pick it up, then longer again before he removed the lid. It was quite a surprise when he found himself smiling. Oliver had stood by his side throughout. Mr Bell wasn't sure he could have done it without him. The dog gave him a strength nobody else ever had.

Mr Bell took a deep breath, then knocked on the door. He stood tall and straight, just like the soldier he had once been, with the little box firmly held in his hand.

When Mother opened the door to welcome him, her first thought was how uncomfortable he looked and how difficult this must be for him. When she had been told he would attend the party, she'd been startled. 'Well, it must be another of this year's miracles,' she told Nancy. 'I never would have believed it.' Yet here he was.

Mother chatted all the way to the nursery department to cover any embarrassment he might feel and he walked silently beside her to the television room. There was a squeal of excitement as he came in and stood just inside the doorway, not knowing what to say or do.

Nancy hurried over and brought him to the table. 'Don't crowd Mr Bell like that, children,' she said, laughing. He was relaxing, she thought. It's the children. He's quite at home with them now. He was offered a seat but before he sat down he looked at Josephine. He saw the sparkle in her eyes and the beautiful ringlets, and smiled, knowing the decision he had made was the right one. He coughed, then looked again at Josephine, who had come stand in front of him.

'You look ever so smart, Mr Bell,' she said.

He nodded.

'Do you like my ringlets?'

Mr Bell nodded again.

'Would you like some cake now?'

There was a pause as Mr Bell looked down at the tin box in his hand. Everyone watched as he held it out towards Josephine. 'For you,' he said.

The children all gathered round to see what it was.

Nancy thought her knees would give way. Can't be, she thought. She sat down quickly, knowing somehow that this moment was creating a memory she would treasure for the rest of her life.

Mr Bell placed the tin box in Josephine's hand and the room fell silent.

Slowly Josephine pulled at the lid, lifted it off and gasped.

There in Mr Bell's treasure box lay the most beautiful pale blue ribbons.

'Happy birthday, Josephine,' he said.

Nancy caught Mr Bell's eye and smiled at him. 'Perfect,' she whispered. There were tears running down her face and she didn't care one bit.

The birthday party was held up for a moment while the blue ribbons were tied in bows in Josephine's hair and once again there were 'oooohs' and 'aaaaaahs'.

There was further excitement when Cook turned up with Mr Bell's special birthday cake, which said, 'Happy Birthday, Welcome Home' on the top.

Cook was praised. 'Oh, it was nothing, nothing at all,' she said, then told everyone how she had toiled over it. Nancy thought the whole thing was hilarious.

Nancy decided the children could stay up late tonight. This was the best birthday party ever and it would be enjoyed until the very last second.

By six o'clock, however, the children were getting tired and the younger ones had already been bathed and put to bed. Thank goodness for all the extra helpers today, Nancy thought.

At seven o'clock Nancy, Josephine and Billy walked with Mr Bell back to his cottage. They took Oliver for a quick run, then made sure Mr Bell was comfortable and the fire banked up for the evening. They returned to the house and the two children got ready for bed. Billy was asleep before his head hit the pillow. He was dreaming of special sandwiches, cake, games in the garden and running around the wood with Oliver.

Josephine was sitting perfectly still in bed thinking about her best birthday ever. Nancy glanced at her and couldn't help laughing. She wasn't moving a muscle yet those ringlets seemed to have a life of their own. ('Quivering, they were,' she told Sister Mary Joseph later.) She busied herself with the socks to be hung at the ends of the beds, then prepared the dining room for Christmas

Day breakfast. Thank goodness I don't have chairs to drag up and down the corridor this year, she thought.

That night as the children slept the stars in the sky twinkled as they looked down upon the dormitory, the little room with the holy pictures and the cottage in the wood.

'Thank you,' they said. 'God bless you.'

Puppy Dog Eyes

Jennifer had no idea what time it was and cared even less. One foot in front of the other, she walked home. Her head was spinning and she felt more alive than she had done in such a long time. She wanted to skip, scream or even dance, and felt an excitement bubbling inside her that she was struggling to contain. She had to talk to Michael and there were hours to go before he was due home. Never had she wished away time as impatiently as she did today.

When she arrived home she shovelled more coal onto the fire. Then she went into the kitchen and spent the next few hours preparing everything that needed to be ready for Christmas Day. She switched on the wireless. Another children's choir, but this time there were no tears as Jennifer sang with them. At four o'clock she ran upstairs, had a bath and washed her hair. Everything must be perfect. She sat in front of the fire drying her hair, then ran back upstairs to choose something pretty to wear. She thought six o'clock would never come, but eventually she heard Michael's key in the front door.

The moment Michael walked through the front door he knew something was different. Happiness hung in the air, and his wife was smiling at him. Her hair looked different and she was dressed up prettily. Was she wearing rouge on her cheeks? he wondered. No, he thought it's natural: she's flushed with what looks like joy. 'Jenny,' he said.

There was only a moment's pause before she threw herself into his arms. 'Oh, Michael, oh, Michael,' she kept saying.

'Well,' he said, 'this must be some very special occasion. You usually send me straight upstairs to clean up before you start hugging me.'

Jennifer laughed. 'Go on then, get yourself upstairs. Then come down and let's have a wonderful Christmas Eve,' she said, hitting him with the tea towel.

Michael couldn't have hoped for more. He had no idea what had brought this about, but as long as his Jenny was happy, that was good enough for him. Maybe God had answered his prayers after all.

By eight o'clock they were settled together on the chair in front of the fire. Michael stroked Jennifer's hair. She didn't know how to start telling him what the day had brought. What she had to say could possibly change their whole life, and she had no idea whether or not Michael would go along with it, so she continued to sit curled up on his knee, feeling the joy in her heart that had been absent for so long.

The heat of the fire and the excitement of the day were taking their toll and her eyes closed. It was more than an hour before she stirred. 'Oh, Michael! It's Christmas Eve and I fell asleep.' She climbed off his knee and straightened her dress. 'Come here, silly,' he said, pulling her back, but she resisted him. 'Leave go,' she laughed. 'I will go and make us a drink. What would you like?' Michael looked at her. 'I'd like to know what you have to tell me.'

'What do you mean?'

Michael winked at her. 'Do I have a rival? Something's put that flush in your cheeks today.'

'Michael Harrison, how dare you!'

'Are you going to tell me then?'

'It's just . . . Well, today it just happened. Oh, Michael.'

'Unless you want to worry me to death on Christmas Eve, Jenny, darling, you're really going to have to spit it out,' he said, and waited.

Jennifer walked over to the fire and sat down, staring into the flames. 'I went for a walk today because I could no longer face the way my life was going. Constantly crying on my own and making sure you didn't know. Watching people with children and feeling a pain so raw it simply wouldn't go away, wondering whether you'd be better off without me. I felt useless as a wife and a woman and empty inside without a baby. So I went out, with no idea where I was going; it was enough to just put one foot in front of the other and breathe in as much fresh air as I could. Something had to change – *I* had to change, Michael. Nobody could help me but myself. I ended up at Jesmond parish church staring at the nativity crib.'

Michael couldn't have interrupted even if he had wanted to. His heart was breaking for her, so much so that his throat hurt, so he continued to watch her and listen. It was all he could do. If he reached out for her, she might stop. He, too, stared into the flames and waited for her to continue.

'I looked at the baby boy in the crib and asked God why he took my baby. If there was a good reason I would accept it, but I wanted to know why. You work in mysterious ways, I said to Him, and it's Christmas, a time for miracles. I wanted to ask Him just one more time to send me a child to love. I don't know why I went that way but I left the church and found myself on Sandyford Road. I heard the orphanage children playing in a little wood inside the grounds. Michael, you're not going to believe this, but I also heard a dog barking. I hid behind the trees and watched the children play with it. It was a yellow Labrador, about the same age as our puppy would have been. I found out later that it had arrived on Christmas Day and nobody knew who it belonged to. There was a little boy the dog kept running to. Oh, Michael, I wanted to scoop him up in my arms and run away with him.'

'You didn't, did you?' said Michael, looking worried.

'Don't be ridiculous! Of course not,' Jennifer replied. 'It's just those eyes, Michael. The most beautiful eyes I've even seen. My heart melted. I could see him here, running around, going crazy with the presents under the Christmas tree. Oh, Michael!' Jennifer cried. 'I must have him.'

Michael knelt beside her and took her face in his hands. 'Listen to me,' he said. 'Christmas Day or not, tomorrow we'll go to that orphanage and bring him back here where he belongs.'

'Pardon?'

'I said, we'll bring him back here with us.'

'We couldn't possibly do that! Don't be ridiculous, Michael.'

'I don't see why not. He's ours, after all.'

'Well, I rather think we have to ask first.'

'Why on earth should we? Do you want him or not? Remember those big puppy eyes?'

'Puppy eyes?'

'Jennifer, pull yourself together. You do want to bring the dog home, don't you?'

Jennifer smiled and looked back into the fire. 'Oh, no,' she said quietly. 'I wasn't talking about the dog. I meant the child – his name is Billy. He had the most beautiful eyes I've ever seen. I fell in love with him the moment I saw him.'

Christmas Magic

It had been a strange Christmas Eve, not at all like the one they had planned. Michael had been shocked when Jennifer had blurted out that she wanted the little boy. He'd thought she was talking about the puppy. When Michael had thought about adopting, he'd imagined they'd take a baby, but Jennifer had told him they didn't look after babies at Nazareth House, only children of two years old and upwards. She had also talked him about Nancy in the nursery and how kind she had been.

'Well, the one thing I didn't expect to hear was that my wife had been hiding in a wood on Christmas Eve.' Michael had laughed to cover the jumble of thoughts that were running through his mind.

Together they had sat in front of the fire, mostly in silence, until Jennifer really couldn't think of anything more to say so she left Michael to busy herself in the kitchen, making sure everything was ready for tomorrow.

Michael was marvelling at how life could change in the blink of an eye. He hadn't seen his wife so happy since before she'd lost the baby. There was a bounce in her step, a sparkle in her eyes and a flush in her cheeks. It was almost as though she was actually carrying a baby. Maybe she's preparing to be a mother, he thought, not that he really understood about such things. All he wanted was for her to be happy. It had been a heart-breaking time for her and she had suffered so much. He believed she would tell him now, if he asked her, what had happened at work that day and they would move on with their life.

The child was called Billy – Dad would like that, Michael thought, then realised he was already thinking along the same lines as Jennifer. Of course, the main worry was that the child wasn't available for adoption. He might already have parents. There was really only one way to find out and that was to ask.

Michael went into the kitchen and stopped in the doorway to watch his wife. She was bustling about, humming to herself, and for a moment he could pic-ture her laughing with Billy, telling him to calm the dog down and get themselves out of her clean kitchen. It was a perfect picture of a perfect family.

Jenny turned and laughed. 'What are you doing skulking in doorways, Michael Harrison? Do you want something?' she asked.

Michael walked over to her and gave her a kiss. 'I want the same as you do, of course. We always want the same thing and that's why we have such a good mar-riage. Just, please, don't get your hopes up in case Billy isn't free for adoption.'

'You mean we can go and ask? Really, Michael? Are you happy about this?'

'You know what? I am, Jenny, truly I am.'

The rest of Christmas Eve passed in a blur. Jennifer was so exhausted that by ten o'clock she was asleep in front of the fire. Michael continued to think about the child. This house was far too quiet when he came home . . . That wouldn't last for much longer. He began to dream about the little boy on his shoulders and the very first place he would take him . . . He jumped when Jenny shook his shoulders.

'Let's go tomorrow.'

'Go where?'

'To the orphanage, of course!'

'Jenny, darling, we can't possibly go tomorrow. In case you've forgotten, it's Christmas Day.'

'What better time to go? I feel like marching back in there right this very minute – it's bad enough having to wait until tomorrow. If you don't want to come, I'll go alone.'

Michael sat up, laughing. 'You should see the look on your face – like a stubborn little girl who's about to stamp her feet.'

'Well, are you coming or not?' Jennifer demanded.

'Of course I'm coming,' Michael replied.

Jennifer woke Michael at six, wishing him happy Christmas and saying it was going to be their best one ever.

Michael's heart sank. What sort of reception they would get, bursting into Nazareth House on Christmas Day, he couldn't imagine. Jennifer was calling him to get up. 'Have you gone back to being a child, waking me up at six when all I want to do is lie in bed?' he joked.

'You have to get ready and put your best suit on. I'm going to wear my prettiest dress and shoes for going out.'

It's going to be a long morning, Michael thought, as he lay back and wondered what the day would bring. He stayed in bed for a little longer, praying that the whole thing wouldn't come crashing down around them. God only knows what that would do to Jenny, he thought. The dog, of course, was theirs and they could have it back, but what would that do to the children, especially Billy? From what Nancy had told Jennifer they were inseparable. Let's hope they can come together, Michael thought. He was extremely nervous, to tell the truth, and wanted the day to be over. He sighed. So much for a relaxing Christmas Day.

Michael had bought Jennifer a new coat, with a matching hat and gloves, for Christmas. She would wear them today. They had discussed what time they should arrive at Nazareth House. Nine o'clock was too early because they would probably be at Mass. Between twelve and three they would be preparing lunch and eating it. But Jennifer couldn't possibly wait for teatime. They finally decided on eleven, and if that was inconvenient, they would ask when they might come back.

Eventually they set off to walk to the orphanage. It seemed like an awfully long way today, and Jennifer thought they would never get there. Twice Michael asked her not to squeeze his hand so tightly. 'If you break my fingers I won't be able to pick him up,' he said.

At last they arrived and stood at the iron gates. 'Ready?' Michael asked, but Jennifer needed a moment.

Michael looked around him and saw that just inside the gates to his left there was a wooded area. This is where Jennifer must have hidden behind the tree, Michael thought, greatly amused. At this moment Jennifer, like many before her, closed her eyes: 'Please, God, please, God,' she was praying. She couldn't think of anything else to say and felt a little light-headed. This was it, then. 'Ready, Michael,' she said. They began to walk down the driveway. Although they had almost sprinted to Nazareth House their footsteps were slow now.

For the second time in two days Jennifer went to the great oak door and knocked. Then she grabbed Michael's hand and they stood like a couple of statues, hardly moving. Over to the right of them the statue of Our Lady of Lourdes was watching them.

That Christmas Day in Newcastle upon Tyne, a few lives were about to change for ever. It was Christmas after all. A time for magic and miracles, according to Nancy.

Trains Indeed

The bell rang out at six a.m., heralding the start of Christmas Day, and most of the occupants of Nazareth House were still asleep. Nancy, though, had been up and dressed since five and was having a quiet cup of tea in her room. It had been impossible to sleep with all that had happened in the last few days. There was a feeling of change in the air and it was a good feeling. Nancy thought she had forgotten how to breathe when Mr Bell gave Josephine the treasure box with the ribbons that had been bought more than thirty-eight years ago for his daughter, Margaret. All that time they had been wrapped in paper, lying in the box, and when he had been in hospital it was the one thing he'd had on his mind: his treasure. It had been such a beautiful gesture. Nancy would make sure that every time Josephine went to visit she would be wearing her ribbons.

Oliver had certainly changed their lives for the better, she thought. And there was Jennifer, still heartbroken over the loss of her child, then her puppy. Nancy knew that Oliver had already healed hearts and was likely to do so again. There was only one problem: how on earth would they all live without him? He was part of them and their lives. The children and Mr Bell would be utterly lost . . . unless this was part of some greater plan.

Nancy picked up her rosary beads and looked at the little cross that dangled at the end. 'Well,' she said, 'I think I'll leave it to you.' She had closed her eyes in prayer until she was suddenly disturbed by the ringing of the six o'clock bell. 'Happy Christmas,' she said. She ran out of her room and along the corridor where she could already hear the children's excited squeals.

Every year, the children made Christmas garlands, which hung all the way down the long corridors. When they had been evacuated to Carlisle, Christmas at home was all they talked about. They planned it down to the last detail, and Nancy had promised that when they got back they would make the longest paper garlands in the world, and indeed they had. Now it was a tradition every year for the garlands to reach all the way down the long corridor. It was a beautiful sight to see the children on Christmas morning, their faces flushed with excitement, walking down the corridor to the dining room for breakfast. Nancy knew Cook only had a few hours' sleep on Christmas Eve, she was always preparing, cooking and baking right up until the early hours of the morning. Once the dinner had been served and cleaned away nobody was allowed to disturb her. She would be sitting snoozing by the big oven in her comfortable chair, a pot of tea beside her. After tea Nancy would have an hour with Cook and together they would enjoy yet another pot of tea and, of course, Christmas cake.

Lunch was to be at one o'clock in the dining room, which would be made ready after breakfast while the children were in the playroom with their new toys. Nancy was so relieved that this year everything was in order. Apart from Jennifer's visit there had been no last-minute panics or new children to worry about. Yet, somehow, she knew there was more to come. She couldn't explain how she knew: she just did. I wish whatever it was would happen, she thought. I can cope with whatever is thrown at me but I don't like not knowing what it will be. I suppose time will tell.

Nancy decided to take Billy and Josephine to see Mr Bell and wish him a happy Christmas. The children had made a card for him, the staff had put together a little parcel of gifts and Cook had sent a basket of goodies. They all laughed when they reached the edge of the wood and Oliver started barking.

The children looked at Nancy. 'Go on then,' she told them, so they ran ahead of her and opened the door. Oliver ran round in circles chasing his tail, then put his paws on Billy's shoulders to lick his face. Josephine went straight to Mr Bell and showed him how lovely her plaits looked with the beautiful blue ribbons tied to the ends. She knew about Margaret, because Nancy had told her, so she walked over to the photograph and said, 'Happy Christmas, Margaret, thank you very much for your ribbons.' Nancy had to look away.

No tears on Christmas Day for goodness' sake, she told herself. Then they all gathered round the fire and watched Mr Bell open his presents. They would do this every year now, Nancy promised herself.

As they waited at the front door of Nazareth House, Michael looked at Jennifer. He was now feeling extremely nervous. What if the child wasn't up for adoption? What if he didn't like them? What if Mother Superior turned them away? What if Nancy was angry with them for disturbing her on what must be a busy day? He turned to Jennifer. 'What if –'

Jennifer stopped him. 'Don't say it, Michael. Let's be brave.' They were standing outside the door and Jennifer suddenly began to lose her bravado. They stood side by side, both lost in their own thoughts. Jennifer looked around her and there to her right stood a beautiful grotto, and the Lady of Lourdes looked back at her. Jennifer smiled then lifted her hand and knocked. They looked at each other and waited.

The door opened and they took a step back. Michael quickly removed his hat.

What on earth is the matter now? Mother wondered. Jennifer and a gentleman, whom Mother presumed was her husband, were standing outside, clearly petrified. 'Come in out of the cold,' she said, ushered them into her room and asked them to take a seat. Jennifer opened her mouth to speak, but Mother raised her hand. 'I

think we need tea. If you'll excuse me for a moment . . .'
She left the room.

'At least she let us in,' Michael whispered.

'Sssh,' Jennifer said. They fell silent again.

'I wish she'd hurry up,' Michael muttered. 'I feel really out of place sitting here.'

'Be quiet, Michael, please,' Jennifer said. 'I am nervous enough to start with.' They continued to wait then Jennifer began to study the room. What a beautiful room, she thought. There was a huge black telephone on Mother's table and she wondered what momentous decisions had been taken on it. The fireplace stretched halfway up the wall and was just as wide. It looked like it was made of marble, and logs were blazing in the grate. When she looked above the mantelpiece, she gasped. Michael followed her gaze – and that was how Mother Superior saw them when she returned. Michael and Jennifer were gazing upwards at the large picture of the Madonna and Child.

'Tea is on its way,' she said, and began to chat about how they had got there, the weather and what they were planning for Christmas. All safe subjects. The tea duly arrived and Mother poured. It was time. 'Well now,' she said, 'what can I do for you?'

The speech had been well prepared. Jennifer had hardly slept all night. Over and over in her head she had said the words until she had them by heart. She opened her mouth to speak, then burst into tears. Mother offered her a handkerchief and waited. 'Maybe I can help a little,' Mother said.

Jennifer was aware that this was a kind voice and felt comforted. 'I'm told by Nancy that Oliver is yours and you lost him on Christmas Day last year, when he decided to make his home in the stable here.' She smiled, then continued: 'A child found him, and managed, with the help of his friends, to keep the puppy hidden for quite a while!' There was laughter in her eyes.

Michael and Jennifer relaxed, glanced at each other, then back to Mother. 'The child?' asked Jennifer. 'Nancy said it was Billy.'

'That's right, little Billy Miller. It was a sad story. He, too, arrived just before Christmas and was grieving for his parents so badly he wouldn't speak. It was due to Oliver and Nancy's love and care that he finally began to heal. He will miss Oliver very much indeed. Perhaps you could visit and let him see the dog. You would both be most welcome.'

Mother was trying to imagine telling Nancy and the children, especially Billy, that Oliver would be leaving them. Then there was Mr Bell.

Jennifer looked up once more at the Madonna and Child, and smiled. 'Oh, Mother Superior, it was those eyes. I looked into them and it just happened.'

'Eyes, my child?'

'Yes! Big eyes that said, "Take me and love me," and, oh, Mother, at that moment all I wanted to do was pick him up and run.'

'Well, of course he is yours to take.'

Michael began to laugh. 'Jennifer, we had this conversation ourselves. Don't you remember what happened then?'

'Oh, yes. I'm not being clear. It's Billy Miller. I saw him running around with Oliver and I saw my life mapped out in front of me, with that little boy at my feet, sitting on my knee, growing up. I saw myself tucking him into bed, reading him stories . . .' Jennifer was breathing rapidly and her hands were shaking.

'Ah, now I think I understand,' Mother said. 'Do you wish to apply for adoption?'

'Yes, Mother! Can we do that? Please tell me we can.'

'Well, the correct procedures must be followed. I can certainly put you in touch with the people who can arrange it for you but they are not available today. I believe they have Christmas Day off,' she said, smiling.

Michael and Jennifer laughed. 'We won't take up any more of your day,' Michael said, and Mother took some details, promising they would be contacted after the holiday by the relevant people, who would discuss the procedures with them.

As they stood at the front door, Mother Superior looked towards the wood. 'I believe if you walk into the trees you will find Billy there with Nancy. You may go and walk with them, if you wish. However, I must ask that you tread carefully with Billy. He has dealt with far too much grief and disappointment already in his young life and you must be patient. I don't want either yourselves or Billy to have any false hope.'

They said goodbye, wished each other a happy Christmas, and when Mother had closed the door, Jennifer grabbed Michael's hand. She almost dragged him towards the wood. Michael had to tell her to slow down.

'What's wrong?' she said, wondering why he wasn't jumping for joy as she was.

'I'm scared,' he said. 'Remember, we haven't to give him false hope and, anyway, he may not like us.'

Jennifer was having none of it. 'Don't be ridiculous. Anyway, Christmas is a time for miracles and it's most definitely our turn for one.' She saw Nancy and waved.

Nancy waved back and shivered, then sent Josephine, who was all smiles today, into the cottage. They were obviously here to take Oliver, and the prospect of losing him terrified her. Jennifer introduced her husband.

'This is Michael and Jennifer, Billy,' Nancy said. 'They're my – my friends.'

'Can we just walk with you a little while, Nancy?' Jennifer asked. Oliver was sniffing Jennifer's hand, then moved to Michael's. Moments later he was running around in circles. Billy laughed and it was the most beautiful sound Jennifer had ever heard. 'He likes you,' he said.

Michael picked up a stick and threw it for Oliver, who tore after it. 'You next,' he said, and there began a competition between him and Billy to see who could throw the stick the furthest. They were not supposed to get too close to the child but it was hard to stop themselves stroking his hair or putting an arm round him. Jennifer ached to do both but Michael gave her a look that said, 'Just don't.'

Nothing wrong with chatting, though, and getting to know him a little. Jennifer bent down to him. 'What's your favourite game, Billy?'

'Trains.'

Michael seemed frozen to the spot until he, too, bent down to Billy. 'Do you mean trains are your favourite toys?'

'No, it's my favourite game.'

'How does it go then, this game of yours?'

'Well, Aunty Nancy gets all the chairs and puts them in a line and I get the whistle and blow it very loud and we can go wherever we want.'

'Where's your favourite place to go?' Michael asked, wondering not only about the child but about the woman who brought magic into his and the other children's lives.

Billy pointed to the sky. 'To the stars.'

'The stars?'

'It's where my mummy and daddy are. They're stars in the sky.'

Jennifer's hand flew to her mouth too late to stop a sob escaping, and Michael had to squeeze his eyes shut.

'Daddy took me to see the big trains once and I

heard the steam hissing. He was going to take me again but he can't now.'

It was too much and, as it turned out, it was Michael, not Jennifer, who threw caution to the wind. He swung little Billy up onto his shoulders.

Nancy was cold as she stood and watched them, pulling her coat tighter around her. However, there was a warmth in her heart. She had played her part and now it was in God's hands. She turned, and saw Mr Bell and Josephine watching from the window and there was a spark of sadness in her heart. Oh, goodness, how they were all going to miss Oliver.

Jennifer and Michael walked home hand in hand, neither of them speaking, both lost in their own thoughts. Jennifer was remembering all the things Billy had told her and her heart broke for him. She could mend that heart, and she hadn't missed the look in Michael's eyes when Billy had told him about the trains.

But how did Michael really feel about all this? Would he want to go ahead with it? Jennifer wanted to ask him but couldn't come up with the right words.

In the end she didn't need to say anything. Michael suddenly stopped, took her in his arms and held her there for a moment. Jennifer thought her heart would burst because the next words Michael said were about to change both of their lives for ever.

'Jenny?'

'Yes, Michael?'

'I want that boy to be our son so much it hurts.'

'Me too, more than anything in the world.'

'Happy Christmas, Jenny.'

'Happy Christmas, Michael.'

They walked to the top of the driveway, hand in hand. At the gates, Michael stopped again. 'Trains indeed,' he said. 'I simply can't believe it.'

A New Mummy and Daddy

Nancy felt out of sorts for weeks, wondering how on earth paperwork could take so long. If this was God's will, she wished He could hurry it up somehow. Yesterday Michael and Jennifer had officially been accepted as adoptive parents for Billy, and Nancy had had to sit down she was so relieved. 'Thank Heaven for that,' she said.

She hurried along the corridor to get little Billy ready to meet his new parents, who had asked if they could tell him themselves. It had all been agreed, although Mother and Nancy had to be present. Nancy didn't know why she was so nervous: she had done this hundreds of times before. Billy sat on the edge of the bed as Nancy put on his best shoes and made sure he was clean and perfectly tidy. The other children were in the playroom and he kept asking if he could go and play, but Nancy said this was a special day and he was to be patient. She combed his hair and Billy complained that it had already been combed. Nancy continued fussing about, waiting for ten o'clock. Finally, she took Billy's hand and smiled.

'Come along, darling. Let's see who's waiting downstairs to take you out for a little while.'

'Aunty Nancy, do you think it's those nice people who played with me and Oliver in the wood? I liked them.

'Well, they are very nice indeed, Billy.'

'And they liked Oliver too. The lady didn't shout when he was sniffing her.'

'Well, that settles it,' Nancy said, laughing.

She paused at the top of the stairs for a moment. Today this little boy's life would change, and she prayed with all her heart that it would be a story with a happy ending. Billy tugged at her hand. 'Can we go now, Aunty Nancy?'

Slowly Nancy walked down the stairs, with the beautiful iron railings, looking towards Mother Superior's room where Michael and Jennifer would be waiting. There was a lump in her throat. This will never do, she thought, but it doesn't get any easier. Alongside the thrill of a happy ending there was always the pain of knowing she might never see the child again. It was her job to love and take care of them until new parents were found. That was God's will, she had to remind herself over and over.

When they reached the bottom of the stairs Nancy took a deep breath. She walked straight to Mother Superior's door and knocked.

As soon as they were inside the room, Nancy saw Jennifer and Michael standing together holding hands tightly. There was a moment's hesitation, then Billy ran over to them. Michael swung him up into his arms and Jennifer reached for his hand.

'Have you come to take me for a walk?'

Michael looked at Mother Superior, who nodded. He put Billy down and took his hand. He opened his mouth to speak and nothing came out. He looked at Nancy, who smiled, so he tried again. 'Well, you see, we'd like to see more of you. In fact, lots more. Like every day and . . .'

Billy was clearly confused and Jennifer laughed. She knelt in front of Billy, taking his hands. 'Billy, darling, I loved you from the moment I set eyes on you, and we would love to be your new mummy and daddy. What do you say, sweetheart?'

Billy Miller stood silently as the people in the room remained perfectly still, like statues, nobody saying anything. He thought Aunty Nancy looked very strange, not smiling like she usually did. Adults could be very strange indeed. When he eventually spoke everyone jumped. 'Like a real mummy and daddy every day?'

'Just like a really mummy and daddy,' Jennifer said.

More silence. Then Billy looked up at Nancy with tears in his eyes.

'Is something worrying you, Billy?' Nancy asked. This wasn't at all how it was supposed to go.

Billy's voice shook as he said, 'You told me it was hard when we had to leave people behind we love and it's just hurting a bit.'

'Oh, Billy, darling,' Nancy said, 'you can come back and see me any time you want.

Jennifer and Michael chipped in: 'Yes, Billy, whenever you like.'

'I didn't mean you, Aunty Nancy,' Billy said. 'I meant Oliver.'

There was only a moment's pause before everyone in the room burst into laughter.

'Well I never,' said Nancy, wiping her eyes with the corner of her apron.

'As if we'd leave without Oliver,' Michael said. 'Let's go and find him, shall we?'

Nancy and Mother watched Billy, who was practically squealing with delight, skipping between his new-mummy-and-daddy-to-be as they walked up the driveway to the caretaker's cottage.

'Cup of tea, Nancy?' Mother said.

'Oh, yes please,' Nancy replied. 'Don't you just love a happy ending, Mother?'

It had been a big day for Billy and, with all the excitement, he had fallen asleep late in the afternoon, which Nancy never usually allowed because it interfered with bedtime. Today, though, she laid him on his bed for a little nap. Once wouldn't do any harm. As he slept she walked over to the window and looked out. Was it only just over a year ago that his little heart had been so laden with grief he couldn't even talk? He had constantly looked up at the stars in the sky from here. Nancy smiled, remembering the first time she had been convinced she thought she heard a dog barking from this very window. Michael and Jennifer's lives were about to change for ever. She prayed with all her heart that life would be good to Billy, Jennifer and Michael. She turned to look at Billy. It was no good, she would have to wake him or he'd never sleep tonight.

It took her some time to rouse him but eventually, with the promise of seeing Oliver, Nancy got him into his hat and coat and they made their way over to the caretaker's cottage. Smoke was billowing out of the chimney so there would be a fire to sit beside. Suddenly Billy shook Aunty Nancy's hand. 'Has anybody told Oliver about my new mummy and daddy?'

'Well, actually, no,' she told him. 'I think that's your job, don't you? It is, after all, a very important one.'

Billy nodded and smiled, very pleased indeed.

Mr Bell was always glad to see them and called for them to come inside. Oliver was standing at the door, whining in welcome. Nancy followed Mr Bell into the kitchen and began helping to make tea. Billy sat in front of the fire and Oliver settled beside him.

'I've got something to tell you, Oliver, and it's very special.' Oliver's tail was wagging furiously. 'I'm going to live with my new mummy and daddy and you're coming too. I could never have left you behind. Mummy is so pretty and Daddy is so strong he can lift me up on his shoulders and run. We can come back here as much as we like, Mummy said, and see all of our friends. What do you think of that then?' Oliver barked, then settled down beside Billy, happily content. He thought it sounded like a marvellous plan.

There had always been a special bond between the child and the dog who had brought him unconditional love, understanding and a friendship that would never be forgotten.

The Special Star

The nativity play for the lady mayor and the dignitaries was eventually taking place. It usually happened just after Christmas but she had been ill and it had been postponed. Nancy had hoped it would be cancelled altogether, but Mother had received a call during the last week in January to say that the lady mayor would like the service to go ahead. 'How completely and utterly pointless,' Nancy had complained. 'You have a Christmas service at Christmas or not at all,' she told everyone.

However, two days before the service was due to take place, Billy's adoption was finalised. Nancy was bubbling with excitement. I should have known there was a good reason for the delay, Lord, she prayed. Mr Bell had been invited to come along and watch. Josephine was going to be an angel this time as another little girl would be Mary, and Nancy's heart had melted when she saw her dressed to play her part: those beautiful ringlets with the pale blue ribbons, a white sheet tied in the middle with a piece of tinsel and a halo on her head. Wings had been made using up all the glitter she had scraped from the Christmas cards. Josephine would steal the show.

Earlier that morning, on spotting Mother, Nancy had called down the stairs, 'Need any polish, Mother?' then burst out laughing. Mother had simply shaken her head and asked Nancy not to shout down the stairs, but when she turned away she was suppressing a smile. There was a thrill in the air this year and Mother could not have been happier.

Everything was in place when the lady mayor arrived and Mother led the guests to chapel with the nuns following. Sister Mary Joseph and Sister Lucy stepped forward and opened the oak doors and the lady mayor gasped.

There they stood on the altar steps, the children of Nazareth House Orphanage. There was the sweetest stable, full of straw, with Mary and Joseph standing at either side. There were shepherds and wise men alongside angels, and a huge Christmas tree to the left of the altar. The Archangel Gabriel stood in front of the tree with a small bouquet in her hand. Very slowly she made her way down the aisle towards the lady mayor.

Everyone held their breath. Josephine had done wonderfully well in a year yet she still walked with a slight limp. The children began to sing 'Away in a Manger' as Josephine continued, eventually stopping in front of the lady mayor. Nancy almost held her breath as the little girl tried to curtsy. A sob escaped the lady mayor, who usually didn't show such emotion.

Josephine handed the bouquet to her, then turned round and placed her hands in the prayer position.

They all began to follow her down the aisle to their pews. Josephine took her place at the altar beside the stable. Nancy looked at her and nodded, mouthing, 'Well done, Josephine.'

Michael and Jennifer sat at the back, thinking their hearts would burst at any moment. They waved at Billy, who beamed back at them.

Just before the end of the service the children went to the back of the chapel to take something out of a basket. Everyone tried to see what it was but nobody knew: this was a secret Nancy had kept to herself. As the children got back into line everyone strained their eyes to see.

The children made their way down the aisle each with a silver star in their hands, which they had spent all week making. Each star bore the words 'God bless Mummy and Daddy'. It was too much for the lady mayor, who now had tears trickling down her cheeks as each child hung their star on the tree.

Little Billy remained standing at the back of the chapel, wearing a huge grin.

'Surely our Billy should be doing that,' Jennifer whispered. 'He was the one who told them all about the stars in the sky after all.'

'Look at you,' Michael murmured, 'getting all protective. I don't think you need worry . . .'

Billy lifted the final star out of the box. This was no ordinary star: this was the Star of Bethlehem. Very carefully, he held it up, then walked to Michael and Jennifer and waited. They looked at Nancy, who nodded at them. With fast-beating hearts, they stepped out of the pew and stood at either side of Billy. He looked up at Jennifer, then Michael, and beamed. The children began to sing 'Silent Night' as they all walked down the aisle to the altar and Billy placed the Star of Bethlehem above the stable. Michael patted Billy's shoulder and Jennifer leaned over to kiss him. Then he returned to his place with the other children, ready to sing the final carol.

'Dear God, thank you for my new mummy and daddy,' Billy whispered.

God looked down on him and smiled. He still had one more surprise for little Billy Miller.

God's Final Surprise

Over the next couple of weeks, when Billy returned from school, he found Jennifer waiting for him at Nazareth House. She would give him a kiss and then they would go to the cottage for Oliver. They would usually play for half an hour in the wood, then visit Mr Bell. Jennifer loved those days when they sat in front of the fire, chatting and laughing. She became fond of Mr Bell, and some mornings, if she had been baking, she would call in, bringing a basket of cake and a few scones. There was really no need, as Cook kept him well supplied, but it was an excuse to see him, which everyone knew. Jennifer loved chatting to him, and they would often take a walk in the wood or he would show her how he mended things. It was hard to know who was gaining the most benefit from their time together. One day they were sitting in front of the fire when Mr Bell told Jennifer about Josephine and the 'thingy', the walking-frame he had made for her, and about how the children had managed to hide Oliver for so long. 'With Nancy and Cook's help,' he told her. 'Those two are a force to be reckoned with, you know, yet they have hearts of gold, but I'm sure you know that already.'

Jennifer told Mr Bell about the forms she and Michael had had to fill in for the adoption and all the questions they'd had to answer. Now it was finalised and they were waiting to be given a date when they could have Billy. 'I know everything's in order,' Jennifer told him. 'Now I just want to take him home.'

As they sat in the cottage one Friday afternoon, waiting for Billy to return from school, there was a knock on the door.

'We've heard!' Nancy shouted, as soon as Jennifer opened the door. 'The children's officer was going to contact you but I asked her to let me tell you and she agreed. The final papers will be brought next Friday and then you can take Billy home.' Jennifer hugged Mr Bell, who looked embarrassed, but Nancy hadn't missed the look in his eyes.

When Nancy and Jennifer had left to hurry down to the house, Mr Bell stood in the doorway of his cottage with Oliver at his side. Sadness had returned to his eyes. 'Things will be changing now,' he told Oliver, as he closed the door. He walked over to his chair, and Oliver curled up in front of the fire. Mr Bell sat down and reached for his photograph of Margaret. 'Be just you and me again soon, lass,' he said sadly.

There was great excitement in Mother Superior's room as she explained to Nancy and Jennifer what the procedure was and when it would take place. Both Jennifer and Michael would have to attend on Friday, when the final papers would be signed. They would then be free to take Billy and Oliver home with them.

Jennifer had no idea what to say, even if she had been able to open her mouth to speak. Instead she grabbed Nancy's hand and squeezed it.

They left Mother and climbed the stairs to the nursery kitchenette. Nancy's answer to everything was a strong cup of tea. When they were sitting comfortably opposite each other, with the teapot and a plate of cakes between them, Jennifer said. 'Nancy, how do you do it? I've seen the way you look at them. If there's one thing I've learned over the last few weeks it's that you know every single one of these children inside and out. I have been told so many stories of the lengths you go to to make sure they're happy. I know all about the Ragdoll Express, the years you made snow buckets and ragdolls for the children when there was little else for them to open on Christmas Day. Mother told me how they survived the upset of evacuation. Your heart must be as big as the world and the hundreds of little children in your care must have felt so loved. How do you do it, Nancy? How do you let them go?'

Nancy smiled. 'It's because I love them that I let them go with a smile, and joy in my heart. God loans them to me for a while to prepare them for a new family like yourself and Michael. It's the greatest job in the world, Jennifer. I'm a mother to many children for a while. My job is to ease the pain in their little hearts and make them happy again. Yet I do admit I've cried. I'll cry when you leave with Billy and Oliver because, for a little while, my heart will hurt because I miss them. Then there will be a new child who needs my help and my heart will heal while I help them learn how to be happy again. Then I'll remember you and I'll smile because I helped to make your dream and Billy's come true. It's the most wonderful feeling, Jennifer.'

'Am I really a mother, Nancy?' asked Jennifer.

'In every single sense of the word,' Nancy replied. 'You grew him in your heart. Do you remember seeing Billy that very first time when you hid behind the tree in the wood? What did you tell me? Can you remember?'

'It was just a feeling, nothing I can really put into words, but when I looked into his eyes I felt like he belonged to me that very moment.' Jennifer laughed, 'Oh, Nancy, it was so funny when I told Michael – he thought I meant Oliver. It wasn't, though. It was Billy. From that moment he was my son and I knew it. How does that happen?'

'I imagine it was quite simply God's will,' Nancy replied, 'and somewhere deep inside you knew that.'

'That day seems so long ago now,' Jennifer said. 'So much has happened. Does he still talk about the stars in the sky? How often should I mention his mummy and daddy? I don't want him to forget them. That's the right thing to do, isn't it, Nancy?'

'What a wonderful mother you're going to be, Jennifer. I think you can take the lead from Billy. If he wants to talk about them, then listen. That's all you can do.'

A little later, Jennifer stood up. 'Goodness, look at the time!' she exclaimed. 'I must get home – and I want to pop in and see Mr Bell before I go. He seemed a little sad today. I want to make sure he knows Billy and I will be visiting every weekend and during school holidays. Billy loves him so much.'

'I think the feeling is mutual,' Nancy said, 'and I suspect you care for him too.'

'I'm going to tempt him out of that cottage – see if I can get him to come and visit us,' Jennifer said. Then she was gone, almost skipping down the nursery stairs.

Nancy sat for a moment, lost in thought, then began to clear away the tea things. When she'd finished, she set off to see Mother Superior. She paused at the top of the stairs and looked at the huge clock that hung on the wall. The clock ticked and Nancy stood and listened. There was nothing to tell her that another day, in the not-too-distant future, she would stand there and watch a tiny baby being handed over at the big oak door. That child would change her life in a way she could never have dreamed of.

Nancy jumped when she heard Mother call up to her. She hurried down the staircase – Mother was gesturing for her to come into her room. Dear God, please, don't let anything be wrong, she thought. Not now, when they had all come so far. That would be too cruel. She entered the room. Mother Superior had a piece of paper in her hand and looked shocked.

'Dear God in Heaven, what now, Mother?'

'Nancy, you're really not going to believe this.'

'Believe what? Is something wrong? Please, Mother, just tell me.'

'God, it seems, had one more surprise up His sleeve, Nancy.' She held up the piece of paper.

Nancy went to her. She was puzzled until Mother pointed to the middle of the page. She gasped, then had to reach for a chair and sit down. 'Let me see that again, please,' she said, and Mother handed her the paper. Above the fireplace the Madonna and Child gazed down on them, smiling.

Adoption Papers

Father's Name: Michael Harrison

Occupation: Train Driver

Nancy handed the paper back to Mother and almost ran along the corridor to the chapel where she opened the doors and raced down the aisle. A little out of breath, she looked up at Our Lord. 'A train driver! A train driver – oh, my goodness, a train driver.' Nancy laughed and knelt at the altar. 'Oh, dear God, what a wonderful surprise.'

The Ragdoll Express

Finally the day had arrived. There had been one or two hold-ups that nobody had foreseen, throwing everyone into panic. Jennifer had cried, Michael had soothed and Nancy had given everyone a piece of her mind, but eventually everything was in order. It had been a long process but now everything was in place and little Billy Miller was sitting in bed, unable to sleep. The children were dreaming their dreams but he was wide awake. Somewhere outside he could hear Oliver barking and he smiled. Nancy had told him his parents would not have been angry that he had hidden the puppy. 'Maybe the stars in the sky sent Oliver to you. Imagine that,' she told him.

Billy asked if the stars had sent him his new mummy and daddy, and Aunty Nancy had said, 'Oh, yes, without a doubt.'

'Will my first mummy and daddy forget me now?' Billy had asked, and that was when Aunty Nancy had lifted him up and carried him to the window.

'Never ever will they forget you, darling,' she told him. 'The stars in the sky are there for ever and will never fade or disappear. Every time you look at them they will send you love and you can talk to them and send your love back to them. They must be very happy indeed to have specially handpicked new parents for you.'

'What does handpicked mean?' Billy had asked.

'Well,' she said, 'it means chosen just for you. How does that make you feel, Billy?'

'All special and tickly inside,' Billy answered.

'Well, that's just about perfect, Billy,' Nancy said.

'I wish I could take my train with me, Aunty Nancy. Do you think I could ever come back and play?'

'You can come back as often as you wish, my darling. I've never known a better game than the train game you all play. I'll ask your mummy if you can come and play during the school holidays. Would you like that?'

'Oh, I would, Aunty Nancy,' said Billy. For the last time he looked out of the dormitory window at the stars in the sky.

'Make a wish, darling,' whispered Nancy.

'I wish . . . I wish that I was sitting in Mr Bell's cottage with Oliver beside me, listening to him telling me stories.'

'Well, Billy, sometimes dreams come true even when we never believe they can.'

'Really?' said Billy.

'Promise,' she said, as she produced his slippers and dressing gown.

Nancy took him down the long corridor and into her room, where she sat him on her bed. She put on her hat and coat, and wrapped a blanket around Billy. Then she led him down the nursery stairs and out into the garden.

Smoke was drifting out of the cottage chimney. Thank goodness there's a fire burning in there, thought Nancy.

Oliver alerted Mr Bell to the fact that visitors were approaching and they were welcomed inside. Mr Bell was delighted that Billy wanted to spend his last evening with him. 'It's all going to be different now,' Mr Bell said, 'and I'll miss you, little man. In fact, I have something for you. I was going to keep it until tomorrow but as you're here I think you should have it now.'

'Oh, but I couldn't possibly not see you again,' Billy told him. 'Mummy said she's going to bring me every weekend and some nights after school and you have to come to our house for Sunday lunch. Daddy said she's the best cook in the world and you can sit in front of our fire with me and Oliver. Mummy said that Granddad Harrison has a car and can pick you up and take you home. Then sometimes, when we have to go places, she's going to leave Oliver with you until she can collect him again. Will that be all right, do you think?'

Mr Bell thought it was more than all right. It sounded perfect. He got to his feet, went into his workshop and picked up a parcel. It was just as well Billy hadn't gone any sooner. It would never have been finished in time. Mr Bell remembered when he had first had the idea. It had taken time and a lot of effort. Some days he'd still felt weak from his illness, but it was a labour of love, something he had wanted to do, especially now Billy was leaving. In all these years he had never felt happiness, just a sense of doing what was right, giving to the children of Nazareth House something he had never been able to give his own child. He would be there at all times, no matter what they needed, and there was a sense of peace in knowing that his small labours helped. Yet in all that time there had never been the love and companionship he felt now. He had been forgiven, he knew that. Maybe losing his wife and child was God's way of sending him here to make a difference, and if that was the case, then maybe it was time to be happy again. It had been a long time since he had felt happy and yet this last year he had smiled more than he had ever smiled in his whole life. 'God's will has been done,' Nancy had told him. Well he didn't know or understand about all that but he wanted so much to believe her.

For the last few weeks he had been in his workshop sawing, hammering and carving until it was perfect. He prayed it meant little Billy wouldn't forget him or the orphanage that had been his home this year. He picked up his gift, wrapped in old newspaper with a bit of string around the middle, and carried it into the room.

'For you,' he said awkwardly, handing it to Billy.

'What is it?' Billy asked.

'Best open it and find out,' Nancy told him, leaning forward.

Billy slowly unwrapped the parcel. Both he and

Nancy gasped when the newspaper fell away. Billy placed it on the floor and looked at it.

It was the most beautiful train, made of wood, with 'Ragdoll Express' carved into the sides. 'Knew you'd miss your train,' Mr Bell said, shuffling from foot to foot.

There wasn't a sound in the room. Nancy and Billy continued to stare at the train as the fire crackled in the grate.

Suddenly Billy jumped up and ran to Mr Bell. He threw his arms around him and began to sob. Mr Bell's eyes filled with tears and, for the first time in thirty-eight years, he bent down and held a child in his arms.

When it was time to leave, Billy hugged Oliver, then Mr Bell waved them off and returned to sit beside the fire. He closed his eyes and began to doze as the dog lay down on the hearthrug for the evening.

'I think it's going to be all right after all,' Mr Bell told Margaret, just before he fell asleep.

The moonbeams shone in through the window and fell on the photograph. Margaret, it seemed, agreed wholeheartedly.

The Blue Room

It had been an extremely busy few days for Jennifer, and for Michael, who had managed to take a little holiday from work. Although he now had the job he dreamed of and didn't want to let them down by being away, when he had told his boss the reason for his absence, there had been slaps on the back and congratulations. Jennifer had been thrilled. After all, when they collected Billy they should do so together.

Then there was Billy's bedroom, which Jennifer insisted had to be just right for their son. 'A dream come true,' she told Michael, who had agreed. They had known each other such a long time, yet never had Michael seen Jennifer so excited. Billy's bedroom was out of bounds to him. It was to be a surprise, and Jennifer's father was helping. Both sets of grandparents had got carried away with the excitement and had been brought to Nazareth House to meet their new grandson. Billy had been overwhelmed, as had they, but when Jennifer had told Billy to tell them about the stars in the sky, they had cried and that was it. He was their grandson and they were going to make up for all that he had lost.

They had all howled with laughter when Billy told

them about hiding Oliver. 'We'll have to keep an eye on you, my lad,' Michael's father had joked.

There had been such activity in the house today. Both sets of grandparents, Michael and Jennifer had been bumping into each other with paint pots, brushes and glue in their hands. There were shouts of 'Is anyone going to make a brew? This is thirsty work, you know,' and Jennifer had had to keep stopping what she was doing to make tea.

The house had fallen quiet now and Jennifer was glad because she had one more thing to do.

As evening drew in, she sat on the floor in Billy's new room, cutting and gluing for what seemed like hours. Michael was not allowed in until she had finished, she told him. It was nearly nine o'clock before it was complete and there was a knock on the door. 'You almost done?' Michael called.

'Be down in a minute,' she said. She stood up and admired her handiwork. 'Lovely,' she said.

She made her way downstairs to the kitchen, where Michael had supper ready for them. 'Last night on our own, Jenny,' he said. They imagined tomorrow night when they would have a child to tuck into his bed. There were no worries about Billy being happy: they had grown close as a family in the last few weeks – Billy's eyes had lit up every time he was told they were there to see him.

'I've got a surprise for him,' Jennifer said, taking Michael's hand. 'Come and look.' Together they walked up the stairs and she threw open Billy's bedroom door. The walls were painted pastel blue and there was a blue rug on the floor beside his bed. The bedside cabinet and chest of drawers were all painted blue. The curtains that hung at the window were pale cream with blue stripes. Jennifer waited. 'It's all very . . . very blue,' Michael laughed. Jennifer waited. Michael looked up. Jennifer had cut out silver stars and stuck them all across the ceiling. Michael took his wife's hand and together they lay down on the bed, gazing up at the stars that their son would see every night.

'Thank you,' Jennifer whispered. 'Thank you for giving us your son. We'll take good care of him, I promise.'

All Aboard

The next morning Jennifer woke early. She could hardly believe that the day had actually arrived. Today they were going to collect their son, with Oliver, of course, from Nazareth House and finally bring them home. At last Jennifer would be a mother. She had not forgotten Nancy's words and, indeed, would never forget Nancy. She had a feeling they would be seeing a lot of each other in the future. It had been agreed that Billy would visit Mr Bell during the school holidays and at weekends. Every third Sunday, Mr Bell would come for lunch. Sunday Mass was held every week at nine o'clock and Billy, Jennifer and Michael would attend while Mr Bell looked after Oliver.

Michael was doing well at his new job. He was one of the youngest train drivers and had worked hard for his promotion. No matter what shift they offered him he took it. 'Got a hungry lad at home to feed now,' he told them.

Jennifer had asked for permission to bring Josephine to their home every few weekends. Billy and Josephine had become close over the last year and Jennifer wanted them to stay friends.

She was ready by ten even though they weren't due

to collect Billy until noon. She had made sure that everything was ready for him. Billy's favourite meal was in the oven, ready to be heated up when they arrived home. She couldn't wait to tuck him into bed for the first time and read stories. I do hope he likes his room, she thought.

Billy sat in the parlour with a brown suitcase beside him. He was wearing his best clothes and cap, waiting for his mummy and daddy to come and collect him. Nancy was sitting beside him, chatting. She had done this many times so why she was feeling nervous today, goodness only knew.

There was a knock on the door and Billy reached for Nancy's hand. She squeezed his and continued chatting. 'Your new clothes are in the case, Billy, along with your books and the train. You can put your train in your new room tonight and remember us all. Your new mummy and daddy are bringing you to chapel on Sunday so it's only a few days before we see you again. Mr Bell is coming to lunch at your house afterwards. Did you know that?'

Now Michael and Jennifer were walking towards him. 'There you go now. Give me a hug, then off you go and have fun.'

Jennifer ran over and took her hands. 'I don't know what to say.'

'Best say nothing,' Nancy said. 'Go on, get away with you and have a wonderful life together.' She reached for the corner of her apron but it was for herself. Today there were only happy children and no tears to be dried.

Michael looked down at his son. 'You all right, Billy? Is there anything you want before we go?'

Billy thought for a moment. 'Can I ride on your shoulders?' he asked.

'Indeed you can, son,' he said, and swung Billy up. They collected Oliver from the cottage and told Mr Bell they would come back tomorrow when Michael returned to work. Billy would be off school for another couple of days to let him settle in at home so he, Jennifer and Oliver would pop over.

As they made their way up the driveway, Nancy stood at the window with Josephine whose plaits were standing perfectly still.

Halfway up the driveway, Jennifer paused and looked back and saw Nancy and Josephine were watching them leave. Michael stopped and turned, following her gaze.

'Michael?'

'Yes?'

'About Josephine . . .'

Michael chuckled. 'One at a time, darling,' he said, 'one at a time.'

They jumped on the trolley bus at the end of Sandyford Road. 'Where are we going, Daddy?' Billy asked.

'It's a surprise, son,' he told him. 'Just you wait and see.' On the way there Billy told his mummy and daddy all about the day he'd run away to Central Station.

Michael smiled but Jennifer began to fret about keeping an eye on him.

They got off, to Billy's surprise, opposite the station and once more Michael hoisted Billy onto his shoulders. As soon as they got into the station there were cries of 'Hello there, Michael! Is this the young lad then?'

'Give them a wave,' Michael said, and Billy waved at all the people who were calling to them.

'How does everyone know your name, Daddy?' Billy asked.

'Just you wait and see, son,' Michael replied.

They walked onto a platform, hearing the trains hissing and smelling the smoke. 'Want to look even closer?' Michael said.

'Yes, please, Daddy,' Billy replied.

Michael felt choked. He would never tire of being called 'Daddy'.

The train in the station was billowing smoke and Billy heard a whistle blow somewhere. Just like his own train, he thought. They walked all the way down the platform to the locomotive. Billy's eyes were as wide as saucers. He was so thrilled he wasn't sure he could speak.

'Want an even closer look, Billy?' Michael said. Then, when Billy didn't answer, he lifted him into the driver's compartment and jumped up beside him. Jennifer and Oliver climbed up, too, and they all stood together.

Billy looked at Jennifer, who smiled at him, then at

Oliver. Finally he looked at his daddy. 'You're a train driver, a real train driver?'

'So they tell me, young man.'

'My daddy is a train driver!' Billy yelled at the top of his voice.

Michael took off his hat and placed it on Billy's head. 'Well, son,' he said, 'where in the world would you like to go?'

Billy smiled at his parents and patted Oliver. 'You know,' he said, 'I rather think I would like to go home.'

Afterword

For this book, there are two groups of people I wish to thank. First, there are the mothers who, for whatever reason, had to hand over their child for adoption, which gave another family the chance to be parents. My mother, Nancy, always told me that giving up a child was one of life's greatest sacrifices. Her heart hurt for those who had no choice other than to relinquish their child. She prayed constantly that somehow the future would bring such mothers more understanding, kindness and solace.

People called Nancy a remarkable woman but to me she was just my mother. She was the most kind, loving, giving soul I have ever met, and I loved her for every single moment of our lives together. Had it not been for the sacrifice my birth mother made, Nancy would never have been a mother. I hope they both got a huge high-five from God when they returned home.

The second group of people includes my wonderful friends, who have shared their stories of love and friendship. May God bless you and your furry friends. Over the years, as I listened to people sharing stories about their animals, my heart was always warmed as they told me all about the joy, fun, companionship and unconditional love those animals offer every day.

The wagging tail they see and the bark they hear when they arrive home that say, 'I love you, and I'm thrilled to see you because you are my world', have brought joy to so many hearts.'

I would like to share some stories with you from people whose lives have been not only changed but saved by these beautiful animals we call dogs. I read recently that 'dog' is 'God' spelled backwards. How appropriate.

I dedicate this book to all of the furry friends who have brought comfort, joy and love into their lives.

Max

Some years ago, before my daughter, Gemah, was married to her husband, John, they often stayed with John's grandparents, Norma and Brian, who had a dog called Max. Gemah's fondness for Max quickly turned to love, and Max would follow her everywhere. I was amazed to learn that when Gemah was working late (it would sometimes be two in the morning before she got home), Max would leap up, bound down the stairs and be at the door waiting for her about five minutes before she arrived. When Gemah was carrying her first child, Seamus, Max would sit beside her and lay his head gently on her stomach, gazing up at her. Gemah wept when Max crossed

the Rainbow Bridge, and remembers him with love
today.

Monty

Nicola's story of unconditional love began when she
was twenty-three. She was living with her boyfriend
when Monty, a Pomeranian, came into her life. The
moment Nicola saw him for the first time she was in
love. They say Pomeranians are immensely protective
and possessive of their family and Nicola was told,
'You don't own a Pomeranian, they own you.' It was
absolutely true.

'It's hard to describe the bond,' Nicola said. 'There
simply aren't words to begin to explain the unconditional love that we shared. He was my best friend. He
was there to share the joys and a constant by my side to
see me through my challenges.'

When Nicola was expecting her first child, many
people wondered how he would react to sharing her,
but Nicola ignored them. She knew better, and she was
right. When Gracie came along, Monty extended his
protection to the baby, and again when Harvey arrived.

As the children grew up he became as much a part
of their lives as Nicola and Ian, their parents, were.
Wherever the family went, Monty went too. In the
summer of August 2016, after a visit to the vet to have
some teeth out, a routine blood test showed signs of

kidney failure. Monty's time with his family was drawing to an end. It was a devastating blow. As Christmas approached Nicola knew this would be the last they would share together. For fifteen years he had brought her happiness, love and understanding.

On 4 January 2017, Monty was in Nicola's arms as he took his first steps onto the Rainbow Bridge to skip in the fields of Heaven, leaving his heartbroken family behind. They will never forget him. God bless you, Monty.

On 18 January 2017, after Nicola had spent the morning talking about her beloved Monty to me, she returned home to find a piece of Monty's fluffy hair on the landing, where he would sit and wait for her to return home. The carpet in that spot had been vacuumed many times since his passing. I hope it helps to ease her pain to know that Monty really is still around, popping in to remind her of how much he still loves her.

Lola

The first time Gillian saw Lola, a British bulldog, she reached down and stroked her. 'Hello,' she said. Lola lifted her head and her big sad eyes looked directly into Gillian's. There and then their journey of love began. Lola was suffering quite a few health problems and wasn't expected to live much longer, the vet told Gillian, but they hadn't reckoned on the healing power of love. Gillian had never before owned a dog and had little idea of how to look after one. However, she is not one to give up easily and she got the expert advice she needed. Lola not only received the necessary treatment but the kind of love every animal should experience. Lola, I have to say, had been well looked after previously but in Gillian's care she began to thrive. Ruby, a sweet little Shih-tzu, lived with Lola, so naturally they both moved into Mama Gillian's home. Ruby was fun and bouncy but Lola was getting old and often Gillian wondered how long she would have her.

As time passed, Lola became slower and slower. The vet said it was only due to Gillian's love and constant care that Lola was still with them. There were nights when Gillian would lie beside her on the floor, comforting, stroking and talking to her. 'I'm here,' she would whisper. 'Mama loves you.' Lola would lie there quietly looking straight into Gillian's eyes.

Early one morning, Gillian was upstairs in the bath, getting ready for the day ahead, when there was an almighty howl from Ruby downstairs. Gillian called down to Ruby saying Mama was on her way down in a moment. It was then Ruby began to cry, a heart-rending sound that made Gillian's heart freeze. Her heart was racing as she hurried down the stairs to find Ruby sitting crying next to Lola. Gillian took a deep breath, went to Lola and lay down beside her. 'Mama loves you,' she whispered, as Lola took her last breath and crossed the Rainbow Bridge.

Dottie and Rocky, Murdo, Paddy, Bodie & Doyle and Solo, always remembering Colin the bulldog who has now crossed the rainbow bridge

When I hear these stories my thoughts always turn to my friend Sandra Hopper. Sandra has been sent many angels disguised as dogs. Never have I seen such complete dedication to animals as I have seen from Sandra. At one time she and her husband, Theo, had many cats and a Scottish terrier, Murdo. She knew all of their characters, their likes and dislikes, and would happily have gone without to ensure her animals were always taken care of. Her family has grown now and she has more dogs: Dottie and Rocky, the pugs, Colin, the bulldog, Murdo, the Scottish terrier, Paddy, the yellow Labrador, Bodie & Doyle, British bulldogs and Solo the spocker, who all live in a home filled with love, understanding and compassion.

Sandra's furry friends not only changed her life, they saved it. Sandra had suffered loss, grief, fear, deep loneliness and, at one point, had almost given up hope. That day she had woken and felt a deep need not to go on; the pain was too great. The dogs and cats she loved so much had other ideas, though: they decided to invade her bedroom. The cats purred and jumped up beside her and the dogs wagged their tails and gazed into her eyes. They knew how she felt and they not only cared about her, they loved her. Sandra's soul was warmed that day as she got out of bed surrounded by her furry friends who loved her so much.

Hunni and Brewster

This pair came into Caryl's life at a time when she was struggling with health issues and brought fun when she needed it most. Holding Hunni and Brewster comforted her, and soon the whole family loved them too. Their little acts of love moved Caryl beyond words.

Caryl's eyes sparkle when she tells her stories of their antics. It is plain to see the love they have for her and how much she loves them too.

To our beautiful furry friends: you are angels disguised as animals and we thank God for you every single day. This poem is for you.

As God looked down upon us,
He watched his angels fly
To every corner of the world,
Then slowly, by and by,

He saw the sad and grieving,
Alone and saddened too,
Praying for a friendly hand
To guide and see them through.

Those lonely days with no one
To share a thought or talk,
To sit awhile beside them
Or simply take a walk.

So many hearts were damaged,
Too many souls cried out,
'Is anybody listening?'
Such disbelief and doubt.

Too many tears from children;
It wasn't what He'd planned,
To see the grief of these young souls
On His beloved land.

God gathered all the angels –
He stilled the Heavens too.
'We all must think together
And see what we can do.

'I need something quite special,
Gentle and yet tough,
To bring back love and laughter.
I haven't done enough.'

A young boy crept upon God's knee.
'Got just the thing.' He smiled.
The angels gathered round; God said,
'Come tell me now, my child.'

'Something really cuddly
That stays right by your side.
It makes your heart go warm
And then all tickly inside.

'Eyes so big and loving,
You simply couldn't fail
To laugh out loud and then, I think,
A strong and waggy tail.'

The angels gathered round him.
'How wonderful it sounds,
A sweet and happy creature
That skips and jumps and bounds,

'With eyes that see for others,
To guide and watch each day,
Then gently steer them onwards
And help them on their way.

'Then most of all a heart so big
To conquer all their fears,
Take and throw them far away
And dry up all their tears.'

They all looked up and waited.
God paused and then agreed
It sounded rather wonderful.
'Let's do it,' God decreed.

A drop of love and laughter,
A bucketful of love,
A heart and soul of gentleness,
To you from God above.

A sprinkle of enchantment,
Then mixed into the bowl
A drop of pure compassion
To heal your very soul.

A waggy tail as promised,
A love that knows no end,
Eyes that look into your own,
A soft and furry friend.

God looked and He was happy,
'I quite like what I see.
Hello there, little fellow,
Come here and sit by me.

'Well now, what can I call you?
I've many newts and frogs,
Horses, zebras, lots of cats –
I know, I'll call you dogs.'

Then over earth from Heaven
There came a shooting star.
'Now make a wish,' God whispered,
'No matter where you are.'

The tiny little puppy
Looked up, and with a bark,
Said, 'God, I think I'm ready.
It sounds like quite a lark.

'Except when I grow tired
And can no longer roam.
After all my work is done,
How then will I get home?'

'Little one, I've made for you
A Rainbow Bridge so bright,
A million different colours,
A truly wondrous light.

'The moment that you fall asleep,
The colours that you see
Will dance before your very eyes
And lead you back to me.'

AFTERWORD

The stars were shining brightly,
The moonlight and the sun
Rejoiced alongside angels,
And so God's will was done.

Acknowledgements

To Fiona Crosby, editor, with grateful thanks for your belief in me and my storytelling. Your constant support and encouragement help to make the writing process a joy. Again, I wish to thank Daniel Bunyard and Punteha Van Terheyden: I will be eternally grateful for your belief in me and my stories. I wish to thank Frank McChrystal for his technical wizardry and infinite patience with me. You really do deserve a medal.

Many thanks to Beatrix McIntyre for all your help and guidance through the editing process and for your kind words which helped keep me on track and eased the process.

I would also like to say thank you to Carol Anderson for making my story flow and her thoughtful and kind words along the way.

To my wonderful daughter Gemah, son-in-law John, and my precious grandchildren, Séamus and Finláy, how loved you all make me feel. I cannot help but think how extremely proud your grandma and great-grandma, Nancy, would be of you all.

Grateful thanks to my husband, Harry, who sat patiently for hours, helping me edit. More importantly, while I have been glued to the laptop, he has done all the washing, ironing, cooking and cleaning – oh, and made sure I stopped to eat. Where would I be without you?